History Of Assamese Literature

History Of Assamese Literature

Birinchi Kumar Barua

GYAN

Published by

Gyan Publishing House
5, Ansari Road
Daryaganj, New Delhi-110002
Phone: 011-47034999, 9811692060
E-mail: books@gyanbooks.com

Distribution Network
gyanbooks.com
India, USA, Canada, UK, Australia

ISBN: 978-93-6280-111-1 (HB)
First Published, 1964

2nd Impression 2024

Printed at: Gyan Press, Delhi.

History Of Assamese Literature

Author: Birinchi Kumar Barua

HISTORY OF ASSAMESE LITERATURE

HISTORY OF ASSAMESE LITERATURE

BY

BIRINCHI KUMAR BARUA

M. A., PH. D.

LATE PROFESSOR OF ASSAMESE AND DEAN OF THE FACULTY OF ARTS,
GAUHATI UNIVERSITY

SAHITYA AKADEMI
NEW DELHI

FOREWORD

THE present volume is the fifth in the series of Histories of Literature, which the Sahitya Akademi has sponsored for publication. The four earlier volumes, namely, *History of Bengali Literature* by Dr. Sukumar Sen and *History of Oriya Literature* by Dr. Mayadhar Mansinha (both in English), History of Malayalam Literature by Sri P.K. Parameswaran Nair in Malayalam and History of Kannada Literature by Dr. R.S. Mugali in Kannada were published earlier and have been well received by discerning critics. *History of Telugu Literature* by Dr. G.V. Sitapati in English and an English translation of the History of Malayalam Literature are now in Press and are expected to be published shortly. Other volumes are under preparation.

These volumes have been planned in uniform size and aim at a standard quality. The Sahitya Akademi hopes in course of time to publish their translation in all major Indian languages of the country so as to make available to the reader authentic surveys of Indian literature, not only of his own region but of the other regions as well. For Indian literature is one though written in many languages. Though the contribution of Assamese to the literature of India is not inconsiderable, very little is known of it outside the Assamese-reading public. It is hoped that this volume will help to introduce the wealth of Assamese literature to the Indian reader in general and will prove of as much interest to the general reader as to the scholar.

The selection of authors of these Histories is made by the Sahitya Akademi in consultation with its Advisory Board in the language concerned and the manuscripts are read and approved by a committee of its literary advisers before they are published. No History of Literature, unless it is a mere chronological catalogue of names, can wholly avoid critical estimates and qualitative preferences. These critical estimates are necessarily the author's and it is not unlikely that there will be difference of opinion amongst the readers in this matter. The publisher (in this case the Sahitya Akademi) need not be identified with these estimates.

It is deeply regretted that the learned author of this History who was himself a creative writer of distinction passed away suddenly while the book was in Press. His premature death cut off a career of great promise and is an irreparable loss to Indian Literature.

SAHITYA AKADEMI

CONTENTS

CHAPTER I

ASSAM AND THE ASSAMESE LANGUAGE

THE part of India now called Assam was known in the epic age as Prāgjyotiṣa. In classical Sanskrit literature, e.g., in the works of Kālidāsa, Prāgjyotiṣa is also called Kāmarūpa. The first available epigraphic record mentioning the name Kāmarūpa is the Allahabad inscription of Samudra Gupta, belonging to the fifth century of the Christian era. A graphic account of the geography of Prāgjyotiṣa or Kāmarūpa is to be found in the *Kālikā Purāṇa* (10th century A.D.) and the *Yoginī Tantra* (16th century A.D.), both of which dwell upon the religio-geographical history of mediaeval Assam. The *Yoginī Tantra* traces the frontiers of Kāmarūpa thus:

> nepālasya kāncanādriṁ brahmaputrasya saṅgamam
> karatoyāṁ samārabhya yāvat dikkaravāsinīm
> uttarasyāṁ kañjagiriḥ karatoyā tu paścime
> tīrthasresṭḥa dikṣunadī pūrvasyāṁ girikanyake
> dakṣine brahmaputrasya lakṣāvah saṅgamāvadhi
> kāmarūpa iti khyātaḥ sarvaśāstreṣu niścitaḥ

"From the mountain of Kāncana in Nepal up to the confluence of the Brahmaputra, from the Karatoyā to Dikkaravāsinī, in the north the mount Kañja, in the west the Karatoyā, in the east the Dikṣu, in the south the confluence of the Lakṣā with the Brahmaputra; this, daughter of the mountains, is the territory which all scriptures call by the name Kāmarūpa." Thus, the ancient Kāmarūpa embraced, besides the districts of modern Assam, the whole of North Bengal including Cooch-Behar, Rangpur, Jalpaiguri, and Dinajpur.

The modern name of the province, Assam, is of recent origin. It is connected with the Ahoms or the Shan invaders who entered the Brahmaputra valley in the beginning of the thirteenth century A.D. The tradition of the Ahoms themselves is that the present name is derived from 'Asama' in the sense of 'unequalled' or 'peerless'. They say that this was the term applied to them by the native tribes at the time of their invasion of the valley, and was an index of the awe and admiration with which the latter regarded the Ahom conqueror who conciliated them. Dr. Banikanta Kakati suggests that 'Asama', 'peerless', may be a later-day Sanskritization of an earlier form, 'Acham'. In Tai the root 'cham' means 'to be vanquished'. With the Assamese prefix 'a', 'Asam' or 'Acham' would mean 'undefeated', 'victorious'. It is argued that the name of the victor passed to the country in due course. Another derivation, however, has been suggested. "The name Asam", observes Baden-Powell, "is most probably traceable to (the Bodo) 'Ha-com', the low or level country."

The earliest inhabitants of Assam, according to the epics and the Purāṇas, were the Niṣādas, Kirātas, Cīnas and other tribes commonly designated 'Mlecchas' and 'Asūras'. Linguistic and ethnographic evidences including some ancient place names of the province indicate that the earliest inhabitants of Assam spoke an Indo-Chinese language of the Mon-Khmer family, which is, according to Schimdt, a branch of the Austric family of languages. The date when the Austric speakers began to infiltrate into Assam is not known, but it must have occurred several hundred years B.C. and certainly long before the advent of the Aryans from the West. It is hard to define the contribution of the Austric-speaking Mongolian peoples to the enthnological structure of Assam; but it is manifest in many existing cultural institutions, customs and manners of the Assamese.

The next wave of Indo-Chinese invasion comprised various peoples speaking Tibeto-Burman tongues. The original abode of these invaders was the land near the Yang-tse-kiang and the Hwang-ho river basins in north west China. From there they went down the courses of the Brahmaputra, the Chindwin and the Irrawaddy, and entered India and Burma. The swarm which came to Assam proceeded down to the crescent of the river Brahmaputra near Dhubri. From this vantage point, some drove south and occupied first the Garo Hills and the State of Hill Tippera. Others appear to have ascended the valley of the Kapili and the neighbouring streams into the highlands of North Cachar, but they failed to occupy the mountainous tract between these highlands and the Garo Hills, now known as the Khasi and Jaintia Hills, and this ever remained the home of the original Mon-Khmer settlers. Other members of this Tibeto-Burman horde halted at the head of the Brahmaputra Valley and turned south. They took possession of the Naga Hills, and from them descended that confused sample-bag of tribes whose speeches are classed as the Naga-group. Another of the swarms that settled in the upper basins of the Chindwin and the Irrawaddy gradually advanced towards the south of Assam and colonised in the Lushai, the Cachar, and even in some parts of the Manipur and Naga Hills. Of the Tibeto-Burman races who settled in Assam, the Bodo tribe is at once the largest and the most important of the non-Aryan strata. The Bodo group includes the Koc, the Kachari, the Lalung, the Dimacha, the Garo, the Rabha, the Tipura, the Chutiya and the Maran tribes. The Bodos who live to the west of the present Kamrup district are called 'Mec' by their Hindu neighbours. This word is probably a corruption of the Sanskrit word '*mleccha*'. The Bodos who live in and to the west of the district of Kamrup are called Kacharis. Various guesses are made about the origin of the word *Kachāri;* possibly the word is connected with *Kakṣāṭa*, a hypothetical formation parallell to the Sanskrit *Kirāta*.

Linguistic evidence shows that at one time the Bodo people occupied the whole of the present province west of Manipur and the Naga Hills, excluding only the Khasi and Jaintia Hills. In fact, they have lent their own names to many of the most prominent features of the province. The Bodos established their colonies in the vicinity of rivers, and so most of the river names in eastern Assam are of Bodo origin. They even rechristened river names of earlier Austric origin by prefixing them with 'Di', their own equivalent for water, e.g., Di-hong, where Bodo 'Di' was placed before Austric 'hong' (water), which perhaps was the name of the river in older times.

The Bodos built strong kingdoms and under various tribal names, the Chutiya, the Kachari, the Koc, etc., held sway over one part or the other of Assam at different times. In the course of centuries the Bodos yielded to external pressure, from the east by the Ahoms of the great Tai race and from the west by the Aryans.

The Tais or Shans first appeared in history in Yunnan, and from thence they migrated into upper Burma. In the 6th century A.D. they migrated from the mountains of Southern Yunnan into the valley of the Sheweli and the adjacent regions. In the 13th century one of their tribes, the Ahoms, overran, conquered Assam itself, and blazed the trail for other Shan tribes to follow. These were the Khamtis, Phakiyals, Naras and Aitaniyas, who mostly inhabit the eastern part of Assam.

It is difficult to ascertain precisely when the Aryans came into the Brahmaputra valley. But there is hardly any doubt that they settled in Assam at a fairly early period either by successful invasion or by peaceful colonisation. The earliest references to Assam's cultural and military contacts with Aryavarta are found in the *Rāmāyaṇa* and the *Mahābhārata.* In the study of the Aryanisation of the province the Naraka[1] legend is of particular interest. Early inscriptions show that high-caste Aryans, such as Brahmanas, Kayasthas and Kalitas, came and settled in Assam at the beginning of the Christian era. The Nidhanpur Copperplate grant records that King Bhutivarman (6th century A.D.) granted special *Agrahāra*[2] settlements to more than two hundred Brahmanas of various *gotras*[3] and *vedasākhās*[4] for promotion of Vedic religion and scholarship. They not only established their own settlements, but absorbed without obliterating the earlier inhabitants in their hierarchy by giving them Aryan religion, ritual and language. In the process of Aryanisation and consolidation even the names of tribes were changed to

[1] Naraka was an adopted son of Janaka, an Aryan king of Videha. Janaka brought up the child in his court along with the royal princes till he was sixteen years old. Naraka excelled the royal princes in the arts of war and peace, and this frightened his foster-father Janaka, who feared that this child would one day wrest the kingdom from his own sons and usurp the throne. Naraka's nurse Kātyāyanī, scented trouble, and slipped out of Janaka's palace and came to the bank of the Ganges. Then both of them came by water to Prāgjyotiṣa, modern Assam, which was then ruled by the Kirātas, a group of the Mongoloid people. Naraka raised an army, fought and conquered the Kirātas. In due course, Naraka brought Brahmanas and other high-caste people from Videha, and, introduced Hindu faiths and religion in the country.

[2] Religious gift of land to Brahmanas.

[3] Family.

[4] Pertaining to various branches of the Vedas.

Aryan caste names. Thus the Koc, a name which was originally used to designate a tribe, was metamorphosed into a recognised Aryan caste embracing all converts from the Kachari, the Lalung, the Mikir and other aboriginal tribes.

Geography is very important in shaping the linguistic and cultural history of a country. A glance at the physical map of Assam may well illustrate this point. Assam is surrounded on three sides by countries of different races and tongues, separated by mountains with passes which are not difficult to traverse. These passes from the earliest times to the present day have been serving as trade and cultural routes between Assam, Burma, Tibet, Bhutan and China.

Another noticeable geographical factor is the river Brahmaputra, which runs through the heart of the province. It has been the chief artery and highway linking Assam with Bengal and other parts of India from ancient times. Its waters have rendered the basin of Assam fertile and the harvest rich and copious. In a sense it is the life-giving blood of Assam, as the Nile is that of Egypt; and Assam's whole history and culture are intimately connected with the Brahmaputra. Nature is also so generous to the people that little do they have to bother about their daily bread and butter. In earlier ages, even gold was found in the sands of the Brahmaputra and other big rivers of the country.

These geographical factors have contributed towards the making of the Assamese people in several ways. The vast terrain of the Brahmaputra valley has an alluring quality that has invited people from neighbouring countries to come and settle there. Each influx has brought in its train the staple of its own culture only to be woven into the general texture of the culture of the soil. The abundant supply of food and the bracing climate have made the people of both the plains and the hills simple, cheerful, easily contented, and indolent. These factors have further encouraged them to live a colourful open-air life throbbing with the rhythms of art, music and dance.

The Assamese language developed out of the Sanskrit language as early as in the 7th century A.D. Its direct ancestor, however, is Magadhi Apabhramsa. According to Grierson, "Magadhi was the principal dialect which corresponded to the Eastern Prakrit. East of Magadhi was spoken Pracya Apabhramsa. It spread to the south and south-east and here became the parent of modern Bengali. Besides spreading southward, Pracya Apabhramsa also spread to the East keeping north of the Ganges and reached the valley of Assam where it is represented by Assamese. Each of the three descendants of Magadhi Apabhramsa, Oriya, modern Bengali and Assamese, is equally directly connected with the common immediate parent" (*Linguistic Survey of India*, Vol. I, Part I, pp. 125-126). Dr. S. K. Chatterji divides Eastern Magadhi Apabhramsa into four dialect groups. Three of these are related to the dialects current in Western, Central and Eastern Bengal and Orissa, and the fourth is related to dialects prevalent in Assam and the neighbouring parts which are to-day in North Bengal. Dr. Banikanta Kákati has shown that in a pre-Bengali and pre-Assamese period there were certain dialect groups which may be designated Eastern Magadhi Apabhramsa. Each dialect group, in due time, became clearly demarcated, and so Assamese, under the independent kings of Assam and her 'entirely self-contained,' social life, 'became established as an independent speech'.

The antiquity of the Assamese language, as already mentioned, goes back to the 7th century A.D. During the first half of the 7th century A.D., on the invitation of the then Assam king Bhaskaravarman, the Chinese pilgrim Hieun Tsang visited the province. In his account of the kingdom of Kāmarūpa he speaks of the language as slightly differing from that of mid-India. This account of Hieun Tsang shows that by the 7th century A.D. the Indo-Aryan language had penetrated into Assam, and that the Aryan language spoken in the province differed to a certain extent from the Magadhi dialects then current in mid-India. The archaic specimens of the Assamese language are discoverable in the place-names and proper-names occurring in the old inscriptions. Other specimens of the language in its formative period are manifest in the songs and aphorisms composed by the Buddhist Siddhācāryas[1] between the 8th and 12th centuries A.D. and commonly known as *Caryās* and *Dohās* found in *Hājār Bacharer*

[1] A preceptor, being supposed to be of great purity and holiness, and said to be characterised by eight magical or supernatural faculties called *siddhi*.

Purāno Bāṅglā Bhāsāy Bauddha Gān O Dohā and in *Dohākoṣa* first compiled by MM. Haraprasad Sastri. Bengali scholars consider these *Caryās* and *Dohās* to be specimens of the early Bengali language only. But careful scrutiny will make it clear that their language, commonly called *sandhyābhāṣā* ('twilight tongue'), represents the latest phase of the Magadhi Apabhramsa, and as such it includes to a considerable extent the earliest forms of the eastern group of modern Indo-Aryan languages, namely Bengali, Assamese and Oriya. Dr. Banikanta Kakati has ably shown how certain phonological and morphological traits registered in these songs have come down in unbroken continuity to modern Assamese. We have stated earlier that the people of Assam represent a mixture of different races speaking various languages like Austric or Mon-Khmer (one of which is Khasi), Sino-Tibetan representing Bodo or Kachari speeches, and the Tai or the Ahom. It is, therefore, natural that these languages would greatly influence the phonological and morphological traits of Assamese, a branch of Indo-Aryan. Dr. Kakati traces Austric elements in Assamese and holds that the vocables that are regarded in Assamese as indigenous have mostly been taken over from the Austric speakers. The Bodo and the Ahom sovereigns ruled over Assam at different times and their rule led to the enrichment of Assamese vocables. Of all the modern Indo-Aryan languages, Assamese is at once the most compact and complex, being influenced by a large number of Austric and Indo-Tibetan tongues and dialects.

Because of multi-racial contacts it was inevitable that some original Indo-Aryan sounds should undergo transformation in Assamese. The old Indo-Aryan cerebrals and dentals have changed to alveolars; and three sibilants have lost their original character and developed peculiar sound traits. The process of spontaneous nasalisation, an active phenomenon in non-Aryan languages, greatly operates in Assamese sound systems. Other special phonological peculiarities of the language are less use of conjunct consonants, preponderance of vowel sounds, and abundant use of fond endings, Sanskrit conjoint consonants being generally mutilated by insertion of vowels.

It is noteworthy, however, that the extent of non-Aryan

influences does not appear to be so great as to change the Aryan structure of the language. This seems, as pointed out by Dr. Kakati, due to several salient historical facts. Assam always lay on the highway for all Indian emigrants to the Far East, and this kept Assam in perpetual contact with the rest of Aryan India and effectively checked the non-Aryan tendencies from making any radical change in the main structure of Assamese. Then, there was the rise of a standard literature based mainly on Sanskrit in the 13th century, which exercised a stabilising influence upon the speech and resisted the incursion of non-Aryan idioms to an appreciable degree. The Assamese script also developed out of the pan-Indian Gupta script.

The vocabulary of Assamese is largely derived from that of Sanskrit, and its morphological structure is also based on Sanskrit grammar. In speech, however, the original Sanskrit words are sparingly used, and they are mostly replaced by *tadbhava*[1] or *ardhatatsama*[2] words. Further, Assamese, being a living and growing language, has borrowed a great number of words from other new Indo-Aryan languages. It has also received some Persian and Arabic words, chiefly administrative and legal terms. In recent years English words and expressions are percolating into Assamese. All these factors have contributed towards the full-fledged development of the Assamese language, and made it a subtle and powerful medium of expression.

[1] Words originated from Sanskrit.
[2] Half-Sanskrit.

CHAPTER II

THE EARLY PERIOD

THE rise of the Crescent is the great fact of the Middle Ages and its impact was felt even in Assam in the thirteenth century A.D. An inscription on a rock at Kanaibarashi, near North Gauhati, records that in 1205 the Turaskas (Turks or Muslims), invading Kāmarūpa, were routed. This probably refers to an engagement between the royal sovereign of Assam and Muhammad Bakhtyar Khiliji, who invaded Assam after his Tibetan expedition, as stated by the Muslim chronicler, Minhaj. Again, in A.D. 1227, Ghiyas-ud-din Iwaj of Lakhnavati made an abortive attempt to conquer Kāmarūpa. In 1257 Ikhtiyas-ud-din Yuzbak Tughril Khan attacked Kāmarūpa, but he was defeated and his army destroyed. The invasion of Kāmarūpa by Muhamud Shah also ended in disaster for the Muslim army.

These successive Muslim invasions, though abortive, shook the very foundations of the old kingdom of Kāmarūpa and gradually led to its disintegration. During this period the Shan invaders entered Assam from the North-East. All these factors led to political dissensions and formation of a number of independent principalities. The Ahoms, a group of the Shan invaders, under the leadership of Sukapha conquered the eastern portion of the country (A.D. 1215) and ruled it from their first capital at Charaideo (near modern Jorhat town). The Kacharis, a section of the Tibeto-Burman peoples, who came to Assam in prehistoric times, presently carved out a kingdom along the south bank of the Brahmaputra bounded by the rivers, Dikhau and Kalong (in the present Nowgong district), with its capital at Dimapur. Their kingdom included also the valley of the Dhansiri river and the Cachar district. The old kingdom of Kāmarūpa was thus dismembered and reduced to a small territory comprising the extreme west up to the river Karatoyā, and including the present districts of Rangpur, Cooch-Behar, Goalpara and Kamarup. With the narrowing down of frontiers, its earlier name also changed from Kāmarūpa to Kamatā, although the Muhammadan historians speak as if the names Kāmarūpa and Kamatā were synonymous. The capital of the country was at Kamatāpur, about eighteen miles from modern Cooch-Behar.

One of the notable kings of Kamatā was Durlabhanārāyaṇa, who ruled possibly at the end of the 13th century A.D. Durlabhanārāyaṇa was an indefatigable patron of poets and scholars. It was in his court that the Assamese language found a trellis to lean on for the first time. The king encouraged poets to write verses in Assamese. Harivara Vipra, one of the court poets of the king, says in a benedictory verse in his *Babrubāhanar Yuddha*, "Glory to King Durlabhanārāyaṇa, the hero of Kāmarūpa. May he in happiness reign a thousand years, in the company of his sons and admirers. Living (happily) in his kingdom, Vipra Harivara pays homage to Goddess Gaurī and renders into verse the spirit of the *Aśvamedhaparva*[1] which is appraised only by the pious." Harivara's chief works are *Babrubāhanar Yuddha* and *Lava-Kuśar Yuddha*; the legendary stories of both the works were taken from the *Jaiminiya Mahābhārata*. *Babrubāhanar Yuddha* contains about 600 couplets. It narrates the exciting conflict between a father and his son. It begins with the entrance of the sacrificial horse into the State of Manipur followed by Arjuna, the third Pāndava. Babrubāhana, the king of Manipur, captured the horse, but learning from his Queen-mother Citrāṅgadā that Arjuna was his father, Babrubāhana went to meet Arjuna with the intention of returning the horse with apology. Arjuna, in his utter forgetfulness of his union with Citrāṅgadā, not only disclaimed any relationship with Babrubāhana but questioned the chastity of his mother and ascribed his submissiveness to abject fear. He remarked tauntingly that a Pāndava prince should be made of firmer clay. This enraged Babrubāhana so much that he fought a most sanguinary battle with Arjuna, killing his father in the doleful encounter. Then Śrīkṛṣṇa appeared in the battle-field, restored Arjuna to life,

[1]*Aśvamedhaparva* is the fourteenth book of the *Mahābhārata*, which describes the horse sacrifice of the Pāndavas after the great war.

and explained to him how he had married Citrāṅgadā during his travels in Manipur on a previous occasion and begot Babrubāhana. Arjuna now remembered his visit to Manipur and acknowledged Babrubāhana as his most worthy son, embraced him and marched away with the horse.

This work is not a literal translation of the Sanskrit original. The author only borrowed the main plot but has embellished the theme with exquisite descriptions and dramatic situations. Nowhere in these innovations does he disclose any lack of literary taste. The description of the royal court at Manipur is picturesque and magnificent. The altercation between Babrubāhana and Arjuna, the exciting repartees between the insolent father and the humiliated son, reveal the author's power of characterisation. The battle scenes are graphic and exude heroic sentiments. Harivara's work is adorned with a variety of flamboyant figures and pleasant precepts and aphorisms. In his *Lava-Kuśar Yuddha* the poet narrates at length the fight between Rāma and his two sons as recounted by Jaimini. The abduction of Sītā, the battle with Rāvana, Sītā's fire-ordeal, and Rāma's return to his capital, Ayodhyā, are summarily mentioned.

As the work was intended for the laity, its language is wry and spare, although spiced with popular idioms. Further, to catch the popular fancy, the emphasis and situations of the original story were changed, and consequently the old martial spirit and heroic ideals were toned down to popular sentimentalism.

Hema Sarasvatī, a contemporary of Harivara, also praised his patron king, Durlabhanārāyaṇa, in *Prahlād-carita*. Though Hema Sarasvatī admitted that he had taken the story from the *Vāmana Purāṇa*, he took much liberty with the original. His narration is not attractive; nor did he aspire after a chaste vocabulary; but his work is inspired by devotional fervour. Sarasvatī's *Hara-Gaurī Saṁvāda* is a bigger work running to 900 verses. He collected the stories of this *kāvya* from both the Purāṇas and the folklore of the land. Though it has some verses on Yogic practices, this large popular treatise catered to the unquenchable thirst of mankind for the obvious and the trite.

Two other celebrated poets who enjoyed royal patronage

from the Kamatā kings were Kaviratna-Sarasvatī and Rudra Kandalī, authors respectively of *Jayadratha-vadha* and *Sātyaki-praveśa.* The plots of both the works were taken from the *Mahābhārata.*

In the same period, another centre of learning throve in what is now the Nowgong district, under the patronage of the Kachari kings. Here with the encouragement of the Kachari king, Mahāmāṇikya (about the fourteenth century A.D.), the greatest of the pre-Vaiṣṇavite poets, Mādhava Kandalī, undertook the stupendous task of translating the whole of the Sanskrit epic *Rāmāyāṇa* into Assamese verse. Mādhava Kandalī, who sang of a life dedicated to the service of God and man through his *Rāmāyāṇa,* was the court-poet of the Kachari king, Mahāmāṇikya, and was known as Kavirāj Kandalī (Kandalī, King of Poets), a well-deserved sobriquet. He was a great Sanskrit scholar and, unlike other poets of the time, was never subjective and never interspersed his works with autobiographical fragments. Śaṅkaradeva, who gave the greatest impetus to the cause of Assamese literature in the succeeding century, held him in high esteem and was charmed with his graceful and moving rendering of the *Rāmāyaṇa.* An immense number of Assamese words were first recorded in Kandalī's *Rāmāyaṇa*; he gave many of the colloquial expressions literary currency, used them in a new sense, or formed fresh derivatives and compounds from them. The legacy of a rich and beautiful diction which Mādhava Kandalī left in his *Rāmāyaṇa* exercised a tremendous influence on Śaṅkaradeva and his immediate successors. Its diction is —

> Though deep, yet clear : though gentle, yet not dull :
> Strong without rage : without overflowing full.

It is worth noting that of all modern Indian vernacular translations of Vālmīki's *Rāmāyaṇa,* Mādhava Kandalī's is the earliest. Hindi, Bengali and Oriya versions appeared about a century and a half later. Though so early, Mādhava Kandalī's translation is not at all raw but done in a bright and elevated literary style. Mādhava Kandalī constantly kept two things before him—literary beauty and popular taste.

He never allowed communal, sectarian or religious matters to override the artistic compulsions. His imagination, therefore, had a free and unfettered play in the selection of words, figures and images.

In the original *Rāmāyaṇa* of Vālmīki, from which stems the Assamese version, artistic beauty seems to be the predominant passion of the poet, devotion or ethics becoming only a secondary interest. The Assamese poet also subordinates homiletic materials to literary beauty. In the Assamese version, the *Rāmāyaṇa* undergoes almost a generic transformation. An idyllic beauty replaces the heroic tone of the original. Where there was martial atmosphere and heroism, we now have the charm of the sweet domestic life of an ideal father, mother, son, daughter and brother. Much emphasis has, therefore, been laid in Kandalī's *Rāmāyaṇa* on homely virtues like devotion to parents and husbands, veneration for the *guru*, affection for wife, brothers and friends, kindly feelings, and courtesy to common man. It also holds chastity to be the highest virtue for both man and woman. In short, it is redolent of the temper and genius of the Assamese people.

Broadly following the plot of Vālmīki, Kandalī has woven popular elements into its artistic web and dyed it in local colour. Local customs, habits and manners have been drawn on to lend subtle nuances to the epic. Even the minutest details are noted, which shows how full the poet's vision was. The Assamese version portrays the frailty of the elderly Kunji. She pines for Bharata's love. She approaches him in her finest attire after the prince's return from his maternal uncle's house—an episode not found in the dignified Sanskrit text. Through it the Assamese poet panders to the common taste. Further, the heroic bearing and mighty pronouncements of Rāma before his father, tongue-tied through Kaikeyī's villainy, and his brave undertaking to implement the king's promises to his step-mother, as found in Vālmīki, are finer than the sentiments of vanity expressed by the proud hero in the Assamese version. These, however, are minor flaws in an otherwise admirable translation.

Kandalī has shown considerable skill in providing the background, depicting natural scenery, rousing appropriate emotions, and selecting apt phrases and lively imagery. In the picture of merry Ayodhya, the portrait of Daśaratha, heart-broken at Rāma's exile, Rāma's harangue to Sītā on the perils of an exiled life, their sojourn in the Citrakuta forest, the tranquillizing beauty of the river Mandākinī—everywhere there are projections of contemporary Assam with her picturesque peoples and radiant landscapes. The greatest contribution of this gifted poet was the forging of a literary diction of a kind of its own, with harmonious blending of Sanskrit and Assamese vocables, a diction which was beyond the reach of his contemporaries and was to serve as model and pattern for subsequent writers. The poet possessed a cornucopia of words to describe diverse situations and modes of life. Whether he is describing a town, a country or a forest-glade, as mentioned in the original, imagination and words come to him naturally and gracefully as leaves to a tree and song to a nightingale. When he begins describing a wood, the names of trees, shrubs, flowers, birds come in unwearied succession. Along with such plenty, the poet possessed an instinct for the right word. Another distinctive feature of the poetry of Mādhava Kandalī is his original imagery wherewith he reinforces and diversifies classical ones. In addition he also incorporates scenes from everyday domestic life, making his poetry easy of acceptance for the cleric, the divine and the churl alike, a practice later emulated by Vaiṣṇavite writers.

Devajit is another poetic composition commonly ascribed to Mādhava Kandalī. In this poem, Kandalī seeks to establish the superiority of Kṛṣṇa and other incarnations of Viṣṇu to all other gods.

Another poet who worked on the *Rāmāyaṇa* theme was Durgābar. He lived at the Nilacala Hill during the reign of his patron king, Viśvasiṁha of Kamatā, sometime in the 16th century A.D. Durgābar rendered some cantos of the *Rāmāyaṇa* into melodies and dainty refrains. He was familiar with Kandalī's *Rāmāyaṇa*, and in his *Gīti-Rāmāyaṇa* he incorporated some verses from the latter with slight alterations of words to suit musical tunes.

It has been already shown that the Assamese people are made of diverse elements, speaking Aryan, Mon-Khmer, Tibeto-Burman, Tai or Shan languages. An inevitable consequence of this mixture was that many of the customs, religious rites, beliefs, oral traditions and folklore of the non-Aryan peoples were Aryanised and gradually incorporated into the Hindu Pantheon. One such Aryanised cult is the snake-cult. The Assamese worship the serpent as the goddess Manasā. A cycle of narrative poems was composed glorifying her deeds. These are sung even today on the occasion of Manasā worship.

The poems relating to Manasā worship can be divided into three parts. The first part starts with the mythical story of Śiva and Durgā, and describes the birth of the snake-goddess Manasā, her quarrel with Candī, and her marriage. In the second part is described how the devotees Halika and Jalika worshipped the goddess Manasā. The third part, the most popular of all, recounts the contest between the goddess Manasā and the irreverent Śaivite merchant Chānd who deliberately refused to bow down before her and was intolerant even of the mere mention of her name. The wrathful goddess avenged herself by killing his six sons and getting his fourteen merchandise-laden boats sunk. She did not rest content even with this. She got Lakhindar, the merchant's seventh son, stung mortally by a serpent on the nuptial night. The helpless newly-wedded bride, Behulā, took the corpse of her husband on a rafter down a stream and after floating down a great distance arrived at a landing of the river near Kailāsa. With the help of Netāi, the washerwoman of Śiva, Behulā got an audience with the mighty god who kindly intervened in her favour and asked Manasā to restore to life the seven sons of Chānd and also to return to him the fourteen merchandise-laden boats intact; the merchant in return would worship Manasā at least once. Behulā returned with her husband, now restored to life, and prevailed upon her father-in-law to worship Manasā. Chānd did worship Manasā, but instead of doing it with grace, he offered the oblations in disdain with his left hand. Yet this was something. Chānd got back the things he had lost.

This story has been built on myths and superstitions of both the Assamese and the neighbouring tribes. Some people find in it an echo of the ancient conflict between Śaivism (worship of Śiva) and other religious faiths. This explains the presence in the Manasā poems of many popular gods and goddesses. Human characters have been very ingeniously woven into the texture of the poems, which renders it interesting as a human document.

Mankar is the first poet of the Manasā theme. He flourished about the end of the 15th century. Durgābar, who rendered the *Rāmāyaṇa* into songs, also dwelt on the Manasā theme. Like Mankar, Durgābar also wove into the tapestry of the Behulā theme vignettes of contemporary social life.

Nārāyaṇadeva is the greatest Manasā poet of Assamese literature. He is also known as Sukavi (Poet *par excellence*). His Behulā-Lakhindar-songs known as *Sukanānni* were probably written in the seventeenth century in the court of King Dharmanārāyaṇ of Darangi-rājya. In Nārāyaṇadeva's hands the Behulā episode assumed tremendous popularity and a fresh form. He brought to it a social consciousness that was altogether new to mediaeval Assamese literature. He tried to recapture in his songs the very atmosphere of the simple home life of his time with its joys and cares. In characterisation and portrayal of emotions the poet is true to life. His Cāndsadāgar is a man of indomitable will, inflexible resolution, and unimpeachable integrity. But even he was prevailed upon, at last, to admit the goddesshood of Padmā (Manasā) by Behulā. This is a victory for Behulā's pure devotion, conjugal purity and faith that moves mountains. As an ideal wife she is second neither to Sītā nor to Sāvitrī. Before the pure chastity and deep devotion of Behulā, even heavenly powers bend and break. With a few bold strokes, Sonekā, wife of Cāndsadāgar, has been made into a moving portrait of a forlorn mother, matchless in tragic intensity like Synge's Maurya in *The Riders to the Sea*. Though a goddess in name, Padmā is jealous, vindictive and mean. In the Behulā poems, men have risen to godly heights whilst gods have fallen down to mundane pettiness. Whatever may be the literary merits of the Manasā poems, they have the great value of preserving our cultural heritage, sustaining an interest in the old myths and legends and in strengthening the ties of our cultural life and literature.

CHAPTER III

THE VAIṢṆAVITE PERIOD

THE sixteenth century marked the meteoric and simultaneous rise of two great powers in Assam, the Kochas and the Ahoms, and the entire country was shared between them. The old kingdom of Kamatapur was destroyed by the invasion of Ala-ud-din Hussain Shah about 1498, and after a brief interregnum of confusion, a new kingdom rose from the ashes of the old. The chief of the Koch tribe, Viśva Siṁha, established this new kingdom, about A.D. 1515 with Koch-Behar (modern Cooch-Behar) as capital. The greatest ruler of the Kochas was Viśva Siṁha's illustrious son and successor, Naranārāyaṇa, a worthy contemporary of Akbar, the Great Mogul. Naranārāyaṇa was educated at Banaras and was distinguished for his Sanskrit scholarship. Naranārāyaṇa and his brother Sukladhvaja or Chilārāi invited to their court Brahmanas and learned men from Banaras and other centres of learning. Both of them espoused the cause of Hinduism, patronized learning, and did much to raise the cultural level of Naranārāyaṇa's subjects. The English traveller, Ralph Fitch, visited the Koch country during Naranārāyaṇa's reign, and he speaks with admiration of veterinary hospitals in Assam and the aversion of the Assamese to violence. Naranārāyaṇa invited the great Vaiṣṇavite saint-poet Śaṅkaradeva and his colleagues to his court and bestowed munificent gifts on them. Naranārāyaṇa desired to become Śaṅkaradeva's disciple, but the saint refused to give initiation to a sovereign. King Naranārāyaṇa's brother, Chilārāi, married Śaṅkaradeva's niece Kamalāpriya, and this union advanced the cause of Vaiṣṇavism in the Koch kingdom.

During the same period, the Ahoms were also busy in consolidating their power in the eastern part of the country. The Ahom king, Suhungmung or Dihingiya Raja (1497-

1539), annexed the kingdom of the Chutiyas which centred round their capital Sadiya. The same king drove the Kacharis from their stronghold at Dimapur, and subjugated the Bhuya chieftains on the north bank of the Brahmaputra. Suhungmung forged cordial ties with the Koch king, Viśva Siṁha, and received in 1537 a friendly visit from the latter. Amongst the Ahom kings, Suhungmung was the first to embrace Hinduism, assume a Hindu name, Svarga Nārāyaṇa, and adopt the Hindu way of life. The great Assamese thinker, poet and reformer, Śaṅkaradeva, was born during his reign. His rule synchronised with the Vaiṣṇava Renaissance which struck deep roots in the religious, cultural and social life of Assam.

Śaṅkaradeva (1449-1569) was born in a Bhuya family at Alipukhuri, a village on the south bank of the Brahmaputra, about sixteen miles from the present town of Nowgong. The Bhuyas at that time were powerful feudal lords, enjoying social privileges granted by the king. Śaṅkara's family was called the Śiromaṇi Bhuya, being the chief among the Bhuyas. His father was Kusumbara. Śaṅkara's mother died within three days of his birth, and he was brought up by his grandmother, Khersuti. When Śaṅkara was twelve years old he was sent to a village school maintained by Mahendra Kandalī, an erudite Sanskrit scholar.

Śaṅkara completed his studies at the age of twenty-two and emerged a full-fledged scholar. Soon after he left school heavy domestic responsibilities fell upon his young shoulders. He was married to Sūryavatī, a Kayastha bride. Sūryavatī died four years after her marriage, leaving an infant daughter. About the same time Śaṅkara lost his father. These two bereavements filled his youthful mind with overwhelming sorrow and he thought of renouncing the world. After performing his daughter's marriage, Śaṅkara set out on a long and arduous pilgrimage (A.D. 1491.) He was accompanied by seventeen companions including his teacher Mahendra Kandalī. A detailed account of this pilgrimage has been recorded in the biographies of Śaṅkaradeva compiled by his disciples. He visited most of the sacred places and temples of northern and southern India. Among the sacred places and shrines that he visited were Gaya, Puri, Vṛndāvana, Mathura,

Dvaraka, Kasi, Prayaga, Sitakunda, Varahakunda, Ayodhya and Vadarikasrama. At these holy places he came into contact with Vaiṣṇavite teachers of various schools, and had many learned and theological discussions with them. The results of these discussions and the influence they exercised over his mind were reflected in the Vaiṣṇavite movement which he subsequently started in Assam. After twelve years of such wanderings in many hallowed seminaries of Vaiṣṇavite learning, Śaṅkaradeva returned home a much-travelled man, equipped with first-hand knowledge of Vaiṣṇavite theology, texts, liturgy, and management of institutions.

At the time of the appearance of Śaṅkaradeva, the Śākta[1] and the Tāntrik[2] forms of worship dominated the country. Śaṅkaradeva's ancestors were all Śāktas, and one of them was named Devīdās (the Servant of the Goddess) because of his devotion to the goddess of the Śākta cult. Mādhavadeva, Śaṅkara's devout disciple, and Bhaṭṭadeva, another Vaiṣṇava saint of the period, were Śāktas before their conversion to Vaiṣṇavism. The Kāmākhyā temple at Gauhati, the Tāmreśvari temple at Sadiya, the Parihareśvara temple at Doobi, the Mahādeva temple at Dergaon, were the main centres of Śākta worship in the country and from them spread a tremendous influence over the secular and monastic clergy and all orders in the social scale. In course of time, the Śākta forms of worship absorbed many of the rites and rituals of the aboriginal tribes and thus gave rise to the fascinating Tāntrik cult. Tāntrik rituals with many abominable corruptions were also practised in Assam in the centuries before the birth of Śaṅkaradeva. The Tāntrik mode of worship consisted of elaborate rituals including occasionally human sacrifices. Magic, *mantra* (the word of power), and other esoteric practices were considered the easiest means of attaining salvation. Whatever may be the efficacy of Tāntrik worship as a means of salvation, there can be no denying the fact that it led eventually to moral decadence, social corruption, perversion, and blasphemy.

[1] A religious faith in which the *Śakti* or divine energy under its female personification, especially the goddess Durgā, Kālī, Kāmākhyā, and Candī, is worshipped.

[2] Associated with Śākta religious faith in which magic, mystical formularies, and many rites and rituals are used for the worship of the deities.

Śaṅkaradeva, after his return from pilgrimage, waged a relentless crusade against Śākta worship and Tāntrik practices. His stature grew to its full height against the spiritual barrenness of Śaktaism. With utter contempt for cant and supreme faith in the spirit, he vigorously launched the Vaiṣṇavite Renaissance. Śaṅkaradeva dispensed with the Vedic rituals and worship of diverse gods and goddesses. He enjoined adoration of one God and named his new faith *Ekaśaraṇanāmadharma*, the religion of supreme surrender to the One, and that One is Viṣṇu who in the form of Nārāyaṇa manifests himself in various incarnations from age to age. The most beloved incarnation of Viṣṇu is Kṛṣṇa. Śaṅkaradeva says: "There is one God and one devotion, and there is none else." The surrender to the One is very rigorously enjoined in his religion. For an Ekaśaraṇiyā, the worship of other gods and goddesses is strictly prohibited. It has been said by the saint himself that a "Vaiṣṇava should not worship any other god's temple, nor should he partake of offerings made to any other god. *Bhakti* (devotion) would be vitiated by such fickleness."

The exaltation of *bhakti* in Śaṅkaradeva's religion is well shown by the following passage in his translation of the *Bhāgavata:* "People interpret the *Bhāgavata*," says Śrī Kṛṣṇa, "according to their own whims. They find sanction for everything except *bhakti.* Some make it out that the Vedas inculcate ceremonials, sacrifices, gifts, and oblations; others, that the Vedas prescribe the worship of smaller gods, pilgrimages, and bathing in sacred waters; others, again, that the supreme bliss comes through knowledge. Their interpretations are coloured by the dominant attributes of their minds. But know thou this, oh, my friend, I am not accessible through knowledge, nor through penance, nor through renunciation, nor through gifts. I am not accessible by yoga nor by knowledge, I am accessible by *bhakti* alone."

Śaṅkaradeva, it should be noted, advocated neither a religion of extreme asceticism nor complete renunciation of family life. He upheld the golden mean between the two. He believed that renunciation should be internal, not external. He realised that men and women have to live in the world and to pursue their professions. The saint himself led a full family life and took a second wife after the death of the first one, on his return from pilgrimage. His religion upheld the ideal of a chaste and devoted domestic life and offered a simple way to salvation based on ethico-devotional codes; accordingly, like the gospel of the Buddha, it won over the entire population of the country in no time.

The main argument stressed by Śaṅkaradeva for *gṛhastha*-stage (household) of life was that the man in this stage of life could do many welfare works of the society by supporting one's own family and relatives, giving gifts to the needy and the poor, and performing religious duty. In upholding this view, Śaṅkaradeva was more influenced by the *Mahābhārata* and the *pravṛtti mārga* or *Karma-yoga* (path of action) of the *Gītā*. He occasionally referred to the utterances of the Sage Syumarasmi in the *Mahābhārata* where the sage favouring the house-hold life says: "To achieve a proper equilibrium of mind in misery as well as happiness, is a necessary step towards achieving salvation, it should also be noted that without taking resort to the house-hold life, one does not achieve this state of mind. Just as all the creatures are dependent on their mother for their life, so all the other *āśramas* (stages of life) are dependent upon the house-hold stage of life."

Śaṅkaradeva's religion, further, brought a new meaning and depth to social and cultural life. For the first time in Assam's history, he asserted the dignity of man in society independent of the accidents of birth and social rank, and established the spiritual equality of all men. In his fraternity, Brahmanas, Sudras and men of lower birth enjoyed equal liberty of worship, devotion and prayer. "Why need one be a Brahmaṇa," says Śaṅkara, "to devoutly recite the name of Kṛṣṇa? He might be a caṇḍāl or pariah but he is far superior to any man who does not utter the name of God." Śaṅkaradeva admitted into his fold people from all social orders, and among his chief disciples there were Brahmanas, tribals, and even Muhammedans.

For some years, Śaṅkaradeva made his native place, Bardowa (Nowgong district), the radiating centre of his missionary activities. Here he set up a *Satra* (monastery) and erected a *Nāmghar* or congregational prayer hall for daily devotional recitations (*nām-kirtan*). It was a place for the performance of religious dramas and evangelical services.

With these new methods of propagation, he started mass conversions, and the universal appeal of his religion with its simple tenets immediately brought around him a large number of disciples. As in the case of Martin Luther, Śaṅkaradeva's simple faith and democratic teachings were, however, not liked by the Brahmanas, the priestly class. They vehemently opposed his religion, first because he discarded the rites, ceremonies and modes of worship of the time-honoured religion preached by the Brahmanas, and secondly because he made the Sanskrit scriptures, which were so long the monopoly of Brahmanas, accessible to all people by rendering them into Assamese. The Brahmanas were so alarmed at finding themselves eclipsed by the genius of Śaṅkaradeva, whose teachings spread like wild fire amongst the masses, that they accused him before the Ahom king, Suhungmung Dihingiya Raja (1497-1539), of bringing disaster to the country by preaching an unorthodox religion not envisaged by the Vedas. The Ahom monarch summoned Śaṅkaradeva to argue with the Brahmanas of his court. Śaṅkara defeated them and got off from the trial with credit. He, however, felt that his life would be precarious in the Ahom territory and so he left the place. He then journeyed to Barpeta (1543) in the present district of Kamrup, then under the Hindu King Naranārāyaṇa of Koch Behar. In Barpeta, he laid the foundations of the Pathbausi Satra, erected a Nāmghar, began propagation of his gospel, and fortified the spirit of the people. He spent the remaining years of his life in Barpeta, under the patronage of the enlightened Koch king, in comparative peace. The major portion of his writings, lyrics, dramas and epics, were composed here. After three years of residence at Barpeta, Śaṅkaradeva set out again on a pilgrimage at the ripe age of ninety-seven (1546). He was accompanied by one hundred and twenty devotees. During this journey he met Caitanya Deva at Puri and is said to have met the granddaughter of Kabīr.

In his later years, on several occasions, Śaṅkaradeva was invited by King Naranārāyaṇa to his court to interpret the Śāstras and to participate in religious discussions. These visits to Naranārāyaṇa's court brought him added glory, and he carved for himself a permanent niche in the temple of fame for his scholarship, saintliness, and poetry. King Naranārāyaṇa's brother, Cilārāi, built a Satra near the capital called Bheladanga where Śaṅkaradeva used to stay during his visit to Cooch-Behar. Here the great saint, who gave to Assam a new way of thinking about God and man, passed away in 1569.

The Śaṅkarite movement produced far-reaching religious and social effects. It gave a great impetus to the advancement of learning and literature in Assam. Śaṅkaradeva, though a distinguished Sanskrit scholar, wrote mainly in Assamese, with the aim of bringing Sanskrit lore within the reach of the uneducated masses. He wrote and did a number of textual commentaries and translations to expound his creed, and he transformed whatever he touched into gold. These writings had also a practical utility; they were constantly required for guidance in the performance of one's duties. A versatile genius, he also wrote poetry, songs and plays which gave a new impulse to Assamese literature.

Śaṅkaradeva drew inspiration chiefly from the *Bhāgavata*, which distilled the quintessence of the Vedānta philosophy into a receptacle of popular and unforgettable legends. An early attempt was, therefore, made to translate the book into Assamese. It was really a very bold and extraordinary undertaking to render into a provincial language a venerable text written in the grand style of a classical tongue. In this connection it is interesting to note that Śaṅkaradeva was accused before the Koch king, Naranārāyaṇa, by the Brahmans as an ardent reader, teacher and translator of the *Bhāgavata*.

The translation of the entire text was not a light job for one man; so Śaṅkaradeva allotted different sections for translation to his disciples. He himself undertook the rendering of the major portion, namely Books I, II, III, VII, VIII, IX, X and XII. Besides Śaṅkaradeva, other writers who undertook the translation of different sections were Ananta Kandalī (Books IV, VI and a section of Book X), Keśavacaraṇa (Books VII and IX), Gopālacaraṇa Dvija (Book III), Kavi Kalāpcandra (sections of Book IV), Śrī Viṣṇu Bhāratī (sections of Book IV), Ratnākara Miśra (sections of Book V), Śrī Candradeva (sections of Book IV), Aniruddha Kāyastha (sections of Books IV & V), and Hari (sections of Book V).

The rendering of the *Bhāgavata* marks an era of renaissance in Assamese poetry. Its literary influence on Saṅkarite literature was manifold. It remoulded the faith and the conscience of the Assamese. Śaṅkaradeva was indebted to the *Bhāgavata* not only for its Kṛṣṇaite legends but also for its metres, expressions and traditions. The greatness of Śaṅkara's translation lies not merely in the flowing Assamese version but in its vital use of the Assamese idiom.

Of all the books of the *Bhāgavata*, the Adi Daśama (the first part of Book X) enjoys universal popularity. This Book describes the incidents of Kṛṣṇa's early life, such as Child Kṛṣṇa's killing of demons, his sports, his tending of cattle with his friends in forest glades, his childish pranks such as stealing of butter, milk and curd, his quarrels with the milk-maids, and the various chastisements he had from his foster-mother Yaśodā. Though permeated with religious emotion, the Daśama gives an intensely human and realistic picture of child life, a mother's love and grief for her little son, and other themes that eternally move the human heart. It should however be noted that, unlike as in the Vaiṣṇavite literature of other provinces, Rādhā does not appear in these scenes, nor does she find a place in the whole of Śaṅkarite literature.

The *Bhāgavata* was an inexhaustible source of knowledge from which Śaṅkaradeva drew again and again. Besides the translation, he composed a large number of works with materials from Sanskrit scriptures. His *Nimi Nava Sidha Saṁvāda* is a doctrinal treatise based on Book XI of the *Bhāgavata*. Nārada here recounts before Vāsudeva the discussions which took place between King Nimi and the nine sages on various moot points in Hindu theology. Each sage expounds one of these points, namely, the nature of the religion of the *Bhāgavata*, Devotion (*Bhakti*), Illusion (*Māyā*), way of escape from Illusion (Salvation), *Brahma-yoga* (The System of Meditation) and *Karma-yoga* (The Metaphysics of Action), demerits of the uninitiated (*abhakta*), and the nature of a Divine Incarnation. Here a number of abstruse metaphysical problems are expounded in the Assamese language with a clarity of expression unique of its kind. From its very nature the work does not strive to reach any high level of poetry, though some of its verses bear mark of literary excellence. The merits of *bhakti* are expressed in popular homilies with apt illustrative similes:

> He who meditates on the Word of God, Mādhava,
> Finds at once all his three needs gratified.
> First he finds lust, ebbing out, a sure sign of devotion,
> then grows an indifference to his abode and body,
> And love swells for the Form of the Lord (Kṛṣṇa),
> The centre of love.
> The three assets come to one,
> Like food to the hungry.
> And each morsel (of meditation) gives the soul fulfilment.
> Pleasure grows, the body is restored,
> And the soul's hunger vanishes.
> Listen, O King, to the nature of love and devotion,
> Even a little of devotion sustains love well,
> Just as a morsel satisfies some.

Bhakti-pradipa, another metaphysical work of Śaṅkara, gives a reflective analysis of the nature of devotion (*bhakti*). Though the work is said to have been compiled from the *Garuḍa Purāṇa*, in fact its contents tally more with the materials of Book XI of the *Bhāgavata*. His *Anādi Pātana* is mainly an adaptation from Book III of the *Bhāgavata*, though a few episodes are introduced from the *Vāmana Purāṇa*. The book deals with cosmological matters and is poor in literary merit. *Guṇamālā* (*Garland of Praises*) is one of the last works of Śaṅkaradeva composed at the request of Koch king, Naranārāyaṇa. In essence, *Guṇamālā* is a little handbook based on Books X and XI of the *Bhāgavata*. It is a *stotra* or *stuti* type of psalm with six small sections containing hymns of praise to Viṣṇu and Kṛṣṇa. Within the compass of a single laudatory verse, the poet recounts many incidents from Kṛṣṇa's life, making them easy to remember. In fact, there is not a Vaiṣṇavite in Assam who has not learnt the *Guṇamālā* by rote. Superabundance of alliteration with sonorous rhymes makes the poem suitable for recitation.

The next outstanding literary production of Śaṅkaradeva is the *Kīrtana-ghoṣā* (the lyric in praise of God's Glory), which even today fills the mind and heart of every Assamese with a lofty spiritual elation. It is looked upon with the same fond reverence as *Rāmacaritamānasa* of Tulasīdāsa in northern India. There is no Assamese Hindu home which does not possess a copy of *Kīrtana-ghoṣā* either in manuscript written on sanchi-leaves or in print, none where some of its verses are not recited on religious occasions and during illness.

The date of composition of the *Kīrtana-ghoṣā* is not known. Some biographers say that Śaṅkaradeva did not write the book during one particular period, and that the composition was spread over several years. From the methodical arrangement of the chapters it may be said that though the book was written at different periods, the entire opus could have been projected only in his late years. Furthermore, the *Kīrtana-ghoṣā* is not a single poem but a selective collection of twenty-six poems comprising about 2261 couplets in diverse metres. General names for these narrative poems are *ākhyāna*, *upākhyāna*, *kīrtana*, *varṇanā*, and *vṛttānta*. Poems of elegiac type are called *prayāṇa-gītā*. Most of the poems are adaptations from the *Bhāgavata Purāṇa*. Two of the poems, *Sahasra Nāma Vṛttānta* and *Ghunucā-kīrtana*, were contributions by other writers. They were written respectively by two of his disciples, Ratnākara Kandalī and Śrīdhar Kandalī, and were incorporated in the anthology at the desire of the authors. Each poem included in the *Kīrtana* is of the nature of an independent work modelled after Sanskrit homiletic *kāvyas* and illuminative of many didactic and doctrinal points. The very name *Kīrtana* is suggestive of the fact that the poems were intended for chanting in congregational prayers. Each poem bears a *ghoṣā*, a refrain. These poems are recited by the leader of the religious congregation. After reading a couplet, the leader repeats the *ghoṣā* or refrain, and the rest of the party takes it up with rhythmic clapping of hands.

Kīrtana-ghoṣā was a mature product of Śaṅkaradeva's mind. A number of episodes from the *Bhāgavata* are presented in it with the specific intention of enlightening the people, in a clear and straightforward style, on the rudiments of the doctrine of *bhakti* and the ethics and spiritual discipline of a devotee: such episodes as the simple devotion of the child Dhruva, the fearless devotion of Prahlāda, the adoration of

Kubji, the friendship of the cowboys, the sincere devotion of Bipra Dāmodar and Uddhava, the ardent supplication of Gajendra, the salvation of Ajāmila merely by uttering the name of God, etc. Thus, in *Kīrtana*, we find a string of stories first of their kind in Assamese literature, charmingly told, combining instruction and entertainment, and couched in a moving language. But to a modern reader the merits of *Kīrtana* do not depend so much upon its didacticism and moral or theological content as upon its literary form, picturesque descriptions, originality of treatment, and rhythmic felicities, which make the work loved at home and revered abroad. Śaṅkaradeva's poetry fell upon Assamese ears with a cadence and music as familiar as their dialect. As for its popularity, Shri Jnananath Bora rightly says: "All the sentiments—pleasure and pain, love and separation, anger and forgiveness, are equally blended in *Kīrtana*. It affords pleasure to all classes of readers. To children it gives stories and songs for amusement, it delights the young with true poetic beauty, and the elderly people find here religious instruction; and *Kīrtana-ghoṣā* stands out not only for its religious outlook but also for largeness of heart and breadth of vision that transcend all religions." We find such striking passages of universal appeal as the following:

> Numbered are the years that measure your life;
> Half the life slips away in the hours of sleep;
> A score of years fly in the winds of boyish pranks;
> Ten more years go in counting coins on the finger-tip.
> Think of the twenty years at the other end of it
> When life shall grow too heavy to drag on;
> Each hour in the sand-glass shall be an eternity of aches,
> Each sunrise bringing dullness and diseases unknown.
> And shall melt away the dreams of your eyes and starry hues;
> Confined in a cabin it shall pile up a welter of woes.
>
> (*Prahlād Caritra*)

We have such pious humility as enshrined in the following lines:

Insensible and arrogant
I wander about with thoughts of the world.
You being devoid of arrogance destroy me anon,
Just as a serpent kills a rat.

(*Mucukuṇḍa Stuti*)

such metaphysical meditations as:

'My intellect is clouded as I identify myself with my body;
Alas! You are within me, and in vain I search without'.

(*Śiśulilā*)

and such noble thoughts as

Him indeed all call a wise man who does not distinguish between the caste of a Brāhmaṇa and that of a Caṇḍāla; who looks at a donor and a thief with an equal eye and who does not differentiate between a debased man and an honest person.

(*Śrī Kṛṣṇar Vaikuṇtha Prayāṇa*)

also:

God is also the soul of the dog, the ass and the outcaste. Knowing this, pay reverence to all living creatures.

Limitations of space preclude further quoting.

Of his other works, *Hariścandra-upākhyāna* was composed while Śaṅkara was a student at Mahendra Kandalī's school. The materials of the poem were collected mainly from the epic, *Mārkaṇḍeya Purāṇa*. All through the poem the author has extolled the merits of *bhakti*.

Another poem of his younger days is *Rukmiṇī-haraṇa* (*Abduction of Rukmiṇī*): a work of idyllic beauty based on the *Bhāgavata* and *Harivaṁśa*. In the opening verses, the poet admits his debt to both these texts. Yet the poem has enough touch of realism in it to transform the scriptural story into an exciting narrative of popular experience.

Balichalan (*The Discomfiture of Bali*) was written while Śaṅkara was at Patbausi. This is mainly an adaptation of the well-known episode of Bāli from Book VIII of the *Bhāgavata Purāṇa*. The poem is surcharged with an intense devotion, particularly of the *dāsya* type, i.e., devotion as of a servant to his Master. There is also a series of pregnant precepts and aphorisms bearing on the use of gifts, wealth a hindrance to spiritual progress, the evils of desire, and the peace of contentment arising out of the control of the senses.

Śaṅkaradeva did not confine himself to Kṛṣṇaite legends alone but dwelt also on themes from the *Rāmāyaṇa*. He rendered into Assamese the *Uttara Kāṇḍa* (the last canto) of the *Rāmāyaṇa*. Mādhava Kandalī's Assamese version of the *Rāmāyaṇa* existed only in five cantos without the first and the last. The *Uttara Kāṇḍa* may, however, be called an independent *Rāmāyaṇa* as most of the incidents of the epic are narrated in this canto through songs sung by Lava and Kuśa in the court of Rāma. Unlike, however, as in his translation of the *Bhāgavata*, where the original, being a sacred text, was faithfully followed, in the *Uttara Kāṇḍa*, fidelity to the original, whether in respect of the ideal, character or incident, was not the main concern of the translator. The central figure is not an epic hero but a man-god, an incarnation of Viṣṇu. For, in one of the *bhanitās*[1] Śaṅkara says of Rāma:

> Thou art the Lord of the three worlds, and the way of the universe.
> Thou art the unthinkable virtue, unlimited power.
> Beyond Prakṛti[2] thou art the supreme secret.
> None knows the beginning or the end of Thy glory.
> Thou relievest the burden of the world, incarnating thyself ever and anon,
> To chastise the wicked and protect the pious.
> Thou art Iśvara,[3] Whom gods and demons revere.
> To the last Thou alone stayest and, alas, none else.

In two other branches of Assamese literature Śaṅkaradeva was the pioneer, namely, in *Bargīt*, devotional song, and *Aṅkīyā nāṭ*, one-act play. Both were new literary types in Assamese. These compositions were not couched in homely Assamese as the poems of *Kīrtana* or the *kāvyas*. These were written in an archaic speech called Brajabuli, a mixed Mai-

[1] Colophon. [2] The natural condition. [3] God.

thili-Assamese dialect said to have been used by Kṛṣṇa and the Gopīs in the epic age. This literary medium was in vogue among the mediaeval Vaiṣṇavite poets of Bengal, Bihar and Orissa. It is difficult to guess why Śaṅkaradeva made a departure from the popular language of his poems and chose Brajabuli for his devotional lyrics and plays. The reason may be that Brajabuli as a language had less use of compound consonants, a preponderance of vowels, an alliterative fineness of texture, and a subtlety of implication, and these phonetic and other traits may be said to have made it a more flexible medium for lyric compositions. In addition to this flexibility, some element of sacredness was associated with this artificial language, as it was traditionally considered to be the hallowed language of Vraja (Vṛndāvana). This archaic language with a deeper tone and feeling was employed to "meet requirements which do not arise in ordinary speech", and it immensely succeeded in interpreting the Vaiṣṇavite renaissance. Śaṅkaradeva was our first great poet to use this artificial language, and superb was the use he made of it in his *Bargīts* and *Aṅkīyā nāṭs*. The Buddhist *Caryāpadas* may be said to have served for structural models of these *Bargīts*.

The *Bargīts* are far more poetical than the *kāvyas* and more passionate even than the *ākhyānas* of *Kīrtana*. The growing popularity of music and the requirements of the devotional services made Śaṅkaradeva compose a large number of *Bargīts*, the most beautiful psalms in Assamese literature even today. Śaṅkaradeva's *Bargīts* have for their principal matter religious experience, philosophic reflection on the world and on morality, poignant introspection of the self, spiritual anguish, and yearning for illumination. Some of them speculate on the nature of God, His relation to man, His boundless compassion, the burden of human existence, the way of liberation, and so forth. Others are exhortatory, urging men to 'chant the name of Hari', to 'think of Govinda', 'to rest on the feet of Rāma,' 'to leave the illusory pleasures of the world', and so on. Each one of the *Bargīts* invariably concludes with a fervent prayer for shelter at the feet of Govinda and deliverance from suffering.

In the *Bargīts* we find Śaṅkaradeva at his most exalted

moments. Here he exhibits his power of fusing philosophical thought with lyrical feeling in a language at once felicitous and graceful. Numerous are the similes, metaphors, alliterations and other figures of speech used in these hymns making them enjoyable and appealing. The popularity of *Bargīts* grew rapidly and a large number of such hymns were composed by later poets. Among these writers, there are also women. The best compositions are those of Mādhavadeva, who himself was a master musician.

Another type of Śaṅkaradeva's poetry is known as *Catihā.* During his pilgrimage at Banaras, Śaṅkaradeva probably met some disciples of Kabīr and heard their recital of Kabīr's *Cautisā* verses, which might have impressed him much. The *Cautisā* is an exposition of the religious significance of the consonants of the alphabet. Just as in Chaucer's A B C, the verses begin with the successive letters of the Latin alphabet, the lines in this form of composition begin with the successive consonants of the Sanskrit alphabet. Their reproduction in Assamese resulted in the *Catihās.*

The *Aṅkīyā nāṭs* have both a sensuous and an intellectual appeal. These plays exercised a tremendous influence on the national and cultural life of Assam; they led to the growth of the popular stage, and development of music and dancing. The drama represents a spectacle and its appeal in an age when printing was unknown was profound. Although first used mainly as a means of promoting the cause of Assamese Vaiṣṇvism by their spectacular appeal to the people at large, these plays of Śaṅkaradeva have continued to exercise an abiding influence on the common folk of Assam to this day. They have inspired Assamese poetry and led to the creation of a special type of narrative poem called *Bhaṭimā.* Further in the *Aṅkīyā nāṭs* is found the first Assamese prose: a prose sinewy, musical and elevated.

Of Śaṅkaradeva's dramas *Kālī-damana* (*Subjugation of the serpent Kālī*), composed at Bardova about 1518, *Patnī-prasāda* (*Favour to Wives*), written about 1521 at Dhuvahata, *Rāsa-krīḍā* or *Kelī-Gopāla* (*Sport with the milkmaids*) (1540), *Rukmiṇī-haraṇa* (*Abduction of Rukmiṇī*), *Pārijāta-haraṇa* (*The theft of the flower Pārijātā*) and *Rāma-vijaya* (*The Conquest of Rāma*), the last composed at Cooch-Behar in 1568 at the request of King Naranārāyaṇa, are now extant. The first three plays were based on scriptural materials drawn mainly from the *Bhāgavata*. *Rukmiṇī-haraṇa* and *Pārijāta-haraṇa* are adaptations respectively from *Harivaṁśa* and *Viṣṇu Purāṇa*; the story of *Rāma-vijaya* is taken mainly from the *Rāmāyaṇa*. The stories of all these plays have a happy ending. The story of each play being pre-determined and presentation being mainly confined to ecclesiastical propaganda rather than artistic representation, the playwright had to work under serious limitations. Śaṅkaradeva was a preacher first and artist afterwards. So he selected the episodes that served his proselytising purpose. Nevertheless, even under these limitations, in some of his plays, particularly in *Rukmiṇī-haraṇa*, *Pārijāta-haraṇa* and *Rāma-vijaya*, he could break new ground. Even in the small canvas of these plays, the main characters stand out in bold relief.

The growth of *Aṅkīyā nāṭs* was influenced by the earlier practice of reciting *kāvyas* and *sāstras* in social and religious congregations. Prior to the composition of the *Aṅkīyā nāṭs*, Śaṅkaradeva himself had written a set of *kāvyas* which were used in such recitals. He realised the effectiveness of the dramatic medium in propagating his cult—an effectiveness greater than that of merely reciting the story as in the *kāvyas* whose appeal was aural and not visual.

It should also be noted that when he wrote his *Aṅkīyā nāṭs*, Śaṅkaradeva was a much-travelled man, having led a pilgrim's life for twelve years, visiting most of the sacred places of northern and southern India. It may be surmised that he had seen the dramatic entertainments like *Rāmlīlā*, *Rāslīlā*, *Yātrā*, *Kathaka*, *Yakṣagāna*, *Bhāgavatam* and *Bhavai*, popular at the time in other parts of India. On his return home, he immediately seized the opportunity of turning the *kāvya* type of entertainment into the dramatic, and put the stories of the *Bhāgavata Purāṇa* into action by living performances.

During Śaṅkaradeva's time, there were other kinds of popular dance and dramatic entertainments in Assam such a temple dance, Deodhani-*nāc*, Putala-*nāc* and Oja-Pali performances. The choral singing of Oja-Pali was extremely popular, and it continues till today as a very common entertainment in our villages. The Oja-Pali party usually consists of four to five singers, and is divided into two groups, each singing in chorus. The leader is called Oja, and his companions are called Palis. One of the Palis is called Daina Pali, the right-hand or the chief assistant of the Oja. The leader extemporises or unfolds the story, recites the refrain, and the Palis repeat the refrain by playing on cymbals and keeping time with the movements of their feet. In interpreting the verse-narrative, the Oja uses dramatic gestures, expressions, and movements. Occasionally, in the middle of the performance, the Oja pauses and converses with the Daina Pali by way of expounding the story in order to give the entertainment the appearance of a dramatic dialogue. This pre-Vaiṣṇavite Oja-Pali dance-recital might have given to Śaṅkaradeva the basic idea for the production of *Ankīyā* plays. It may, therefore, be reasonably presumed that the recital of *kāvyas*, Oja-Pali choral singing, and spectacular shows of other parts of India, might have jointly contributed to the rise of the fully developed drama in Assamese.

Though the *Aṅkīyā* plays[1] have largely been developed out of native and indigenous materials, the influence on it of the Sanskrit drama and dramaturgy is also perceptible to a great extent. Śaṅkaradeva himself styled these dramatic compositions *nāṭ* and *nāṭakas* after the Sanskrit names. Other titles used by the Vaiṣṇava poets for this type of play are *Yātrā*, *Nṛtā*, and *Aṅka*. The shorter plays of Mādhavadeva are called *Jhumurā*. The more popular name, however, is *Aṅkīyā nāṭ*. These plays, however, bear no resemblance to the Aṅka type of Rūpakas[1] in Sanskrit. *Aṅkīyā nāṭ* is a generic term in Assamese and means a dramatic composition in a single act depicting the articles of Vaiṣṇava faith.

In technique, too, these *Aṅkīyā nāṭs* follow to a certain extent the texts on Sanskrit dramatic theory, particularly with reference to use of Sanskrit verses and *nāndī*, the introduction of the role of Sūtradhāra,[2] and performance of the preliminaries (Pūrva-raṅga). Unlike as in Sanskrit plays, the Sūtradhāra is an integral part of an *Aṅkīyā nāṭ*. In

[1] A type of Sanskrit drama.
[2] The stage-manager (lit., the thread-holder).

Sanskrit dramas, the Sūtradhāra disappears altogether after the invocation. But it is different with the Assamese plays. Here, the Sūtradhāra remains all along on the stage. Further, the Sūtradhāra in an *Aṅkīyā* drama combines the functions of the producer and a running commentator. He dances with the orchestra, opens the play by reciting the *nāndi*[1] verse, introduces the characters, gives them directions, announces their exits and entrances, fills in lacunae in the action of the play by song, dance and speech, and delivers brief discourses on the ethical and spiritual points of the plot. Further, there are no acts or scenes in an *Aṅkīyā* play, and changes of scene are either announced by the Sūtradhāra in his dialogue or by orchestral singing. The *Aṅkīyā nāṭs* needed the services of the Sūtradhāra to perform all these roles to heighten and popularise the effect of the *Bhāvanā* or performance, as the audience consisted mainly of unlettered villagers who at every stage of the progress of the play required explanations. The role of the Sūtradhāra is therefore very important in an Assamese *Bhāvanā*, and even today he is necessarily a man of no mean talents. He is an actor, a trained musician, and an accomplished dancer. Wherever possible, the most artistically gifted man of the village is chosen as the Sūtradhāra to guide and conduct the play. He is trained from childhood in music, dancing and dramatic technique.

The other noteworthy characteristic of an *Aṅkīyā nāṭ* is its essentially lyrical nature. In these plays, songs and verses greatly preponderate, and the playwrights largely use them to bring home the message inculcated in the play. Many situations and incidents are suggested by mere descriptive verses uttered by the Sūtradhāra instead of being represented through action and character. Minor incidents and feelings and sentiments are at places given expression by songs. The dialogue which is introduced mainly to elaborate the lyrical sentiments in prose is very thin, though extremely musical. In these plays, the writer appears more as a poet and composer than as a dramatist. His play is not a drama in the real sense, but a 'lyrico-dramatic spectacle'.

The songs and verses of the plays bear special characteris-

[1] The benedictory verse of a drama.

tics, and they are called *Aṅkar gīt* and *bhaṭimā*. In some plays, *Bargīts*, a special type of devotional songs, are also included. Each *Aṅkiyā gīt* or dramatic song contains a *dhuvā* or refrain, and bears a particular *rāga* (melody), *tāla* (time measure) and *māna* (rhythm).

Like the Sanskrit drama most of the *Aṅkīyā* plays open with preliminaries prescribed in the orthodox *Nāṭya-śāstra* (dramaturgy), namely, *nāndī*, *prarocanā* and *prastāvanā*. In earlier Assamese plays, there are usually two *nāndī* verses with 8 or 12 feet of verse or *caraṇa*; one of this is of a benedictory nature and the other suggests the subject-matter of the play. Some of the later plays totally discarded the *nāndī* verse in Sanskrit and in its place introduced a benedictory poem in Assamese. In Sanskrit drama, the general stage direction, *nāndyante sūtradhāra*, brings the Sūtradhāra after the *nāndī*, which implies that the *nāndī* was not recited by the Sūtradhāra. But in the *Aṅkīyā* plays, the *nāndī* recital is the specific function of the Sūtradhāra.

The *nāndī* being over, the Sūtradhāra announces the subject-matter of the play in a Sanskrit verse (*prarocanā*). This is invariably accompanied by a long poem in Assamese called *bhaṭimā*. Then follows the *prastāvanā*. The Sūtradhāra hears a celestial sound. On this point a discussion arises, and as it progresses the Sūtradhāra announces the names of the approaching personages. At the end of this discussion the companion (*saṇgī*) retires from the stage.

The Sūtradhāra apart, there appear two other additional characters in an Assamese play, namely the *Dūta* and *Bahuvā*. They are, however, outside the category of the dramatic personnel, and they are introduced in actual performances of the play to serve as heralds and to provide comic relief. The Dūta and Bahuvā appear on the stage to explain the reasons for eventual interruptions in the progress of the play. They also announce the change of scene and the entrance of new characters on the stage. The Bahuvā has other duties too; besides filling in gaps in the narration he is to relieve the monotony and amuse the audience as best as he can by his skits and jokes which he himself invents, of course, in rigid conformity with traditional practices. He, however, is never allowed to interfere with the organic part of the play.

Just as the play begins with a characteristic benediction, so it ends with a prayer in Assamese called *mukti-maṅgal bhaṭimā*, where, the Sūtradhāra begs forgiveness of God for any faults of omission or commission in the management of the drama. Lastly, he emphasises the moral effect of the play, and desires his audience to follow the path of righteousness.

The most striking feature of the staging of an *Aṅkīyā nāṭ* is the co-ordination and harmony of the four elements—song, rhythmic representation by dance, melody emanating from appropriate instruments, and dialogue. We have already referred to the lyrical nature of the *Aṅkīyā nāṭ*, which abounds in songs and verses of varied forms. In an Assamese play, *Bhāvanā*, all the characters move rhythmically from the beginning to the end, in the form of dancing with appropriate steps, gestures and *abhinaya* (dramatic) postures. In short, the whole narration of the story progresses through dances, and dancing is considered one of the best arts for awakening feeling. It may be said that the Assamese dramatic performance consists mainly of movements of the limbs, rhythm forming an essential part.

In this dance-drama, the Sūtradhāra is the principal dancer. After the recitation of the *nāndī*, the Sūtradhāra interprets the story and the sentiments embodied in the sloka by appropriate dance. This is done by the Sūtradhāra all through the play. The major three dance-forms of an *Aṅkīyā Bhāvanā* are *Sūtradhāra-nāc* (dance of Sūtradhāra), *Kṛṣṇa-nāc* (dance of Krishna), and *Gopī-nāc* (dance of the milkmaids). Other forms of dances are *Rāsa-nāc*, *Natuvā-nāc* and *Cali-nāc*; all are more or less adapted from classical texts on dancing.

Before the recital of the *nāndī* verse, an Assamese *Bhāvanā* displays a prolonged series of dances by the Gāyan-Bāyan party with the Sūtradhāra as its leader. This is called *Dhemālī* or *Raṅga*. It consists of singing and dancing of an invocative and devotional nature by the orchestra or Gāyan-Bāyan with accompaniment, mainly, of *khol* (drum) and *tāla* (cymbal). The essential aim of these preliminary dances known as *saru-dhemāli*, *bara-dhemāli*, *deva-dhemāli*, *ghoṣā-dhemāli*, and so on and so forth, is to secure the favour of God for the play to be presented. Sometimes these preliminaries continue unceasingly for several hours before the actual performance of the play.

The *dhemāli* or musical prelude very much resembles the *pūrvaraṅga*, the preliminaries mentioned in Bharata's *Nāṭya-śāstra*, and as in the Sanskrit plays it does not form a part of the drama proper. According to Bharata, the *pūrvaraṅga* has twenty different constituent elements of which nine are performed behind the curtain and the rest on the stage. In later dramatic practice, this elaborate procedure underwent a considerable cut. This happened in the Assamese performances also; the occurrence in *Aṅkīyā nāṭ* of the expression *alam ativistreṇa* (no use elaborating) after the recitation of the *nāndī* is a pointer to the fact. At the end of the performance the instrumental music and dance are repeated. The end of an incident in the play is also marked by the playing of the orchestral music and dance of the Sūtradhāra, which serve as a welcome relief.

The *Aṅkīyā nāṭs* were written more with a religious motive than for secular enjoyment. Hence they were staged in the village Nāmghar (the prayer-hall), on occasions like Janmāṣṭamī, Dolyātrā and Rāsa-Pūrṇimā. Later on, they came to be staged on festive occasions, for example, on full-moon nights, during seed-time and harvest, and whenever the villagers were free from agricultural work. Sometimes special houses and temporary sheds or *rabhās* are constructed for such dramatic performances. Mādhavadeva is said to have set up at Barpeta a big hall called *barghara* or *raṅgiyāl-ghara* to stage his plays *Bhojana Vihāra* and *Dadhi Mathana*.

The Nāmghar is the common property of the villagers, where they meet each evening to listen to the recitations of the sacred scriptures by the Pāṭhaka, and to join the evening prayer. During the day, the Nāmghar becomes a seat of justice where major village disputes are settled and topics of local interest are discussed by the leading villagers. On festive occasions, it converts itself into a public theatre. So the Nāmghar plays a significant part in the social and religious life of the Assamese people. It has not only preserved the cultural traditions of Assam but immeasurably helped the growth and development of Assamese music, dance and drama.

The Nāmghar is a two-roofed thatched structure generally measuring more than fifty feet in length, and is rectangular in shape (like the *vikṛiṣṭa* type of play-house mentioned in the *Nāṭya-śāstra*). Close to it, at one end, is built a small house called the *Maṇikuṭ* (*garbhagṛha* of a Hindu temple), where an image or a copy of a religious scripture is placed on a *siṁhāsana*, a wooden throne. Except the initiated few, others are not allowed inside the Maṇikuṭ. The Nāmghar consists of two wings. The one near the Maṇikuṭ is reserved for the Adhikār, the pontiff, who usually presides over the performance, and for the Brahmanas; and the other for the actors. The side close to the entrance forms the general auditorium (*raṅga-maṇḍapa*) where the audience sit on mats or on the bare ground. There are two rows of pillars in the middle of the hall, and seats near some are reserved for distinguished visitors. About two-thirds of the space between the rows of pillars make the stage or *raṅga-bhūmi*, which has no raised platform. The orchestra and the actors sit surrounding the space meant for the stage. There is no other special arrangement for the stage than an *ārkāpor* (*paṭī* or *apaṭī* of a Sanskrit play), a white curtain which is used when the principal actors come out from the *cho-ghar* (Skt. *chadma-gṛha*), the green room, situated near the Nāmghar. All the actors do not appear on the stage at the same time; they wait in the *cho-ghar* till their presence on the stage is announced by the Sūtradhāra. Sometimes, after playing their parts in a particular scene, they do not leave the stage but sit with the orchestra awaiting their next appearance.

The general term for actors in Assamese is *Bhāvarīyā* (from Skt. *bhāvatā*), i.e., one who produces *bhāva* or emotion in the mind of the audience. Those who play the dance-roles are called *nartaka*, *naṭuvā* or *naṭa* (as they represent the actions of others). Those who supply the orchestra are called *gāyan*, the singer, and *bāyan*, the instrumental musician.

Then, as now, there were no professional actors; they were recruited from the villagers. Assamese acting is thus the work of amateurs. The roles of the principal characters of Kṛṣṇa and Rāma and their consorts are played by handsome young men specially of the higher castes, as they in their dramatic roles have to receive the obeisance of the other actors and of the audience. These actors are supposed to observe a fast before the *Bhāvanā* is presented. Female roles are performed generally by teen-agers having a feminine appearance.

Unlike, however, as with the earlier Sanskrit theatre, the reputation of actors of an Assamese *Bhāvanā* was never low nor dishonourable. Even men of erudition, great artistic attainments and high social, religious, and political status played roles in an Assamese *Bhāvanā* without loss of prestige and honour.

The Adhikār, when present at a performance, becomes *prekṣapati*, the guest of honour or *sabhāpati*. He receives obeisance from the actors as well from the audience. The audience is addressed as *sabhāsad* or *sāmājik*.

The actors have special sets of dresses. These are preserved in the house of the *khanikar*, a painter and maker of wooden and earthen images by profession. His services are indispensable to the actors. He makes the image of God for worship, prepares the effigies (*cho*) and masks (*mukhā*), makes arrangements for necessary costumes required in different performances, constructs the weapons of battle, such as sword, shield, bow and arrow, discus, club, etc., helps in the general make-up of the actors in the green-room, and has to provide *āriyā* and *matā*, that is, the torches, when the performance takes place at night. The *khanikar* or the maker of the masks is a man of many attainments, and his services are used mainly for the prerequisites outside the stage. He derives his inspiration and his skill in the arts from an accumulated fund of hereditary knowledge. He has not only imagination and ability required to make grotesque and fantastic life-size masks, but has also, to execute them properly, an accurate knowledge of human physiognomy and of the nature of the animal world, and, above all, a full acquaintance with the dramatic requirements.

Besides masks, the dress and appearance of the characters are very carefully made up as regards both design and colour. The Sūtradhāra wears a *ghuri* or crinoline with broad lace-buttons and flowing to the ankle; a *phatau* or a vest with or without sleeves, and a colourful *karadhani* or waist-band. He ties a particular type of turban (*pāg*) to his head. The gāyan-bāyan troupe wear a costume like that of the Sūtradhāra but of simpler designs and homelier materials. The other male characters put on *dhuti* coming down to the knee and a waist-coat. These may be colourful and embroidered according to the rank of the character who wears them. The costumes for female roles are carefully chosen, their main dress consisting of *mekhelā* (flowing skirt), *rihā* (breast-cloth) and *chādar* (shawl). They wear ornaments in profusion, of course, of tinsel.

The actors use paints for their make-up, befitting their roles. The conspicuous paints are generally prepared by mixing *heṅgul* (cinnabar) and *hāitāl* (yellow-orpiment). The different colours, whether used singly or in combination, have traditional significance; for example, Kṛṣṇa, with his long head-dress, called *kiriṭī*, is painted in *śyāma* i.e., blue-black, a Brahman or mendicant in white, a violent and brutal man in red, the devils in black.

Effigies and masks were probably in use in Assam, especially in popular dancing, prior to the introduction of the drama by Śaṅkaradeva. We have a reference to that effect in the first show, namely, *Chihnayātrā*, produced by Śaṅkaradeva and his companions, where a mask was worn by Garuḍa, the vehicle of Viṣṇu. The variety of masks that are used in Assamese *Bhāvanā* may be classified into three types: (i) those representing grotesque forms or hideous persons, such as Rāvaṇa, the king of the Rākṣasas; Kumbhakarṇa, his brother; Yama, the god of death; Hanumān, the lord of monkeys, etc.; (ii) those for different animal-actors such as Garuḍa, Kālīya-serpent, boar, monkeys, Jatāyu-bird, etc.; (iii) the comic masks of the buffoons and the jesters.

Masks that cover the head and the face are generally in use. But in many performances elaborate life-size effigies are indispensable, particularly in *Rāvaṇa-badh*, *Kālīya-daman*, and *Syamanta-haraṇ*. In *Rāvaṇa-badh Bhāvanā*, a life-size mask with ten heads and as many as a hundred hands is worn by Rāvaṇa; Kumbhakarṇa and Hanumān have also respective life-size masks. In *Kālīya-daman* and in *Syamanta-haraṇ* life-size masks are worn by Kālīya-serpent and by Jambuvanta, the bear-king with whom Kṛṣṇa fought to rescue the gem *syamanta*.

To make them light in weight and make movements easy with them on, large-size masks are made of bamboo splinter-bars and cloth. The buffoons wear small masks prepared from clay, cloth, rough paper and tree-bark; the bark of the plaintain tree is also used to serve temporary purposes. Head-dresses and upper masks, i.e., masks for head and face, are carved out of wood and hard bark-sheet.

In most cases, the time of performance of a *Bhāvanā* is in the evening, and it continues all through the night. Sometimes it starts in the afternoon and then goes on till night. The presentation of smaller plays such as Mādhavadeva's *Cor-dharā* or *Pimparā Guchuvā* is of shorter duration and ends before nightfall. No play, however, is presented in the early hours of the morning. Further, *Bhāvanās* are mostly presented during the winter months beginning from Māgha (mid-January) to Vaiśākha (mid-April), i.e., after the harvesting and before the commencement of ploughing season, a period when the villagers are practically free from work in the fields. On occasions, a number of villages assemble together and for several days continuously present different plays both day and night. They are called *Bāra-kheliyā Bhāvanās*, i.e., *Bhāvanās* performed by several *khels* (guilds).

Thus this new genre of literature, combining different forms of art and giving them a composite expression of its own, happens to be the most remarkable phenomenon in the history of Assamese literature. Although an ethico-religious mood is the dominant note of the *Aṅkīyā nāṭs*, they have admirably dovetailed the dance-tradition of the soil into the classical tradition of drama and music along with occasional gleanings of art-fragments from different parts of India.

It is true that the Vaiṣṇavite movement gave a tremendous impetus to the development of Assamese literature in various directions, but the personality and the genius of Śaṅkaradeva gave it a galloping momentum. Śaṅkaradeva was himself a source of infinite inspiration to contemporary writers. His devout disciple Mādhavadeva, another literary luminary of the time, composed lyrics and dramas at the suggestion of his guru. The circumstances of the compilation of *Nāma-ghoṣā* or *Hājāri-ghoṣā* by Mādhavadeva, a treatise of philosophical verses, are vividly described in *Kathā-guru-carit*. Mādhavadeva undertook the translation of Viṣṇupurī Sannyāsī's *Bhakti-Ratnāvalī* and composed the *kāvya*, *Rājasūya*, at the request of Śaṅkaradeva. According to tradition, the first couplet of each of the texts of *Nāma-ghoṣā* and *Bhakti-Ratnāvalī* was composed by Śaṅkaradeva as a mark of his kind regard for his disciple. Rāma Sarasvatī, another prodigious contemporary writer, undertook to translate the *Mahābhārata* at the suggestion of Śaṅkaradeva. His indebtedness to Śankara was very great. An interesting story is told regarding the translation of some sections of Book X of the *Bhāgavata Purāṇa* by the Brahmana Ananta Kandalī. In a dream Ananta Kandalī was directed to partake of the remains of Śaṅkara's meals; when the Brahmana asked Śaṅkara for them, the latter refused to offer them but instead, entrusted Ananta Kandalī with the rendering of the remaining sections of Book X of the *Bhāgavata Purāṇa*, which Śaṅkara himself had previously undertaken to translate. Most of the other poets who translated different books of the *Bhāgavata* were either directly commissioned by Śaṅkaradeva or inspired by his immediate disciples to undertake the translations.

After all that has been said above, any special treatment of the dominant motif of Śaṅkaradeva's writings is hardly needed. His literature was meant chiefly for didactic ends and was intended to propagate the Vaiṣṇavite movement. In tone, colour and form, it is predominantly religious and, therefore, suffers from certain limitations. As religion and morality are inseparable, his writings give much emphasis on the ethical aspects of religion. Śaṅkaradeva, at many places with apt illustrations from the epics and the *Purāṇas*, extolled such virtues as *satya*, truth, *dayā* or *kṛpā*, mercy, *dāna*, charity, *ahiṁsā*, non-injury, *kṣamā*, forgiveness, *anasuyatā*, absence of envy, *dhṛti*, patience, *śraddhā*, respect and *dama*, control of senses. The vices that lead to misery and destruction are enumerated as follows: *kāma*, sensual pleasure, *krodha*, anger, *lobha*, desire, *moha*, delusion, *māna*, pride, *mātsarya* or *asūyā*, envy and jealousy. In spite of the predominance of these religious and ethical matters, there are magnificent and inspired utterances that have a universal appeal and touch the chords of every human heart. In many of them we have the true religion of man for all ages.

We have already noticed that Nature too has some place in Śaṅkaradeva's writings. In fact, his brilliant descriptions of Nature were largely instrumental in transmuting much of his religious slag to rich lyrical quartz. The poet took rapturous delight in lingering over the beauties of rivers, oceans, groves, forests, and mountain scenery. He portrayed them as they presented themselves to his eyes, and did not project his own feelings and sentiments into them. Although not attempting to discover any spiritual message, he saw, like Gerard Manley Hopkins, God's grandeur in every beauty of Nature. His famous descriptions of Divya Upavana in the *Haramohana* or the Citrakūṭa in *Gajendra Upākhyāna* are pointers to the fact. Each one of them exhibits the author's penetrating and sensitive observation of Nature and unfolds a kaleidoscopic landscape.

In literary conventions, modes, and figures of speech Śaṅkaradeva closely adhered to the canons of Sanskrit poetics and followed the classical traditions. Most of the images, expressions, and ideas used in his poetry were drawn from the traditional Sanskrit poets; as for instance, the comparison of the lovely suppleness of a body to a flash of lightning (*vijuli rekhā*) or burnt gold (*tapta suvarṇa*), of the thigh to the trunk of an elephant (*kari-kara*) or the stem of a plantain tree, of the neck to a conch (*kambu-kaṇṭha*), of the arms to the rounded body of a serpent (*valita bhujaṅga*), of the forearms to lotus stalk (*mṛṇāla-daṇḍa*), of the fingers to the petals of campaka flower (*campaka-pāpari*) or to sticks of gold (*kanaka-śalākā*), of the eye to a new lotus petal or to a cakova bird, of the eye-brows to Cupid's bow, of the side-long glance to Cupid's arrow, of the face to the moon, of the nose to a sesamum flower, of the redness of the lips to a 'banduli' flower or a ripe bimba fruit (both are as red as ripe cherries), of well-formed teeth to a string of pearls or the seed of a pomegranate, of the breasts to badari fruits or goodly jars, of movement to that of a swan (*rājahaṁsa*) or an elephant (*gajagait*) or a lion's (*mṛgarāja*), of the voice to that of a cuckoo, and hundreds of others of such stereotyped comparisons. Among various figures of speech alliteration, which helps to create impressions of different sounds and produce marvellous melody, permeates all his poetry.

Of the figures of sense, similes of various types are a very favourable device and are frequently employed to elaborate an idea. Sometimes a series of similes run through a stanza to drive home one and the same fact. To suggest Śiśupāla's undeserving desire to marry Rukmiṇī, no less than a dozen similes are piled on each other:

'This Śiśupāla [Rukmiṇī says] comes to marry me: my life has taken a better turn indeed; with what cheek has he come to marry me? As a fox would feed on the lioness, as a baby would snatch at the moon, as the frog in the corner would long for nectar, so would Śiśupāla desire me. As the crow would feed on the offerings made at a yajña, as the degraded Brāhmaṇa would covet great gifts, as the Brāhmaṇa-slayer would aspire for heaven, so would King Śiśupāla desire me. He talks of being husband to Rukmiṇī. But who would shut her eyes setting aside Mādhava, the Lord of the three worlds, and choose Śiśupāla? What man would ignore the lion and ask for the pig? Who would ignore milk and drink the water in which fish has been washed.

Śaṅkaradeva's writings are also rich in other *alaṁkāras*. A feature which made his writings acceptable to the popular mind is the use of proverbs in surprising numbers. These pithy sayings, racy of the soil, are used to illustrate facts of ordinary life, moral precepts and the wisdom of the common man.

Whatever be the merits or limitations of Śaṅkaradeva's writings, they have been for the last five centuries a source of delight, inspiration, consolation and wisdom to the Assamese people. In his own age Śaṅkaradeva was acclaimed as a master poet, and his compositions became the touchstone and criterion of poetic excellence during succeeding generations. The Assamese honour him for greatly developing the resources of their language, for widening the imaginative range of their literature, and for raising it to classical elegance and richness by imparting to it what is good and beautiful in Sanskrit. We may say after Mādhavadeva that "formerly the streams of love-nectar flowed only within the confines of Heaven, until Śaṅkara came and breached the embankments; and lo, now it flows tumultuous through all the world!" Despite change of outlook, shifting of ideals, and birth of new literary forms, Śaṅkaradeva's writings have come to stay with us as a standard and measure of great poetry. Even today his one-act plays are acted, the *bargīts* are sung, and the *kāvyas* are read with enthusiasm. We treasure them as part of our national, cultural and spiritual heritage.

The next outstanding figure in the Assamese Vaiṣṇavite movement is Mādhavadeva, the favourite disciple of Śaṅkaradeva. He blazed across the literary firmament of Assam, a spectacular phenomenon. He was born in 1492 at Letekuphkhuri in Lakhimpur. He was originally a Śākta, but when he came in contact with Śaṅkaradeva, the latter completely won him over to his cult. From then Mādhavadeva became Śaṅkaradeva's shadow, his most accomplished and faithful follower. The Vaiṣṇavite movement gained a great impetus by his conversion, for in him was a remarkable force of intellect and strength of character, imperative requisites for a great social and religious reformer. A master of the traditional learning of the time, he was also a mellifluous singer. Almost against the wishes of Śaṅkaradeva Mādhavadeva remained a celibate throughout his life, and his ideal brought into being a monastic order called Kewaliyas (life-celibates). In fact Mādhavadeva is regarded as the real founder of the Satra institution, for he placed it on a firmer footing and introduced a very rigorous and disciplined monastic code. Further, he advocated complete allegiance to his guru Śaṅkaradeva, and enjoined the vow of chastity and poverty. After Śaṅkaradeva's death, when the apostolic mantle fell on him, the rigorous monastic life strictly enjoined by Mādhavadeva on all *ācāryas*[1] and disciples became a cause of rift and schism in the Mahapurushiyā[2] community.

The first literary work of Mādhavadeva is *Janmarahasya*, a small poem on the creation and destruction of the world based on the Puranic theory. His next work is versification of the *Bhakti-Ratnāvalī* of Viṣṇupurī Sanyāsī. This important book on the Bhakti cult was rendered into Assamese verse by Mādhavadeva at the direction of his master, Śaṅkaradeva, and in his translation the author borrowed materials from

[1] Preceptors. [2] Śaṅkarite sect.

the commentary *Kāntimāla*. Mādhavadeva also rendered the *Ādi-kānda* (Book I) of the *Rāmāyaṇa*. One of his popular works is the *Rājasūya yajña*. The subject-matter of the poem was borrowed from the *Mahābhārata* episode of the Rājasūya sacrifice of the Pāṇḍavas. The book is written in a very popular style and incorporates many interesting episodes. The poet here and there reveals his indebtedness to Māgha and other classical Sanskrit poets.

With the production of these works the genius of Mādhavadeva came of age. His writings ranged from the simplest and sweetest works of poetry to most difficult writings on abstruse metaphysical subjects. He marshalled all his varied powers born of his penetrative intellect, comprehensive knowledge, and deep erudition to establish Śaṅkaradevas' system on a firm and secure foundation. Viewed from this point Mādhavadeva's *magnum opus*, the supreme achievement of Assamese Vaiṣṇavite hymnic rapture, the *Nāma-ghoṣā*, known also as *Hājāri-ghoṣā* (a book of thousand couplets), occupies a unique place in the philosophical literature of Assam, nay of India. It is not only widely read but memorised and freely quoted as scriptural text, and thus, without a doubt, is an enduring prop of Assamese Vaiṣṇavism. The philosophy of Mādhavadeva as revealed in *Nāma-ghoṣā* divides itself into different sections, namely, Māyā, its nature and effects; cosmology; the Brahman; means of self-realisation; psychology of the Jīva; the goal of human life.

At the very outset *Nāma-ghoṣā* explains that just as a dreaming man believes in the dream world which is his own creation, the individual self under the influence of Māyā forgets its true nature—the pure self, and takes the unreal world, a creation of Māyā, as real. That is why Mādhavadeva says, "Thy Avidyā (illusion), Oh Hari, has so bewildered and bewitched me that I do not know Thee in Thy essence (or Reality)." He clearly says all that is seen and extended in forms is nothing but Māyā, and as such all of it should be rooted out from the mind.

According to Hinduism, the creation of the world is not out of nothing. The *Bhāgavata* says that the world is created, made to stay and dissolved by Kṛṣṇa. The *Nāma-ghoṣā* solves the problem by saying that quite distinct from Puruṣa and Prakṛti and yet the cause and upholder of the two is Parameśvara Nārāyaṇa.

In this world, the 'inhabiter' or the 'indweller' (Puruṣa) has two forms; the Kṣara (perishable) and the Akṣara (imperishable). The Supreme (Uttama Puruṣa) is otherwise called Paramātman, the Immutable, and the Lord upholds the three worlds having interpenetrated them.

Thus there exists nothing but Brahman. Brahman alone is true in essence. He is all-pervading, in all space and in all time. Mādhavadeva says, "I bow down to Thee again and again, O Eternal, unstained one! Thou art the Reality, the everlasting Nārāyaṇa, Śiva, the Infinite without beginning, the Absolute without attributes. Thou art Bhagavanta, the Supreme Puruṣa, who has no antecedent or subsequent, neither beginning nor end. Thou art the only consciousness that thinkest out the whole universe." In short, *Nāma-ghoṣā* maintains that the universe is nothing but a manifestation of God.

The *Nāma-ghoṣā* says that Brahman is Eternal, Infinite Good, Benevolent, Permanent, All-pervading, one without a second, and beyond all change. In essence all apparent variety in name and form is nothing but Brahman. Brahman is beyond space, time or causation. It is absolutely pure, perfect, impartite, and indestructible. It is of the nature of pure consciousness. Anything which is not in the beginning and not at the end necessarily does not exist in the middle. Thus Brahman is like the vast expanse of the sky, the beginning or the end of which is unfathomed. It is Brahman that creates, preserves and destroys the universe.

The Brahman is both immanent and transcendental. It pervades all the three worlds and is yet apart from them. It is beyond the three qualities, beyond merit and demerit. It is Sama,[1] Narottama[2], Nirvikāra[3], Nirañjana[4]. Above all, Brahman is Sahajānanda[5], Svarūpānanda[6], and Paramānanda.[7]

Mādhavadeva believed in Incarnations because his unmanifested and unqualified God may be brought to manifest

[1] Equality. [2] Best of men. [3] The unchanged.
[4] The unstained. [5] Whose joy is spontaneous.
[6] Whose very nature is spontaneous. [7] Supreme joy.

Himself by virtue of devotion. *Nāma-ghoṣā* speaks of the following ten Avatāras (Incarnations): viz.,[1] Matsya, Kūrma, Narasiṁha, Vāmana, Paraśurāma, Hālīrāma, Varāha, Śrī Rāma, Buddha, and Kalki. Thus the idea of Brahman of Brahmanising the soul is the keynote of *Nāma-ghoṣā's* thought and religion.

According to *Nāma-ghoṣā*, there are two steps to self-realisation: Bhakti and Grace of Guru. *Nāma-ghoṣā* considers the path of devotion to be the easiest of all. It is even superior to Jñāna (Knowledge), Karma (Action), and Yoga (Contemplation). Knowledge and action cannot save one where devotion does not avail. It further says: "Contemplation is prescribed for Satya-yuga, Jñāna for the Tretā, Pūjā or ceremonial rites for the Dvāpara; in the Kali-yuga,[1] however, there is no other religion than chanting the name of Hari." Devotion alone helps one to cross the ocean of the world. This alone is the path to salvation.

The devotional recitation of the name of Hari is regarded as the supreme religion of the Kali-yuga. He who wears constantly the invulnerable amulet of the name of Rāma and Kṛṣṇa is no more pierced by the strokes of the weapons consisting of the three guṇas, Satva, Rajas and Tamas. The importance of the chanting of the name of Hari may be known from the fact that even the demon king Hiraṇyakaśipu who put his son, Prahlād, to various tortures could not, however, remove a hair from his body because of the magic influence of the great amulet of Harinām. There is no necessity of reading various Śāstras, the Vedas, Tantras etc., neither is there any need of visiting numerous sacred places. If you want to be free from the sufferings of the world, take to this means of your safety and salvation: utter constantly the word, Govinda.[1]

Nāma-ghoṣā lays great stress on the help of the *Guru* (Preceptor). The service of the Guru as the chief cause of self-realisation is emphasised. It lays the highest stress on Guru-Bhakti (devotion to the Guru). The Guru, in fact, is God to his disciples. There is no difference between God and Guru. Both are one, although the Guru appears to have a

[1] *Yuga* is an age of the world. The *yugas* are four: *satya, tretā, dvāpara* and *kali.* The present is *kali*-age.

different bodily existence. The hearts of both are full of sweetness of grace; both always think of the good of the world, are devoid of pride, are pleased with others out of their own virtues.

The Guru visualises the Brahman and it is he who enables the disciple also to visualise it and thus makes him *jīvanmukta* (one who attains salvation in the flesh). Only the Guru is competent to show the extremely subtle path of God-realisation, which is beyond the reach of the scriptures. Real knowledge of the Brahman cannot be had without the Guru. Thus the Guru is the real means to self-realisation.

According to *Nāma-ghoṣā*, the *Jiva* (Creature) is not different from the Brahman. Its inherent power is as infinite as the Brahman itself. But the *Ātman* (Self) fails to experience *Iśvara* (God) because of *Avidyā* (Illusion). It thinks this unreal material body to be the Atmā and commits a great offence, deeply immersed, as it were, in worldly pleasures. When Avidyā is destroyed Kṛṣṇa becomes manifest just like a thing attached to the neck. Enveloped by *Māyā* and imbued with ego, the Jīva undergoes the bondage of *Saṁsāra* (the World). Unless the ego is annihilated there is no release from Saṁsāra. *Nāma-ghoṣā* is replete with prayers to God, supplicating Him to destroy the dread of the world. Man's involvement in the cycle of birth and death is primarily due to desire. Man desires to achieve something, acts accordingly and reaps the fruit of action. That is how he goes on whirling in the endless cycle of birth and death. The only way, therefore, to self-realisation is cessation of desire once for all which alone can pave the way to the attainment of the supreme bliss.

The *sumum bonum* of all this religious quest, according to *Nāma-ghoṣā*, is the attainment of the state of Supreme Bliss. Liberation in *Nāma-ghoṣā* does not mean the realisation of identity between God and the soul. It simply means the attainment of proximity to God, a state where the Jīva continues to chant the name of Hari. As a matter of fact, the devotee does not count liberation as valuable, but remains immersed in the ocean of the joy of Rāma-Kṛṣṇa *nāma*. In other words, devotion to Kṛṣṇa is the ocean of unthinkable infinite bliss. Thus those who are single-minded and intense in their devotion do not desire any other object but remain absorbed in the ocean of great joy consisting of Kṛṣṇa's name, than which there is nothing sweeter, nothing more beneficent or wonderful.

Besides, *Nāma-ghoṣā* contains a large number of hymns on repentance and entreaty, self-discipline and self-reproach. In each of the hymns the lyric cry is predominant and ecstatic. The last few sections of the book serve as a litany consisting of eulogistic names for Lord Kṛṣṇa. *Nāma-ghoṣā* bears a universal appeal and is in perfect accord with the same class of sublime literature as the Upaniṣads and the *Gitā*. Profundity of thought, unity of outlook, and music of diction mark *Nāma-ghoṣā* as an outstanding work of art and a fitting monument to Mādhavadeva's philosophical and poetic genius.

Mādhavadeva also composed a few one-act plays (*Aṅkīyā nāṭs*) : *Cordharā, Pimparā Guchuvā, Kotorā Khelovā, Bhuṣaṅ Herovā, Bhumi Lutivā*, all presenting incidents of Kṛṣṇa's child life. These *Aṅkīyā nāṭs* of Mādhavadeva contain fewer songs and Sanskrit *slokas* than those of Śaṅkaradeva, and are therefore closer to the soil and wider in appeal.

Mādhavadeva came to be a very popular figure in the Vaiṣṇavite movement through his *Bargīts*. His piety found full expression in these impassioned devotional songs. Many of his *Bargīts* strike deep notes of contrition and humility born of knowledge of the original sin, and of the spirit of self-surrender and consecration which alone can purge off the sin. Some of them contain idyllic descriptions of Vṛndāvan with Child Kṛṣṇa as the focus. These lyrics of Mādhavadeva furnish lovely portraits of the childhood and adolescence of Kṛṣṇa, and they reflect the thoughts and sentiments which animate childhood and youth. The supernatural and extraordinary personality of the Lord Kṛṣṇa of the *Bhāgavata* becomes quite human and simple in these *Bargīts*. The incidents in Child Kṛṣṇa's life, associated as they were with Nature's beauty, here become more lively and apposite. The eternal nature of the child is revealed in the boy Kṛṣṇa, who becomes the child of today, absolutely simple, and "his very smile rains a shower of nectar". The magic of Mādhavadeva's pen has worked a renaissance of wonder and given a new import and delight to familiar episodes.

Some lyrics speak with animation of Mother Yaśodā's half-amused tolerance of the pranks and capers of the Child Kṛṣṇa. There are, on the other hand, a few songs that deal with separation too. These songs catch at the restlessness and the vague apprehensions which overtake the mother's mind when, even for a moment, Kṛṣṇa, the apple of her eye, is out of sight. It is natural that Yaśodā's heart should throb with this tremulous all-conquering love; for her child is the fruit of long and arduous penance, prayer and sacrifice, a fruit vouchsafed rather late in life. Kṛṣṇa has escaped in the morning into the streets for playing with his companions. The mother counts impatient hours at the threshold till the boy returns. "The morning is far advanced, and yet my son has not returned home," she mutters to herself. She grows apprehensive, goes into the streets, questions passers-by about Kṛṣṇa, and at last reaches the sands of the Yamunā where her son might be playing. But not discovering him there, she beats her chest, weeps, and faints. Regaining consciousness, she weeps again:

> 'She wept; tears rolled down her cheeks, and she cried,
> "Where can I find my son, the crown of Yadus?"
> And then in despair rolled in the dust.
> Such love is a heavenly sight.'

In describing such scenes of separation, Mādhavadeva has followed the traditional literary practice of laying greater stress on the depth rather than the tumult of feeling. With remarkable economy of words, the saint has woven something of the integrity of his own soul into these songs of the pangs of a mother's separation from her son. The melody, the rhythm and the sweet cadence of these songs not only transport the listener but also lull the senses into the sequent mood, namely, that of expecting her cherub to return to her lap and lisp affectionate and tender words while the mother fondles the dear thing. The Assamese Vaiṣṇavite literature has in this manner enshrined childhood beauties and motherly love in rich verse, which ennobles and exalts tender human relations even to the pitch of apotheosis. Rabindranath Tagore has made a happy remark on this deification of childhood. He says that whenever there is deep and unalloyed love, there is the Lord's true worship. Whenever we love men, there do we realise God. There is something in the small face of the child which captivates one and all. We want to understand the significance of that something, which we may call, for want of an alternative term, Beauty. This attempt to grapple with Beauty has often led men into forest recesses. Yogis have given up food and rest in search of this Beauty. But the mother gets that ambrosial and peerless Beauty in the face of the slip of a thing in her lap. In these songs, therefore, Yaśodā's son becomes merged with one's own son; the universal is reduced to the particular. The Lord of heaven has deliberately merged himself in the human child only to draw us nearer to Himself.

Mādhavadeva outlived Śaṅkaradeva by twenty-eight years, during which he mostly stayed at Ganakkuchi and Sundaridiya Satras close to the principal Satra at Barpeta. Here, Mādhavadeva came into conflict with Raghudeva, king of the Eastern Koch Kingdom. It was reported to the king that Mādhavadeva was preaching against the worship of Kāmākṣyā, the guardian deity of the Koch kings. So Raghudeva brought him to his court at Vijayanagara as a prisoner. The allegations, however, proved false and the preceptor was released with due respect. Mādhavadeva, thereafter, stayed for some time at Hajo, near the present Hayagriva Madhava temple. But here also he could not live in peace on account of the hostile activities of both the King and the Brahmanas, and therefore left for Cooch-Behar, the capital of the Western Koch Kingdom ruled then by Lakṣmīnārāyaṇa, son of Naranārāyaṇa. King Lakṣmīnārāyaṇa received him with due honour and got him and his disciples settled at Bheladuar, a village near the capital. In course of time, with the king's munificence, a Satra was established at Bheladuar, and it is recorded that some principal members of the King's family embraced the Vaiṣṇava faith and were initiated by Mādhavadeva. Mādhavadeva passed three peaceful years in this Satra and gave the final shape to his *magnum opus*, *Nāma-ghoṣā*. He died at Bheladuar in the year 1596.

The *Barīts* and *Aṅkīyā nāṭs* composed by the pioneer Vaiṣṇava leaders Śaṅkaradeva and Mādhavadeva formed the main stream of Assamese devotional writings, which was swelled by several tributaries in the course of two centuries. Śaṅkaradeva established the tradition of singing psalms, chanting hymns and reciting the scriptures during devotional services known as *prasaṅgas*, which were held at different hours of the day from dawn to dusk. Another sagacious policy of Śaṅkaradeva was the propagation of his faith through the pageant of the drama or *Aṅkīyā nāṭs*. He wisely made it a custom with the heads of monasteries or *Satrādhikāras* to compose *gīts* and *Aṅkīyā nāṭs* before their ordination as priests. All these factors not only contributed towards the growth of a rich body of Assamese literature but went a long way to spread literacy in the country. One of the early *Satrādhikārs* who wrote *gīts* and *nāṭs* was Gopāla Ātā, (1547-1611), who was appointed by Mādhavadeva as one of the twelve *Dharmācāryas* (spiritual leaders) and who founded the Kalajhar Satra and the Kalasamhati order in Śaṅkaradeva's fraternity. Śrīrām Ātā, founder of the Ahatguri Satra, and his son Rāmānanda Dvija, who was a contemporary of the Ahom king Chakradhvaj Siṁha (d. 1669), composed a large number of hymns on the earlier models, and they manifest influences of Śaṅkaradeva in feeling, thought, and diction. Echoes of Jayadeva's *Gītagovinda* are also discernible in their compositions: some of these lyrics narrate the love of Kṛṣṇa and Rādhā, a motif unknown in early Assamese Vaiṣṇavite poetry.

One interesting feature of the Vaiṣṇavite renaissance is its democratic spirit, for it encouraged learning not only among men but also among women. Kanaklatā (Lakṣmī Ai), grand-daughter-in-law of Śaṅkaradeva, wrote several hymns of dedication. She was not only the first poetess of Assam but also the first woman to be appointed head of a Satra or religious order.

Next to the *Bhāgavata*, the *Mahābhārata* exercised tremendous influence on the Vaiṣṇavite poets as this epic was also considered a Vaiṣṇavite scripture. The Vaiṣṇavite poets naturally turned it into an instrument for popularisation and propagation of their own doctrines. Many poets either translated a section from the *Mahābhārata* or adopted a story therefrom to inculcate devotion to Viṣṇu or Kṛṣṇa, to promote the study of hagiography, and to celebrate the Vaiṣṇavite ideals of renunciation, simple living, love towards all sentient beings, charity, piety, truthfulness, pilgrimage, and so on and so forth. Amongst the *Mahābhārata* poets in Assamese, Kavi Rāma Sarasvatī was the foremost. Rāma Sarasvatī was a very popular poet and also a voluminous writer who made this period famous by co-ordinating the literary activities of all the contemporary poets under the patronage of King Naranārāyaṇa. Naranārāyaṇa commissioned the poet Rāma Sarasvatī to render the *Mahābhārata* into Assamese. Rāma Sarasvatī, under different names such as Aniruddha, Kavicandra, Bhārat-bhūṣaṇ and Śrīnāth Brāhmaṇ, translated the major portion of the *Mahābhārata*. It is known from the poet himself that he composed thirty thousand verses while the other poets did only three thousand. He translated the entire *Ādi-parva* in 1993 padas. *Sabhā-parva* was done in 1073 padas with the collaboration of his son Gopīnāth Pāṭhak. The translation of *Vana-parva* together with its various *Upa-parvas* was entirely the work of Rāma Sarasvatī. The Assamese version of the *Vana-parva* contains several sections, viz., *Ādi-vana-parva* (833 padas), *Puṣpaharaṇ Vana-parva* (584 padas), *Maṇicandra Ghoṣa-parva* (1085 padas), *Vijaya-parva* (2222 padas), *Śeṣa-vana-parva* (718 padas), and *Sindhuyātrā-parva* (1842 padas). The Assamese version of the *Vana-parva* further includes *Kulāchala vadha* (1847 padas), *Baghāsur-vadha* (4125 padas), *Khatasur vadha* (182 padas), *Kurmavali-vadha* (366 padas), *Asvakarṇa-vadha* (611 padas), *Jaṅghāsur-vadha* (304 padas) and *Bhojakaṭa-vadha*. Each of these sections styled as *vadha-kāvya* is of prodigious length and is independent in conception and execution. These *Badha-kāvyas* are mainly made up of superhuman feats and exploits of the *Pāṇḍavas* mingled with various myths, legends, and fables about gnomes, demons, deities, sages and kings of antiquity. Besides imparting religious instruction and telling wonderful stories, the *Badha-kāvyas* went a great way to educate the common man in morality, truth and righteousness. Naturally, these *kāvyas* deal with problems relating to the clash between good and evil, the oppression of the righteous by the wicked, the ultimate triumph of righteousness over wickedness, and the victory of truth. These sections have very little in common with the original epic.

Besides, Rāma Sarasvatī translated *Udyoga-* and *Karṇa-parvas*, and, in collaboration with a contemporary poet, Vidyā Pañcānan, *Bhīṣma-parva*. The translation of *Droṇa-parva* was the joint work of Rāma Sarasvatī, his son Gopīnāth and Dāmodara. *Virāṭa-parva* was completed in 1321 padas mainly by Kaṁsāri Kāyastha, whose translation is in complete accord with the original. Kaṁsāri was a great Sanskrit scholar, and even Rāma Sarasvatī hails him as a poet (*kavi*) and a seer (*ṛṣi*). Some sections of this *parva* go under the name of Srimanta Gabharu Khan, 'who with great diligence composed the verses'. Other poets who translated the remaining *parvas* were Dāmodar Das (*Śalya-parva*), Jaynārāyan (*Stuṭi-parva*), Lakṣmīnāth Dvija (*Śānti-parva*), Gaṅgādās, Subudhirai and Bhavānīdās (the last three jointly rendered *Aśvamedha-parva*).

It should be mentioned here that the Assamese *Mahābhārata* is not a literal rendering of the original epic. Through compression, omission, alteration, innovation and adaptation, the Assamese version emerged as an epic of the soil. To make the narrative sweet, direct and appealing, particularly to the village people, Assamese poets have deliberately omitted most disquisitions on law, morality and abstruse philosophy. Furthermore, the Assamese recension took on the character of a Vaiṣṇava Śāstra as it was translated by Vaiṣṇava poets to disseminate the Vaiṣṇava creed. Most of the sections of the Assamese version consequently conclude with passages stamped with Vaiṣṇavite tenets, legends and traditions. Even in the principal episodes, the poets interposed several couplets in praise of *Bhakti*.

Moreover, the Assamese version freely incorporates many interludes not found in the original. In this respect its *Vana-parva* is very conspicuous. Sometimes the original incidents are elaborated with the colours of imagination and lingering relish. As an illustration, we may refer to the account of the death of Pāṇḍu. The original text has it that one day in the spring Pāṇḍu, accompanied by the beautiful Mādrī, was moving about in the woods. The king was suddenly caught with passion and forcibly embraced Mādrī. He died in the very act of gratification of his desire. According to the Assamese version, Pāṇḍu was in an assembly of sages and engaged in theological discussion. The sun was about to set and there was no indication that Pāṇḍu would rise to offer his evening prayer (*sandhyā*). Kuntī was perturbed, for Pāṇḍu would not take his evening meal if he could not perform his *sandhyā*. Kuntī, therefore, asked Mādrī to stand in the courtyard facing the sun, for the sun would be enamoured of her beauty and would not drop below the horizon. Mādrī did accordingly. When the assembly broke off, Pāṇḍu came home and was surprised to see the sun on the horizon, though the night had far advanced. On enquiry, he was told by Kuntī that it was Mādrī's beauty which had enchanted the sun to linger on the horizon. Then a fatal longing to possess Mādrī seized Pāṇḍu, and he would not listen to the counsel of Kuntī. Kuntī had to procure Mādrī for her husband, and in the union, Pāṇḍu died.

Instances of introduction of incidents relating to local history and geography are no less numerous. For example, we may cite the incidents in the Assamese versions of *Ādi-parva* and *Droṇa-parva* relating to King Bhagadatta's presence at *svayambara*[1] of Draupadī and the description of his death in the battle of Kurukṣetra.

It is natural that the vernacular recension will abound in materials relating particularly to Assamese life and culture. The instances of local colour are too numerous to be recounted here. They generally consist of vivid delineations of nature, of flora and fauna, of marriage festivities, dress and ornaments, food and drink, feast and revelry, merry-making and musical instruments. Local customs and manners are also depicted. The Assamese elements are far more discernible in the use of homely similes and metaphors, drawn from observation of rural life in Assam. The Assamese recension also offers a unique specimen of the early Assamese language. The poets used words of diverse origins and peculiar formations, many of which have now become either obsolete or obscure.

[1] 'Bride's self-choice' is a form of engagement or betrothal in which king's daughter herself chooses her husband from amongst the assembled princes and heroes (invited by her father) by placing a garland around the neck of the chosen one.

The translation of the *Mahābhārata* gave tremendous impetus to the growth and popularity of Assamese literature. It opened a golden vein of tales, romances, allegories, and myths. Even today, modern Assamese writers are drawing inspiration from its inexhaustible store of wisdom and delight. To rural folk this epic is not only an entertaining *kāvya* but also an authoritative apocalyptic text. Throughout their translations the poets again and again laid stress on the Indian ethical ideas of liberality, truthfulness, tolerance, purity of mind, body and speech, and cultivation of manly virtues. In the *Śalya-parva* it has been rightly observed that this "Śāstra satisfies religious and ethical needs and ensures material prosperity, the joys of life and spiritual deliverance."

Rāma Sarasvatī made an Assamese version of Jayadeva's *Gītagovinda*. This too is not a literal translation. The Assamese poet introduced some episodes from the *Bhāgavata Purāṇa* and elaborated and adorned some verses of the original with flowers culled from other Sanskrit texts. Further, the Assamese version was given a Vaiṣṇava bias, and to tune it with the ideals of Assam Vaiṣṇavism, the intensity of the erotic sentiment of the original was much reduced. Another very widely known and popular *kāvya* of Rāma Sarasvatī is *Bhīm-carit*. Here is an episode of Bhīm's early life as found in the *Ādi-parva* of the *Mahābhārata*. Nowhere else possibly in Assamese literature has the popular figure of Bhīm been more picturesquely drawn; a colossus of a man wielding his usual weapon, the club, exhibiting prowess like Hercules, and endowed with a gluttonous appetite. In this book in which Bhīm is pictured as having been employed by Śiva to tend his bull, Śiva's life is presented in a burlesque. Śiva is portrayed as a hardy cultivator devoid of worldly wisdom. With his consort Pārvatī and two little sons he leads a life of poverty and want. To this pleasant picture here drawn, the book owes its enormous popularity. Besides this the book has another merit; it vividly paints peasant life and the simple joys of the hearth.

Rāma Sarasvatī's son, Kalāpcandra, was also a renowned poet. He translated a portion of the Fourth Book of the *Bhāgavata Purāṇa*. But his outstanding work is *Rādhā-carit*. The book is important not so much for its language and style as for its theme. The amours of Rādhā-Kṛṣṇa are not celebrated in the writings of the Assamese Vaiṣṇavite poets. In his *Rādhā-carit* Kalāpcandra depicts the love of Rādhā-Kṛṣṇa without any of the taint of sensuousness normally attached to the hypothetical romance in the popular imagination. The author illustrates the devotional aspect of Rādhā's character; her dedication — body, mind and soul to Kṛṣṇa; her long-suffering and her undying passion for Kṛṣṇa are admirably described by the poet. In short, *Rādhā-carit* relates the triumph of the ideal of selfless devotion.

The story of the book runs thus: Rukmiṇī, proud of her devotion to Kṛṣṇa, inquired of him the name of his best devotee. Kṛṣṇa mentioned the names of many devotees, adding that none could compare with the maids (*gopīs*) of Vṛndāvan in devotion and that even among them Rādhā was peerless. This naturally aroused a feeling of jealousy in Rukmiṇī. She prayed to Kṛṣṇa that she might have a glimpse of Rādhā, and Uddhava was sent to fetch her. Uddhava found Rādhā incessantly chanting the name of Kṛṣṇa, quite oblivious of the outer world. He announced his object and also the desire of Kṛṣṇa that Rādhā should come in her former shape in all her youthful beauty and glamour. Rādhā then turned into an exquisitely lovely damsel, before whose beauty the loveliness of Rukmiṇī and Kṛṣṇa's other consorts paled into insignificance:

> Just as a lamp or the moon appears dim before the sun, so the wives of Śrī Kṛṣṇa became pale and insignificant before the indescribable refulgence of Rādhā (who shone) like a lotus in the night.'

Then Rukmiṇī and others made many rich presents to Rādhā. She refused them and told them that her only desire was that she might have the privilege of worshipping Kṛṣṇa in all her lives.

Among all the compeers of Rāma Sarasvatī there is one whose name cannot be dismissed by mere mentioning along with a group. He is Kaṁsāri Kāyastha. He enjoyed great reputation in his day as a seer. Kaṁsāri's translation of the *Mahābhārata* retains faithfully in a large measure the letter and the spirit of the original, and it far surpassed the renderings of other poets.

One other bright star of the literary firmament of the age is Ananta Kandalī. He was a Brahman of Hajo in the Kamrup District. His real name is Haricaraṇ; Ananta Kandalī is his scholastic title. But he was more popularly known by his title. A contemporary of Śaṅkaradeva at the court of Naranārāyaṇa, he accepted Śaṅkaradeva as his Guru and embraced his Vaiṣṇavite creed. As a mark of his favour Śaṅkaradeva allowed him to complete the translation of the unfinished half of the tenth canto (*skandha*) of the *Bhāgavata Purāṇa*.

Other poetical works of Ananta Kandalī are *Mahīrāvaṇ-badha*, *Harihar-yuddha*, *Vṛittāsur-badha*, *Bharat-sāvitrī*, *Jīva-stuti*, and *Kumārharaṇ-kāvya*. *Kumārharaṇ* enjoyed as great a popularity as Śaṅkaradeva's *Rukmiṇīharaṇ-kāvya*. In *Kumārharaṇ* the author narrates in a winning manner the happy romance of Uṣā and Aniruddha, a story as famous as the unhappy love of Orpheus and Eurydice or of Lancelot and Guinevere; he also rendered in excellent verse the fourth, fifth, sixth and ninth cantos of the *Bhāgavata Purāṇa*.

Sārvabhauma Bhaṭṭācārya was another great writer of the period. He himself tells us that he resided at Prāgjyotiṣpur where he was well known as a devout Śākta. He entered into a long discussion with Śaṅkaradeva about the merits of the two forms of Vaiṣṇava and Śākta worship. Defeated in dispute, he left crestfallen for Banaras to study the Hindu scriptures under a teacher named Biśveśvar Cakravartī. After five years of close study, he became, as he tells us, well-versed in the *śāstras*. At Banaras, he came across a part of the *Padma Purāṇa* which he afterwards rendered into Assamese verse under the title of *Svarga Khandha Rahasya*. At Banaras he became a worshipper of Hari, and on his return he fell at the feet of Śaṅkaradeva and became one of his disciples. Afterwards he wrote the biography of his Guru, Śaṅkaradeva. He also translated fragments of the *Bhāgavata Purāṇa* and *Bhaviṣyat Purāṇa*.

Sārvabhauma Bhaṭṭācārya's wife also was very learned scholar, and is said to have earned a warm encomium from King Naranārāyaṇa by defeating at his court the famous Bengali scholar of the time, Raghunandan Bhaṭṭācārya, in a discourse connected with the different ways of life advocated in the *Vedas* and the *Smṛtis*.

Śrīdhar Kandalī, a contemporary and a favourite disciple of Śaṅkaradeva, also deserves mention. As a mark of special favour Śaṅkaradeva allowed him to contribute a chapter, *Ghunucā Yātrā*, to his famous *Kīrtan-ghoṣā*. But his prime claim to distinction lies in a short poem called *Kāṇkhovā* (*Ear-eater*), which recants a funny nursery tale from the Kṛṣṇa legend. The Child Kṛṣṇa was crying one day. Mother Yaśodā tried to terrify him into silence by singing of the advent of a fearful demon called Kāṇkhowā. Kṛṣṇa at once took fright and quickly ran to his mother's arms imploring her to tell him what this curious demon looked like; for, as he recalled, he had not come across any such demon in all his former incarnations. Yaśodā was at her wit's end and had to confess that she was lying. Even to this day, in Assam, crying children are hushed into silence by the mention of this fictitious demon who is supposed to bite off the ears of crying children. The story has become so popular and well-known that it is heard in every Assamese nursery at dusk.

The Vaiṣṇava movement of Assam was a fragment of the all-India movement, and as such it accepted the canonical scriptures of the Vaiṣṇavas in general and did not develop a separate set of theological and philosophical scriptures of its own. Further, as Assam Vaiṣṇavism placed emphasis on devotion and self-surrender, it had not much scope for development of doctrinal works in large numbers. Of the few 'synoptic gospels' that dwelt upon Vaiṣṇava thought and theology, Śaṅkaradeva's *Bhakti-ratnākara* and *Bhakti-pradīp* have already been commented upon. Besides *Bhakti-ratnāvalī*, Mādhavadeva's *Nāma-ghoṣā* is regarded as an authoritative treatise on Vaiṣṇava philosophy. Bhaṭṭadeva's *Bhakti-viveka* in Sanskrit, Rāmacaraṇ Thākur's *Bhakti-ratna*, Narottama Thākur's *Bhakti-premāvalī*, and Gopāla Miśra's *Ghoṣā-ratna* have an established place in Assam Vaiṣṇavism because of their scholastic and authoritative expositions.

One contribution of the Vaiṣṇava writers to Assamese philosophical writings is the production of numerous commentaries on the *Gītā*, in both prose and verse. Relevant verses from the *Gītā* were first rendered into Assamese by the two saints, Śaṅkaradeva and Mādhavadeva, to expound their doctrines of devotion, liberation and incarnation. But the entire text was not available in a single comprehensive volume. This was first made available in Assamese prose by Bhaṭṭadeva with the help of Śrīdhara Svāmī's commentary. The first verse rendering was done by Govinda Miśra, a native of Kamarupa. High poetic quality and mastery of forceful Assamese are the salient features of Govinda Miśra's translation. His language is simple, chiselled and beautiful, and is easy to memorise.

Vaikuṇṭhanātha Kaviratna Bhāgavata Bhaṭṭācārya, popularly known as Bhaṭṭadeva, and believed to have flourished between 1558 and 1638, wrote *Kathā-Bhāgavata* (the *Bhāgavata* in prose) and *Kathā-Gītā* (the *Gītā* in prose). Noticing the rather early times in which *Kathā-Gītā* was composed, Acharyya Prafullachandra Ray, the renowned scientist and savant says: "Indeed the prose of *Gītā* of Bhaṭṭadeva composed in the sixteenth century is unique in its kind. . . . It is a priceless treasure. Assamese prose literature developed to a stage in the far distant sixteenth century which no other literature of the world reached except the writings of Hooker and Latimer in England."

Before assessing Bhaṭṭadeva's works it is necessary to know why he discarded the traditional verse form in favour of prose. The guiding influence in his life was Dāmodaradeva at whose behest Bhaṭṭadeva undertook to render these texts, because of their didactic and monitory qualities, into Assamese prose for the benefit of women and the submerged stratum of society. Bhaṭṭadeva was to a great extent crowned with success in his attempt. The spirit of the age, an intense and permeating interest in religion, was with him. Even a casual reader of *Kathā-Bhāgavata* and *Kathā-Gītā* can without demur say that the author has succeeded in making these works intelligible to the common people. By translating these two most sacred and edifying Sanskrit texts into Assamese and by making his language an easy and eloquent vehicle for abstract thought and profound philosophical ideas, Bhaṭṭadeva wins the reader's applause.

Bhaṭṭadeva's learning and scholarship made his style distinguished for dignity and poise. With unparalleled skill the author has employed both Assamese and Sanskrit vocables side by side for exposition of deep spiritual thoughts. His style reveals an astonishing flexibility and variety according to the subject-matter. As one reads *Kathā-Bhāgavata* one feels as if he were in the heart of a religious congregation and the scholar-divine were explaining the text with comments on and answers to possible objections to his interpretations. On the other hand, none can fully appreciate the compositional skill of *Kathā-Gītā* without entering into the atmosphere of dialogue that prevails throughout.

Although Bhaṭṭadeva's works were mainly translations, they have enough of originality in them and make pleasant reading thanks to the author's incomparable style. Further, these texts are not mere renderings from one language to another; the writer assimilated the original materials and interpreted them according to his standpoint. The author never failed to weave into the texts homely similes and familiar maxims from standard commentaries wherever they were considered illustrative of the arguments. From the standpoint of the art of translation, *Kathā-Bhāgavata* is a prominent landmark, overshadowing the other prose translations of mediaeval Assamese literature.

Bhaṭṭadeva had a profound grasp of Sanskrit grammar and literature, which earned for him the title of Bhāgavata Bhaṭṭācārya (versed in the *Bhāgavata*). Bhaṭṭadeva has several original Sanskrit works to his credit. Inevitably, therefore, Sanskrit influences, particularly that of Sanskrit syntax, tinged his Assamese writings. Besides, as these texts are translations from Sanskrit, *tatsama* words naturally creep into them; but the author is nowhere pompous because his works are not intended for the learned only. The judicious use of Sanskrit words has only invested these religious writings with dignity and grace. In syntactical structure also his writings are disciplined by Sanskrit grammar. In his *Kathā-Gītā*, however, the sentences hobble at places running to complex lengths due to the piling up of clause on clause for illustrating knotty points In spite of these occasional lapses, the syntax is regular, the verb is not dropped or shifted at will, the infinitive is not split, and clauses are not thrown in in a higgledy-piggledy fashion with utter disregard of the principles of clarity and precision.

Bhaṭṭadeva's works are a landmark in the evolution of an accomplished philosophical and narrative prose in Assamese literature. He created a sure-footed expository prose-style with an eye to grammatical perfection. His aim was to explain religious matters in a clear and logical manner. The conversational and argumentative prose style of *Kathā-Gītā* served as a model and pattern to the metaphysical Vaiṣṇavite prose-writers of later years, and the simple free light-sailing style of *Kathā-Bhāgavata* greatly influenced the writers of *Carit-puthis*.

Another very important type of literature that developed as an offshoot of the resurgence of the Vaiṣṇava movement under the direct aegis of the Satra institutions was the *Carit-puthis*, the biographies of Śaṅkaradeva. Later this tradition continued in the biographies of many other Vaiṣṇavite saints. Recitations from the biographies of saints as a source of religious inspiration to devotees are made after congregational prayers even to this day. According to *Kathā-Guru-carit* (a prose biography of Śaṅkaradeva and Mādhavadeva), it was Mādhavadeva who first introduced this practice. He was the first to undertake a daily recitation of his Guru's biography.

Biography has been described as "the most delicate and human of all the branches of the art of writing". Indeed it is a delicate art because the biographer has to restore the sense of life to a vanished figure. It is a humane art, as it partakes of all the ambiguities and incongruities of life itself. As such, the *Carit-puthis* still reward the reader and have a secure place in Assamese literature.

Most of the earlier biographies are in versified prose and, as literary productions, of doubtful worth. They are, however, very valuable as the first literary treatment of historical material. Rāmacaraṇ Ṭhākur's *Śaṅkara-carit* is the most voluminous biography in verse. Rāmacaran was the son of Mādhavadeva's sister, Urvaśī. Though contemporaneous with Śaṅkaradeva, Rāmacaraṇ could not sift fact from fiction, and so in certain places in his biography blind apotheosis replaces sober narration of facts. Some sections are considered interpolated because they incorporate incidents which occurred after Rāmacaraṇ's death. Besides narrating many a myth and miracle popularly associated with Śaṅkara-deva's life, Rāmacaraṇ identified the master's early life with that of Child Kṛṣṇa as depicted in the *Bhāgavata Purāṇa*. The Master's personality is amplified to make it identical with a divine incarnation, probably because of the saying that one who has realised God becomes God Himself (*brahma-vit brahmaiva bhavati*). Rāmacaraṇ's son, Daityāri Ṭhākur, wrote *Guru-carit*, a short but sober biography of Śaṅkara-deva. The son avoided the mistakes of his father as a biographer, and tried to give an objective study of the saint. He passed over the nebulous incidents of the saint's early life, and contented himself with narrating the main incidents of his subsequent career. To his *Guru-carit*, Daityāri appended an authentic account of Mādhavadeva's life. Bhūṣaṇ Dvija, grandson of Cakrapāṇi, who was a disciple of Śaṅkaradeva, compiled *Śaṅkara-carit* with traditional materials, and he appears to have freely utilised the works of his predecessors. Rāmānanda Dvija's *Śaṅkara-carit* contains new material on the lives of Śaṅkaradeva and Mādhavadeva, and in places stands at variance with earlier accounts. His biography contains a section on the life of Gopāladeva. Rāmānanda was a pontiff of the Kālasamhati sect and as such he introduced and emphasised many a doctrinal point of his own sect.

After Śaṅkaradeva's death conflicting interpretations of his teachings developed, and as a result four *saṁhatis* or sub-sects arose in the main doctrinal frame-work of the Mahā-puruṣīya religion. These are Brahma Saṁhati, Puruṣa Saṁhati, Nikā Saṁhati, and Kāla Saṁhati started respectively by Dāmodaradeva, Puruṣottama Ṭhākur, Mathurādās Ātā and Gopāl Ātā. In time these Saṁhatis became wholly independent of the original sect; and each gathered its own disciples and followers and set up numerous big and small *satras* under it with an elaborate ecclesiastical order including *Satrādhikār* or *Mahanta*, *Bhāgavatī:* reciter and expounder of the *Bhāgavata*, *Pāthak:* reader of scriptures, *Sravanīs:* specially appointed listeners, *Gāyan-Bāyan:* monasterial orchestra, *Deuri* or *Bilanīyā:* distributor of the *prasad* (the food of grace) to the members of the congregation, *Bharāli:* store-keeper, *Al-dharā:* personal attendant of the

Satrādhikār, *Likhak:* scribe, *Bhakats* and *Sisyas:* lay-disciples. Each of these new Satras created a mass of religious writings for its own *prasaṅgas* or religious services, and a large number of works were compiled on the lives and activities of the principal apostles, and also on the history of the different Satras known as *Satrar Buranji*. We have already referred to the works written on the life of Gopāladeva. Gopāladeva, commonly known as Bhawanipuriya Gopāla Ātā, was nominated by Mādhavadeva as the religious head of the sect after him. He was an erudite scholar in Sanskrit and could interpret and vivify religious and philosophical subjects with appropriate and engaging parables and allegories, for which he was famous as *Kathār Sāgar* (The Ocean of Stories). Gopāla Ātā established a Satra at Kaljhār in Kamrup district, where he died in 1611. Rāmānanda Dvija, Rāmānanda Dās, and Rāmagopāl are his principal biographers. All of them have used traditional accounts.

Dāmodaradeva (1488-1598), a prominent figure in the Vaiṣṇavite movement, was a Brahmin, but it is said that he took initiation from Śaṅkaradeva and became his disciple. Immediately after Śaṅkaradeva's death, however, there was disagreement between Mādhavadeva and Dāmodaradeva. Dāmodara seceded from the orthodox church and established his own sect known as Dāmodarīyā, in which worship of other Hindu gods and Brahmin rituals were permitted. It was for these reasons that Dāmodara's creed attracted a large number of Brahmin adherents. Rāmarāi Dvija, a contemporary of Dāmodara, in his *Gurulīlā*, and Nīlakaṇṭha Dās in his *Dāmodara-carit*, have given detailed accounts of the life and activities of the saint and of the Satras that Dāmodara had established. The historical facts revealed in these two biographies give a dependable picture of the growth of different shades of faith in the main religion and their respective doctrines and theologies. Rāmānanda in his *Vaṁśīgopāladevar-carit* refers also to Dāmodaradeva, who was the spiritual Guru of the missionary Vaṁśīgopāl, whom Dāmodara, before his secession from the main sect, deputed to Eastern Assam to propagate the teachings of the Vaiṣṇava religion. Ramākānta's *Vanamālīdeva-carit* is also indispensable for the history of Vaiṣṇavism in Eastern Assam. Vanamālīdeva (c. 1576 A.D.) was a disciple of Vaṁśīgopāladeva, and was responsible for the spread of the faith in Eastern Assam. In his mission he secured royal patronage for the Ahom monarch Jayadhvaja Siṁha. Ramākānta was not only a devotee but a keen observer of contemporary events and possessed an understanding of the political affairs of the time, and so, besides giving biographical details about his master and his proselytizing activities, particularly in Eastern Assam, he offers ample historical information on Ahom rule. and administration and its relation with the Vaiṣṇava gurus and Satras. *Satsampradāya-kathā*, compiled by Govinda Dās during the reign of the great Ahom ruler Rudra Siṁha (1697-1714), though brief, is a very reliable work on the history of the Satra institutions, particularly under the Ahoms. Besides religious and metaphysical leanings, Govinda Dās shows much historical sense, acuteness of observation and love of truth.

In estimating the value of biographies written in verse, it should be borne in mind that in these works the day-do-day experiences and incidents of the saints' lives personally witnessed by the devotee-compilers or handed down by sacred tradition, have been interwoven into a rich tapestry of religious awe. There is, however, another kind of biography written in prose and known as *Kathā-guru-carit*. These life-histories were not written by a single monk but were compiled by a group of devotees of certain Satras. Two of such *Kathā-guru-carits* were compiled at Barpeta and Bardowa Satras. The *Kathā-guru-carits* are more than biographies; they are a rich treasure-house of the cultural history of the country. Besides the lives of the saints, they describe in encyclopaedic detail the history of the Vaiṣṇavite movement, its tenets and philosophy, rites and rituals, schools and institutions, arts and literature, and the contemporary social life.

These *Carit-puthis* aimed at generating a sense of reverence and devotion in the minds of the laity towards the saints by a recital of incidents from their lives. Hence the prose of these biographies and the manner of their compilation differ widely from those of Bhaṭṭadeva. They were compiled to inspire the masses. Naturally, these writings were in the simple, emotional, homely and informal speech of the people.

It should be noted that the use of a spoken language is dependent mainly on three factors—the structure of the sentences, the peculiar use of pronouns and verbs, and the adequacy or otherwise of the vocabulary. "What particularly characterizes spoken language", says J. Vendryes, "is that it contents itself with emphasizing the main lines of thought. These alone emerge and dominate the sentence, while the logical relations of words, and component parts of a sentence, are either imperfectly indicated, with the help, if necessary, of intonation and gesture, or are not indicated at all and have to be supplied by intuition. This spoken language gushes spontaneously from the mind under the pressure of strong emotion. The striking words are then prominently placed, as the speaker has neither the leisure nor the time to mould his thought according to the strict rules of reflective and organized language." Further, in every spoken style there is always some dramatic quality. Everywhere in the *Carit-puthis* dialogues have been happily woven into descriptive passages. Both short and long sentences occur whereever they are required for balance and poise, for effectiveness and beauty. In the same passage indicative, interrogative and other types of sentences occur as indeed they do so in spontaneous everyday speech—a feature that staves off monotony and affords diversity.

Grammar often loosens its reins in day-to-day informal speech. In Assamese, the subject comes first, and the verb comes last, other parts of speech coming in between the two, if the structure of a sentence is built on the strict rules of grammar. In an irregular sentence the writer uses at the beginning, or at the end, the word which he wants to especially emphasize, no matter what part of speech it is. The *Carit-puthis* contain many such irregular popular sentence-constructions. Further, the use of the right word at the right place makes these writings easily attractive. Although there is no attempt at literary flourish, yet the prose of the *Carit-puthis* is not absolutely free from ornament. Their diction is bedecked with metaphors, similes, and alliterations, which emerge spontaneously without much effort.

As has already been noted, the subject-matter of the *Carit-puthis* is something different from dry religious truths and court feuds. They are something like the diaries of famous and revered masters. Here the reader feels quite at home; for in these writings they find the records of men who are intimately connected with their society. The subject-matter of *Kathā-Gītā* is factual, objective and impersonal—for the most part it consists of dissertations on philosophy. The subject-matter of the *Carit-puthi,* however, is, to some extent, subjective. The writer is himself a devotee and as such he is in spiritual union with his hero. A mere factual statement of events and incidents is never his aim. He must show how the example of his master has touched and inspired him, so that others might feel a similar inspiration. In his pages the hero lives over again with his joys and tears, his vicissitudes of fortune, his fortitude and faith. Here in these writings, we come, for the first time, into really intimate relationship with the great personalities of Assam and see them in the company of contemporary men and women with whom they worked and daily conversed. In this respect the *Carit-puthis* are human documents of irresistible charm, absorbing interest, and wide appeal.

Of special interest in these biographies are the simplicity, deep faith and sincerity of the devotee-compiler, which create a fine and homely atmosphere. This could not have been achieved merely by the adoption of the spoken language. The whole atmosphere is delightfully free and unconventional. It is the spirit of ease and unsophistication which had made it possible even for anecdotes of the supernatural kind to find room in them. While the anecdotes of the supernatural kind associated with the lives of the saints arouse in the hearts of the devotees a sense of reverence for the divinity in man, those of their everyday life help in establishing a sense of kinship and sympathy by bringing out their essential human nature. These human documents are not without an element of humour; in particular, the quaintness of many colloquialisms and the very nâïveté of the authors appeal to the modern reader's sense of humour.

Hagiography was never so important as it is today for the doubt-tormented modern mind. A sense of discrimination is the fruit of our knowledge of true theocentric saints. It is said in the *Bhagavad-Gītā* that men who lack discrimination may quote the letter of the scripture, but they really deny its spirit. They are full of earthly desires and hungry for the gifts of heaven. They use pretty figures of speech; they teach elaborate ritual; but actually they know nothing except the law of Karma that chains men to rebirth. Those who have lost the sense of discrimination are unable to develop that one-pointed concentration of the will which leads a man to absorption in God.

It is surprising that among the cultivated and mentally alert in our day hagiography is rather unpopular. Aldous Huxley attributes this apathy of the modern mind to its insatiable appetite for novelty, diversity and distraction. But the saints are always preoccupied with one thought—that of the Spiritual Reality. Their actions are as monotonously uniform as their simple single-minded thought. They behave in all circumstances "selflessly, patiently and with indefatigable charity". No wonder that their biographies are unread.

The Indian belief that "one should hope for Him whilst one lives because deliverance abides in life" is as old as the *Upaniṣads*. Saint Kabīr wrote:

> If He is found now, He is found then;
> If not, we but go to dwell in the city of Death.

Hence the supreme value of life here as a means of deliverance. And deliverance is possible through devotion, through the Grace of the divine Incarnation. With St. Bernard, a Vaiṣṇavite might say, "I think the chief reason which prompted the invisible God to become visible in the flesh and to hold converse with men was to lead carnal men, who are only able to love carnally, to the healthful love of His flesh, and afterwards, little by little, to spiritual love." The biographies of saints and apostles inculcate this spiritual love in the sincere reader.

The Vaiṣṇavite renaissance ushered in a new era in Assamese literature as in the other phases of Assamese life. It was a spacious period. Young scholars flocked to Banaras, mastered the *Śāstras*, acquired urbane tastes, and carried them back to their own state. People went on pilgrimages to come in touch with holy seers and to enlarge their mental horizons. Often the pilgrimages of poets were triumphal marches, and every eminent poet in those days was sure of royal patronage. The Koch kings were liberal patrons of the arts and learning. One may have an idea about the royal patronage by reading what Rāma Sarasvatī says of King Naranārāyaṇa in one of his *bhaṇitās*. He wrote: "My sovereign commanded me to translate the *Mahābhārata* into Assamese verse. He offered to place before me all the commentaries available at the royal court. He sent cart-loads of texts to my residence and encouraged me in my work with adequate money, clothing, apparel and servants."

History, according to Carlyle, is the biography of great men, and indeed the literary history of this period consists mostly in the spiritual biographies of Śaṅkaradeva and Mādhavadeva. These two writers shone like the sun and the moon in the literary firmament. Others imitated or amplified what they did. Through the imaginative amplitude, syntactical freedom and sweeping cadence of their works, they turned the tide of literary taste in the classical direction and taught the age to value above all else devotion and fortitude in life and scholarly elegance and urbanity in literature.

Most of the other writers of the period are translators or adapters of the Sanskrit classics. Their works are homiletic, didactic or doctrinal, with or without musical elements in the form of solos or songs. In the hands of the psalmists and lyricists, the secular note became predominant. They chose erotic themes such as the marriages of legendary heroines like Sītā, Uṣā or Behulā, and wove with them tapestries of romantic imagination.

In the field of prosody, these writers were renovators rather than innovators. They wrote mostly in rhymed couplets known as *pada*, *dulari* and *chhabi*. Each couplet is clenched, and contains a complete thought. The *pada* is a fourteen-syllabic couplet with a caesura after the eighth syllable. *Dulari* and *chhabi* consist of stanzas of six verses each. In *dulari*, the first, second, fourth and fifth verses contain six syllables; the rest contain eight. As the verses are chanted, the tune fills up the void of syllabic curtailment, if any.

As the poets of this period are classical, we find them ornamenting their diction with similes and metaphors, alliterations and puns, mostly drawn from the Sanskrit classics to display their erudition. Their poetry also abounds in imagery from common life and Nature, which makes it extremely popular.

The Vaiṣṇavite movement sought to raise and to a great extent succeeded in raising the cultural level of the common man. It diffused a high degree of enlightenment among the masses of the people. It should be noted that Vaiṣṇavism in Assam is a religion as well as an institution, and even today it exercises a very great and good influence on the social and communal life of the Assamese people. As an institution, it may be considered mainly in two major aspects: the establishment of Satras for monastic discipline and religious training, and of Nāmghars for carrying out a programme of popular education. The Satras worked both as seats of religious learning and as residential schools. The *bhakats*, monks, lived here under the guardianship of the *satrādhikār*, who was responsible for their temporal and spiritual welfare and progress. The monks received education not only in Vaiṣṇava texts and practice but also in Vedic and Puranic lore. Besides the *satrādhikār*, other teachers and functionaries of the Satras, namely, the *Bhāgavatī* and *Pāṭhak*, also imparted instruction to the monks through discussions and occasional debates. Further, the monks were given written exercises not only in copying out manuscripts and illuminating them with relevant pictures but also in translating Sanskrit scriptures and composing original works in Assamese. After years of education and rigorous training in Vaiṣṇava faith and discipline, these monks were deputed to various parts of the province for the purpose of preaching and propagating their faith. In course of time many of these monks established new Satras at different places, and this network of institutions helped the diffusion of education, learning and culture in the entire country. In this way, the Satras produced successful teachers and missionaries as well as eminent philosophers, scholars and poets.

The Nāmghars, which were set up as central religio-political institutions of the villages, played a great part in their intellectual and cultural activities. Here not only *Śāstras* and literary masterpieces were recited, but great problems of life, philosophy and religion were discussed and debated; and the village people learnt here what they did not know before and received new ideas and experiences. The Nāmghars served, and are serving still now, as a panchayat-hall, where the villagers gather not only for religious purposes but also to discuss many current problems of the village and community life and political as well as economic and social subjects. This institution helps to impart unity to Assamese village life.

Furthermore, both the *satras* and the Nāmghars led to the creation and development of drama, music and the stage. These three are most powerful instruments for popularising culture as they appeal to nearly every one. The *Ankīyā-nāṭs*, which are full of music and dance, are acted even today in the Nāmghars, and the entire village assembles to see on the stage stories from the great works, the *Rāmāyaṇa*, the *Mahābhārata* and the *Bhāgavata Purāṇa*, dealing with deepest problems of human life and religion. The Vaiṣṇavas introduced many new festivals and saints' days in their calendar, and these doubtless widened the scope for dramatic performances and recreations for the mind and spirit of the worry-ridden common man.

We have already referred to the great revival of the study of Sanskrit during the Vaiṣṇavite period that brought about a renaissance in the intellectual life of the country not seen in the earlier ages. This Sanskrit or classical influence proved a great benefit to the cultural life of the people in all respects: it gave the Assamese language a rare distinction, and created in it a literature which is expected to stay for all times; it also tempered, refined and polished the manners and character of the Assamese society, built of diverse elements.

CHAPTER IV

THE AHOMS AND ASSAMESE LITERATURE

In an early chapter we referred to Suhungmung Dihingiya Raja (1497-1539) who consolidated the Ahom power by bringing under its domination the Chutiyas, Kacharis, Bhuyas, Nagas and certain other tribes of the Tai race who had settled in the eastern part of Assam long before the Ahoms. Suhungmung was the first Ahom king to show active leanings towards Hinduism. Apart from the growing influence of Hinduism under royal patronage, his reign witnessed the spread of the Vaiṣṇava revival set in motion by Śaṅkaradeva. Suhungmung's successors, Suklengmung Gargaya Raja (1539-1552), Sukhampha Khora Raja (1552-1603), Pratap Singha (1603-1641), Jayadhvaja Singha (1648-1663), and Chakradhvaj Singha (1663-1669), were all heroic kings and able administrators. They successfully warded off several invasions of the Mughals and resisted the spread of Islam in Eastern India. During their rule, Assam made rapid progress in all domains of life, and Hindu religion and culture began to flourish under their benign care. The arts and Assamese literature were assiduously cultivated in their court.

In 1681, Gadadhar Singha, a prince of the Tungkhungiya dynasty, ascended the throne. Before he became king, Gadadhar Singha had been at one time a fugitive to save himself from the ruling king Lora Raja; and his wife, Jayamati Kuwari, was apprehended and tortured inhumanly to extort information about her husband's whereabouts. Princess Jayamati refused to divulge any information about her husband even when her husband himself came in secret and asked her to do so. Jayamati exhorted her husband to muster an army and save the country and her people from the tyrannical rule of Lora Raja. Jayamati ultimately succumbed to these tortures and is adored as a martyr to wifely devotion

Every year the anniversary of her death is celebrated all through the province. Even today her life inspires our poets and provides them material for poems and plays consecrated to her sacred memory.

Gadadhar Singha was a strong king, and during his reign the Mughals were finally driven from Assam. The king had strong Śākta leanings, and persecuted the Vaiṣṇava *mahāntas*. The great power which the Vaiṣṇava *mahāntas* exercised over their disciples was regarded by the king as a menace to the Ahom sovereignty. Gadadhar Singha, therefore, confiscated the Vaiṣṇava *mahāntas*' properties, drove them from the Satras, killed some, and mutilated others. Gadadhar Singha's successor, Rudra Singha (1696-1714), restored the monasteries to the survivors or their heirs and bestowed royal favours on some Vaiṣṇava *mahāntas*. Yet he also was inclined towards the Śākta faith. Towards the end of his reign, he brought from Nadia (Bengal) Kṛṣṇarām Bhaṭṭācāryya Nyāyavāgīś, a devout Śākta Brahmin, and even on his death-bed he instructed his son and successor, Siva Singha, to take initiation from Kṛṣṇarām. The adoption of Śāktaism by the Ahom monarch, followed by the conversion to that faith of his principal nobles, brought about a breach and conflict with the Vaiṣṇavas.

Rudra Singha was a king of great ability and ambition who strove to form a confederacy of the Hindu States in eastern India to fight the Mughals and to restore Hindu sovereignty in eastern India. Rudra Singha was a great patron of arts, literature and learning. He invited artists, architects, musicians and scholars to Assam. He greatly encouraged development of Assamese literature by patronising poets and scholars liberally. Rudra Singha was succeeded by his four sons one after another—Siva Singha, Pramatta Singha, Rajeswar Singha, and Laksmi Singha. The last-named monarch was succeeded by his son, Gaurinath Singha (1780-95), and later by Kamaleswar Singha (1795-1811). During the reign of Siva Singha, Pramatta Singha and Rajeswar Singha, 1714 to 1769, there was peace and order in the country, and monarchs found time to patronise literature and art; but from 1769 onwards the country was disrupted by civil dissensions, and the government had ultimately to seek outside aid for the suppression of local disturbances.

Kamaleswar Singha was succeeded by his brother Chandrakanta Singha in 1811. Some nobles of his court were dissatisfied with the Ahom Prime Minister, Purnananda Buragohain, and they approached the Burmese king to send an army to put an end to the misrule of the Prime Minister. The Burmese invaded Assam in 1817 but Purnananda died before the invaders entered the capital. Chandrakanta, however, continued to rule till 1818, when he was dethroned by Purandar Singha. Chandrakanta regained his throne in 1821 through Burmese intervention, but being unable to brook the atrocities committed by the Burmese, he entered into hostilities with the invaders, and, on his defeat in 1822, fled to Bengal leaving Assam under the complete domination of the Burmese. But in 1824 the British entered Assam and expelled the Burmese. By the Treaty of Yandaboo, 1826, Assam passed into the hands of the East India Company. Purandar Singha was installed in 1833 as tributary ruler of Upper Assam, but as he failed to pay the stipulated tribute his country was annexed by the company in 1838. This closed for ever the golden chapter of well-nigh six hundred years of Ahom rule in Eastern India.

It is an undeniable fact that the Ahom rule gave Assam for several centuries a good and strong government which, resisting successively several Muhammedan invasions, kept the country in peace, prosperity and order. The Ahoms liquidated all petty principalities, both within Assam and on the tribal frontier; and this led to the emergence of one closely-knit geographical and political unit named Assam. The most notable achievement of Ahom rule was this political unification of the country, which in course of years led to social, cultural and linguistic unity, and awoke the spirit of oneness among the people.

In the beginning, the Ahoms wanted to maintain feudal superiority and separate existence as a ruling community and did not allow its members to have social intercourse with the peasant-population of the country. With the passage of time, they found it impossible to administer the vast country with a small number of their own people who came with the first conqueror Sukapha. They were, therefore, like the far-sighted Akbar, compelled to increase their numbers by marrying in non-Ahom or Hindu families, and by conferring upon some non-Ahom families the privileges and status of the ruling race. These new entrants were thoroughly assimilated with the pure Ahoms, and they and their descendants were not disabled from holding high offices and enjoying privileges to which the older Ahoms were entitled. The Ahoms, in course of years, adopted Hindu manners and customs. Further, by successfully resisting the spread of Islam in Assam, they regarded themselves as protector and defender of the Hindu Faith.

A historical survey of the period would not be complete without some account of the contribution made by the Ahom kings to the spread of Hinduism. Hindu influence first entered the Ahom court during the reign of King Sudangpha Bamuni- onwar (1397-1407), who had been brought up in a Brahmin family. The Hindu influence was more marked in the reign of King Pratap Singha who was personally grateful to Brahmin priests for ridding him of a demon which had possessed him during his princehood. The first Ahom king to accept Hinduism formally was, however, Jayadhvaja Singha. Jayadhvaja Singha and his successors up to Lora Raja were initiated in Vaiṣṇava faith. Gadadhar Singha persecuted the Vaiṣṇavas, and bestowed royal patronage upon the Śāktas and showed great honour and courtesy to Śākta priests. When his son, King Siva Singha, became a disciple of a Śākta Brahmin, the Śāktas got into ascendancy. As a result, rivalry and jealousy began to grow between the Śāktas and the Vaiṣṇavas, the group which enjoyed royal patronage and the group which suffered royal persecution. And when Siva Singha's queen Phuleswari insulted the Vaiṣṇavas of the Mowamariya sect, whom she had invited to a Śakti worship, the Vaiṣṇavas openly revolted against the Ahom king. This religious revolt is one of the causes of the decline and fall of the Ahom power. This discrimination and religious intolerance leading to division of the spirit were reflected in the literature of the period. It is also to be noted that the Ahoms constructed temples dedicated to Śākta gods and goddesses, and these temples became the seats of Śākta culture. Śākta religious texts in both Sanskrit and Assamese were recited and explained in these temples, and thus Śākta literature came to be written and developed in Assamese.

In addition, the Ahoms brought about a cultural synthesis in the country peopled by diverse creeds. It is true that the Ahom kings did not altogether abandon their ancestral religion and practices though they adopted the Hindu religion and the Hindu way of life. Their coronation ceremony was solemnised by both Ahom and Hindu rituals, and the Ahom ceremony, *Rikkhvan*, was always performed at the crowning of a new king. Every king, on ascending the throne, assumed two names, one in Assamese Hindu form and the other in Ahom. The Ahom kings considered themselves descendants of Indra, and the royal dynasty came to be known as *Indra-vaṁśa*. The Ahom gods and legends also came to be identified with Brahmanical ones so that both the Ahom and the Hindu population were made to feel that, after all, the pantheons of the two peoples were essentially the same, the only difference being that of language and of emphasis. Thus, we find that Chaopha, i.e., King of Heaven (*Svarga-deva*), was identified with Leng-dan, i.e., Indra, the progenitor of the Ahom kings; Jaching-pha was identified with Sarasvatī; Lung-chai-net with Vāyu; Khan-pha-pha with Devī; Khuntun with the Sun-god; Khun-ban with the Moon-god, and Lau-khe with Viśva-karman.

In religion and ritual, too, they strove for a synthesis. They held the Hindu scriptures sacred, showed respect and reverence to Brahmins and Vaiṣṇava *mahāntas*, and made grants and endowments for maintenance of shrines and monasteries. At the same time they patronised the Ahom priests, and allowed them to perform their rituals and to officiate at ceremonies like marriage, funerals and coronation as holy men.

This trend towards the growth of one synthetic Assamese culture was discernible also in their language-policy. The language of the Ahoms was of the Tibeto-Burman family while Assamese is an Aryan tongue. The Ahom rulers, in the beginning, tried to make Ahom the language of the court and culture, and *buranjis*, chronicles of the court, and other documents were actually recorded in Ahom. But this practice was fraught with practical difficulties as the bulk of their Assamese subjects did not understand this alien language. Consequently, these records and land-grant charters had to be written in both Ahom and Assamese. Later on, this policy was abandoned and Assamese completely replaced the Ahom language. The Ahom-speaking population merged themselves with the Aryan Assamese-speaking population of the province. Nevertheless, words and expressions from the Ahom language found easy access into Assamese, and the Ahom way of thinking began to influence Assamese writings and literature, particularly the system of writing *buranjis*.

Another notable feature of Ahom history is the successive invasions of Assam by the Muslims. These Muslim invasions indirectly did some good. Prior to the Muslim invasions there was hardly an integrated national life in Assam. The common danger cemented all the rifts and fissures. The Koches, the Kacharis, the Ahoms, the Assamese—all became united under the leadership of one powerful king. Petty, separatist, parochial sensibilities yielded ground to a broad national consciousness. The beginnings of a synthetic Assamese culture were thus laid. The common danger fostered patriotic feelings in the country, and several men and women earned immortal fame by sacrificing their lives in defence of their motherland against the Moghul aggressors. Their stories inspire Assamese men and women even today. At the time of the advent of the Ahoms, not only was the political condition fluid but the social condition was equally chaotic and disconcerting. People had more faith in magic and charms than in effort and work. The Muslim invasions roused the people once again to heroic deeds, self-reliance and patriotic organisation, and indirectly freed their spirit from superstition and idle speculation. The Moghul invasion also brought Assam into contact with the rest of India again—a contact which was lost in the 11th and 12th centuries. With these invasions there came into Assam the cultural impact of other people—notably of the Islamic people on life and art, especially painting and music. There grew up in Assamese the *Jikir* and *Jari* songs, based on Sufi religious teachings. The Pirs and Fakirs made notable contributions.

In this process a large number of Perso-Arabic vocables found their way into the Assamese language.

The Ahoms not only defended the country against external aggression but also fortified it internally on sound lines. They built good and wide roads for communication and transport, organised a postal system, opened markets, built towns and temples, reconstructed villages, and reorganised the social life of the peasant population. The development of communications had important political, social and cultural consequences. It brought separate populations ever closer together, forged some of the strongest bonds of national unity, and awakened in the Assamese the feeling of oneness. It also widened the area of social and commercial intercourse and fostered one composite Assamese culture.

Furthermore, small or big towns built at Gargaon, Rangpur, Jorhat, Gauhati and other places led to the growth of a new urban refinement. The Ahom nobles, of easy fortune and amiable disposition, and the people of these towns reflected an urban culture in their manners, etiquette, dress, living and learning. This new culture distinguished them from the rural people who were dominated by a uniform antique pattern of life, conservatism and inertia. The new urban society, though very small, stirred the imagination of the traditional society so much as to make it adopt new ideas, develop a secular outlook in worldly matters, and forge contacts outside its own social and religious coteries. This urban society began to take a lively interest in the finer graces of life like art, literature and music. Kings, ministers and nobles patronised poets and writers by making land-grants to them, and the recipient-poets and authors eulogised their patrons in their verses. Some changes in emotional complexion doubtless came over the literature devoted to glorification of monarchs and nobles. The first change was seen in panegyric lyrics composed by such poets as Rāma Miśra, Kavirāj Cakravartī, Ruchināth Kandalī, Vidyāchandra Kaviśekhara, all of whom received liberal patronage from the Ahom kings. These eulogistic writings were full of the glitter and sparkle of artificial literary expressions, and cater mostly to the tastes of the class for whom they were written.

Further, the Ahom court was pompous. This pomposity affected the poet's sensibilities, and hence we find a note of artificiality where, in the Vaiṣṇavite era, there were sincerity and austerity. By advocating the ideal of austerity and poverty, the Vaiṣṇavite literature repressed many natural pleasures. Now literature is released from such repression thanks to the baroque extravagance of and the preference for amatory themes of the Ahom courtiers. The court was the centre of love and romance. Kings and queens also preferred love stories to devotional ones. Therefore, the poets composed love stories or added rainbow colours of love to stories otherwise religious. Since the *Purānas* were a rich store-house of love anecdotes, Ahom monarchs encouraged poets and authors to render them into Assamese. A notable distinction between the Vaiṣṇavite and the Ahom period is that whilst in the former the spirit divine was the subject of literary treatment, in the latter man is the centre of literature. Literature now ceases to be other-worldly and idealistic. The shift is towards realism. Even in poems and romances, men and women of the common work-a-day-world now engage the poet's attention.

CHAPTER V

ASSAMESE LITERATURE UNDER THE AHOM PATRONAGE

THERE was much activity during this period in the direction of translating the *Purāṇas*, and of composing *kāvyas* on different themes of these texts. The translation of the *Purāṇas* provided kings and common people with not only a mythology, a magnificent sacramental literature, and a series of love-romances, but also a code of law which the Ahom kings needed very much.

A portion of the *Viṣṇu Purāṇa* was translated at some time in the seventeenth century A.D. by Bhāgavat Miśra who was also known as Raghunāth Miśra. He made metrical renderings of the *Satvata Tantra* also. A complete and literal translation of *Viṣṇu Purāṇa* was made by Paraśu Rām Dvija in the first half of the 19th century (1836). Though the author imitated the Vaiṣṇava poets in language and method of narration, his work on the whole shows no literary skill or accomplishment. The *Viṣṇu Parvan* of the *Harivaṁśa* was rendered into Assamese by Kavi Śekhar Vidyācandra Bhaṭṭacaryya during the reign of the Ahom king, Rajeswar Singha (1751-1769). The work gives an account of Kṛṣṇa's birth and his subsequent doings and exploits amongst the cowherds at Gokula or Vṛndāvana. But one noticeable feature of the work is the presence of Rādhā as the mistress of Kṛṣṇa. In the original Sanskrit version, the *Rāsa-krīḍā* of Kṛṣṇa at Vṛndāvana with the milkmaids is described in the twentieth chapter of *Viṣṇu Purāṇa*, but the name Rādhā is singularly absent there. The Assamese poet, in the course of his description of the *Rāsa-krīḍā* episode, narrates the pangs of separation and the love at first sight of Rādhā and Kṛṣṇa. The introduction of Rādhā as the devoted mistress of Kṛṣṇa was perhaps made under the influence of *Brahmavaivarta Purāṇa*, which gained popularity in the contemporary Ahom Court.

Under the orders of King Siva Singha (1714-1744) and his queen Pramatheswari, *Brahmavaivarta Purāṇa* was translated by the Court Poet, Kavirāj Cakravartī. Kavirāj Cakravartī's work is not a complete translation; the poet adapted only the episodes relating to Kṛṣṇa's early life. His description of the *Rāsa-krīḍā* episode with erotic sentiments and suggestions is rather pleasing.

Kavirāj Cakravartī alias Rām Nārāyaṇ Cakravartī was the most outstanding poet of this period. He was Poet-Laureate under several Ahom Kings. Cakravartī's important literary contributions are *Śaṅkhāsura-vadha, Gītagovinda* and *Śakuntalā-kāvya* The episode of *Śaṅkhāsura-vadha* was taken from the *Prakṛti Khaṇḍa* of the *Brahmavaivarta Purāṇa.* The *Śaṅkhāsura-vadha* begins with the birth of Tulasī and then gives a detailed account of her marriage with Śaṅkhāsura, the demon king, and of the exploits of the latter. The rape of Tulasī by Kṛṣṇa, the fight between Śaṅkhāsura and Mahādeva, and the eventual death of Śaṅkhāsura and his metamorphosis into a conch-shell are narrated in an entertaining manner. Kavirāj Cakravartī's version of the *Gītagovinda* is done in the stereotyped hexametre couplets and does not have the same songs and speeches as in the original. Consequently, it fails to bring out the intense lyrical feeling of the original, and the intimate sentiments of the characters.

Kavirāj Cakravartī is considered to be the translator of the Mādhava-Sulocanā episode occurring in the fifth chapter of *Kriyā-yoga-sāra* appended to the *Uttara Khaṇḍa* of the *Padma Purāṇa.* The story is narrated with a view to showing the merits of bathing in the Gaṅgā-Sāgara-Saṅgama.

It should be noted that a complete translation of the entire *Brahmavaivarta Purāṇa* was made under the patronage of Prince Hayanarayan, a Koch king who ruled in Darrang District. The work was done in collaboration by four poets, namely, Ratikānta Dvija, Nandesvar Dvija, Norottama Dvija and Khargesvar Dvija, at some time in the Śaka era 1717. Rucināth Kandalī is the first translator of the Caṇḍī episode from the *Mārkaṇḍeya Purāṇa.* In this translation, made during the reign of King Rajeswar Singha (1749—), Rucināth introduces episodes from *Kālikā Purāṇa, Vāmana* and *Brahmavaivarta Purāṇas* to fill the rifts in the story narrated in the *Mārkaṇḍeya Purāṇa*. Another book, *Kalki Purāṇa*, is also ascribed to Rucināth Kandalī.

King Siva Singha and his consort Ambika Devi patronised Kavicandra Dvija and set him to translate *Dharma Purāṇa*. *Dharma Purāṇa* is a voluminous work describing eloquently the duties of men and the need of their observance. Along with these, the work narrates many a didactic story. Some of the incidents of this Assamese version, such as the origin of the Ganges, the fight between Andhakāsura and Śiva, the quarrel of Kadru and Vinatā, the stealing of nectar by Garuḍa, are drawn from other Purāṇic lore.

These Assamese versions of the *Purāṇas* are not literal renderings of the originals. Mostly they are epitomes or free adaptations with emphasis on the story (*ākhyāna*) element. Many of the translators and adaptators came from the common people and were in perennial contact with the soil. Therefore they wrote in a simple style and enshrined in their writings many popular myths, legends, folklores, and cultural traditions. Highly philosophical disquisitions were avoided, but, where given, were interpretative. Their works were interspersed with devotional songs to replace the metaphysical elements, and these rendered the *Purāṇas* popular. The authors paid little attention to literary decorations as their principal aim was only to popularise the *Paurāṇikā ākhyānas* and Hindu ideals. Portions of these translations are breezy and racy but not because of quaint humour: a feature rare in earlier literature. These poems may not have high literary merit but they are read by our village people even now with avidity as they are rich in didactic passages and embody popular philosophy.

Very few books were written during this age on themes of the two epics, the *Rāmāyaṇa* and the *Mahābhārata*. One of the leading poets who enjoyed great reputation in the later part of the eighteenth century and who drew on the *Rāmāyaṇa* story was Raghunāth Mahanta. Raghunāth made a prose summary of the *Rāmāyaṇa*. His prose shows, on the one hand, the influence of the *Buranjis* and, on the other, in a still more marked degree, that of the traditional style of the *Carit-puthis* of the Vaiṣṇavas. Raghunāth's fame as a poet rests on his two long narrative poems *Adbhuta-Rāmāyaṇa* and *Santruñjaya*; both appear to have been based on some floating *Rāmāyaṇa* legends.

According to the poet, the source of *Adbhuta-Rāmāyaṇa* is the *Mārkaṇḍeya Purāṇa.* The story relates to Sītā in the Nether World (*Pātāla*) after her final estrangement from her consort, Rāma. Having parted from Rāma for good, Sītā was living in Vidyābilāsinīpura of the Nether World. But she had lost her peace of mind. She had left behind her husband and her two beloved sons, Lava and Kuśa. The pangs of separation pierced her heart day and night. In Ayodhyā, Rāma was pining for the company of his beloved wife. His agony was still deeper. It was because of his unkind innuendos that Sītā had been compelled to beg her mother, the Earth, to rend herself asunder so that she might find solace in her bosom. Sītā asked Vāsuki, the king of Serpents in the Nether World, to abduct Lava and Kuśa from Ayodhyā. Vāsuki made an abortive attempt and reported his failure to Sītā. He found it impossible to break through the hosts of invincible warriors like Hanumanta, Nīla, Nala, Vibhīṣaṇa. Sītā understood his difficulty, but implored him to try again, this time by using his magical power. Accordingly, Vāsuki went in the guise of a Brahmin and, on the pretext of training Lava and Kuśa in archery, brought them from Rāma. Having thus fulfilled his mission, the disguised Brahmin succeeded in persuading the princes to accompany him to Vidyābilāsinīpura where their mother lived. Vāsuki then arrived at Pātāla where the mother and the sons met to their unbounded joy and happiness.

This treachery of Vāsuki infuriated Rāma so much that he at once ordered his courtiers to find out Lava and Kuśa from wherever they might. Everybody tried his utmost but to no avail. At last the task was entrusted to Hanumanta, who, by virtue of his great magical power, adopted many subtle devices. He had very tough fights with the serpents and the Serpent King. At last he defeated all of them, ferocious and frightening as they were, and brought Sītā and her two sons back to Rāma.

Naturally Rāma's joy over the reunion knew no bounds. Sītā made obeisance to Rāma, but urged him not to press her to live with him as she was not destined to do so. She assured him, however, of her daily visit, which would be visible only to Rāma, Lava, Kuśa and Hanumanta. Sītā then vanished into the air.

In *Santruñjaya*, the Rāma legend is treated very briefly as a sequel to another story. The author's intention was not so much to tell the well-known story of Rāma as to narrate the exploits and expeditions of Bālī and Hanumān. The first part of the story which describes these exploits in detail is very amusing, and seems to be the poet's own invention. We give below a summary of the first section of the poem.

The poem begins with the author's invocation to Viṣṇu who in his different incarnations on this Earth did away with corruption, vice and injustice and established the kingdom of justice, truth and virtue. The narrative begins as in a *Purāṇa* with a dialogue between Vālmīki and Bharadvāja, the former relating to the latter how and why the gods became monkeys.

Brahmā, the Preserver, was one day presiding over an assembly of the gods in Manivatipura on Mount Meru. The gods, including Sumeru, King of Meru, attended the assembly accompanied by their daughters. All of them enjoyed the graceful dances of the charming Vidyādharī maids. Sulocanā, daughter of Sumeru, unsurpassed in beauty, made all the gods spellbound with her graceful dance. Everybody wanted to marry her. The wind-god Vāyu, one of the prominent gods, decided to make advances to Sulocanā's father with the intention of asking his daughter's hand and sent a messenger to this end, along with a letter to Sulocanā herself requesting her to accept him in wedlock. The messenger accordingly informed Sumeru of the purpose of his mission, but the latter turned down the proposal flatly. Being at a loss, the messenger prayed to Vāyu to send a puff of gentle breeze. This was sent, and the messenger had the letter borne by the breeze to Sulocanā who, having read the letter, laughed away the strange proposal. At this Vāyu flew into a rage and declared war on Sumeru. A fierce battle broke out. The gods were frightened and prayed to Brahmā to bring about a settlement. Brahmā commissioned Nārada who brought about a compromise between the contending parties.

According to the terms of the compromise, Sumeru gave away to Vāyu one of his summits, the Vihaṅga Śṛṅga, which was blown away by Vāyu to the Milk Ocean (Kṣīra Sāgara) where lay Mount Trikūṭa. On this mountain fell the Vihaṅga Śṛṅga. When Viśvakarmā, the architect of this universe, found this Vihaṅga Śṛṅga, he carved out on it a beautiful city known as the golden city of Laṅkā. In this city lived Mālī, Sumālī and Mālyavanta, the three Rākṣasa brothers. Viṣṇu beheaded Mālī with his disc (*cakra*), and the two other brothers fled for dear life.

Then came on the scene Kuvera, King of Laṅkā. One day Sumālī found Kuvera on the throne, and bewailed the deplorable lot of Rākṣasas who had been driven to recapture Laṅkā. He had given his daughter Naikeṣī in marriage to Viśravā, father of Kuvera, in the belief that Viśravā would restore the lost kingdom. Naikeṣī conceived in her 'unclean period' (during menstruation) and was afraid of the progeny, who, according to popular belief, would be notorious for their violence and evil-doing. During the period of her conception, evil omens were sighted everywhere. Everybody on earth and in heaven got panicky. In view of the universal fear and impending menace, Naikeṣī retained the bitter fruit of her womb for one hundred years. But the panic was all along there. The gods went to Brahmā who told the former that the danger was real and imminent. He then explained how Jaya and Vijaya, the two gatekeepers of Viṣṇu, who were cursed to be born to Diti first, were both of them being cursed by Lakṣmī again, in the womb of Naikeṣī now. He finally told them that the moment they were born there would be no end to the miseries and distress of people and that Viṣṇu alone could overcome the calamity.

Brahmā then lay in a deep trance awaiting the 'unbodied message' of Viṣṇu, the Supreme Power of the universe. The message came that there would be an incarnation of Viṣṇu Himself to put an end to the menace. The gods were ordered to be reborn on earth as monkeys. Brahmā was directed to be reborn as a bear, Vāyu as the monkey Keśarī, Indra as Bālī, the monkey-king of Kiṣkindhyā, and thus all the gods and goddesses were directed to become monkeys. Some of the monkeys would be savage and would plunder and pillage one kingdom after another until at last they would reach Kailāsa where Nandī, God Mahādeva's disciple, would persuade them to assault Kiṣkindhyā, the kingdom of the mighty king, Bālī, who would conquer them.

Brahmā intimated to the gods all that he had heard, and in course of time all were reborn as desired by God.

Bālī went out on world-conquest. In the course of his march he found a tender-aged monkey throwing stones at the fruits of a tall mango-tree. Bālī saw to his great surprise that the monkey-boy was physically too strong to be ignored, and so Bālī, instead of using force, had the monkey persuaded by one of his ministers to be the adopted son of Bālī who pretended that he had no son to call his own. The monkey-boy agreed to the proposal and became his adopted son.

Asked about his birth and name, the monkey replied that he was son of Keśarī. His mother was Añjanā, and his name was Hanumanta. Immediately after his birth,, he climbed the mountain Lokaloka where he saw a huge elephant. He could not check the temptation to mount the elephant, who presently began to groan under the weight of the boy monkey and almost collapsed. But the bushy and pointed hair on the back of the elephant pricked him and caused severe pain. So he jumped down and faced the elephant, challenging him with his tail raised. His attitude frightened the elephant so much that the latter ran for life, and in this way Hanumanta defeated eight such elephants. This act of Hanumanta displeased his father and made him very angry. He admonished Hanumanta; for the elephants whom he had given so much trouble were none other than eight incarnations of God, who had borne this earth on their backs. Hanumanta politely replied that since the earth itself had been borne by God, it was absurd to accuse him as one guilty of mounting them. Moreover, God is all-pervasive and the soul of every living being is an inalienable part of that Supreme Soul. So what one did was done by God Himself. Hence he pleaded not guilty, adding that he was always ready and happy to do whatever his father would bid. Keśarī was moved. As desired by his son, he ordered him to serve pilgrims and devote himself to Rāma heart and soul.

Bālī was much pleased with the story of Hanumanta and

appointed him commander-in-chief of his powerful army. It was now that the real adventure began, and the succeeding verses tell of Hanumanta's deeds. In no time Hanumanta brought one monkey-king after another under the suzerainty of Bālī.

He attacked the demon king Bhauma, son of Dharaṇī. Bhauma got the help of Dhanañjaya, a prominent king of the Nether World. He helped Bhauma with his innumerable serpent-soldiers. Kaṅkaṇa was his great general. This was a formidable alliance. There was an 'unbodied message' from heaven that it would be next to impossible to defeat Dhanañjaya Nāga who possessed 'Śāraṅgadhanu' and 'Nārāyaṇī Astra'. So all was not smooth-sailing with Hanumanta. He, therefore, called upon Rāma to help him. A golden chariot with some invincible weapons in it came down from heaven. Hanumanta got into it and a fierce battle followed resulting in Hanumanta's victory. Thus Hanumanta conquered all the notorious serpent-kings who helped Bhauma.

The news upset Bhauma who immediately went to Maṅgala (the planet Mars) and wanted to know from him if Bhauma should fight with Hanumanta. Maṅgala laughed away the idea of fighting with a petty monkey. Meanwhile, a serpent-king, who had fought with and been defeated by Hanumanta, arrived there and told them that it would be absurd to fight with Hanumanta who had no parallel in warfare. Bhauma realised the situation and withdrew.

In the meantime, Gajaketu encouraged Hanumanta to march to Śakadvipa. Hanumanta ordered his armies to start by Yogapatha. They got down at the mountain Iśāna where they met a large number of very beautiful monkeys. They came to know that Nala was their king and they were the direct descendants of the Gandharba, Citraratha. Hanumanta, along with Śatavalī and Dividha, then went to Nala and told him of their mission. Nala replied that he was a devoted disciple of Rāma. At this Hanumanta's joy knew no bounds, and they became true comrades. Hanumanta now enquired about the kings of Śakadvipa who were to be conquered. Nala supplied all the information. Strengthened by the company of great warrior like Nala, Hanumanta fought with vigour and defeated all the kings concerned and compelled them to surrender. Most of the kings were, however, devotees of Rāma, and so the victory was pleasant and easy.

Then Hanumanta arrived at an island called Baimānika where one Rudrabāhu ruled. The people of that land used to fly in aeroplanes. Passing by Baimānika, Hanumanta at last reached the city of Puṣkalinī which was his birth place. There he bowed to his parents who blessed him, wished him a long life, and inquired about his exploits. Hanumanta told them of all that he had done. Now he sent all the vanquished kings to Bālī. But the monkey-kings of Lokaloka mountain were yet to be conquered. Moreover Bālī desired the company of Hanumanta's parents whom Hanumanta wanted to take with him to Bālī. While the three had such conversations, they welcomed Nārada who expressed joy at the victory of Hanumanta but forbade Hanumanta to attack the monkey-kings of Lokaloka, for they were destined to be conquered by Rāma who was going to incarnate himself very soon. Then Nārada asked Hanumanta and his parents to leave for Bālī's capital. Hanumanta consented and asked his mother Añjanā to take the charge of two princesses, daughters of Suṣena, and train them in such a way that they might be worthy queens. Then along with his father, he went to Bālī, who was naturally much pleased. Hanumanta proposed that Bālī and his brother be pleased to marry the two pretty daughters of Suṣena. Bālī agreed and, after his marriage, left for Kiṣkindyā, where he began to live amidst royal pomp and grandeur.

The story of Bālī's adventures ends here. The author then adds a new chapter describing Rāma's birth and banishment, the abduction of Sītā by Rāvaṇa, Rāma's fight with Rāvaṇa — practically the whole *Rāmāyaṇa* in a nutshell, including the story of Lava and Kuśa.

The long poem ends with a prayer to Viṣṇu. The aim of the poet was, no doubt, to depict Rāma as an incarnation of Viṣṇu and also to propagate the tenets of *Bhakti*. This he certainly achieved. But he also deserves praise for handing down these entertaining Rāma-legends which would otherwise have been consigned to oblivion. The poems reveal the poet's acquaintance with the floating Jaina versions of the *Rāmāyaṇa*.

We have already referred to the growing Śākta influence in the Ahom period. The later Ahom kings adopted Śākta religion and developed the Śākta outlook on life, which was in accord with the militant and epicurean ideals of the ruling class. For this reason and on account of the impact of new urban cultural currents, the influence of Vaiṣṇava poetry began to decline and a new Śākta literature came to be written. In imitation of the Vaiṣṇava *Bargits* the Śākta poets created in Assamese a body of hymns which are even now sung as prayer-psalms. Some of these hymns were said to have been composed by the Ahom kings Rudra Singha and Siva Singha. These Śākta hymns, though impressive in alliteration and metrical perfection, suffer from a certain monotony of theme and phraseology coupled with want of personal feeling. Side by side with these lyrics flourished during this period descriptive verses on Śākta goddesses such as Durgā, Kālī, Śītalā, which are even today chanted in their worship and adoration.

The court poets were encouraged by the Ahom kings to render Śākta scriptures into Assamese. Ananta Ācārya was commissioned by King Siva Singha to write *Ānanda Laharī*. The book begins with a hymn to the goddess Durgā, who has been described as the primordial cause of the universe. It goes on to describe how, in her infinite mercy, she assumes form to please her devotees, and then it dwells on the beauties of her form, adding descriptions of Kailāsa and Lord Śiva. There are devotional hymns to the goddess, and the poem closes with a eulogy of the royal consort, Queen Phuleswari.

Rucināth translated *Chaṇḍī* into easy flowing verse. There is another Assamese version of *Caṇḍī* by Madhusūdan Miśra. Both the poems are descriptive and lack literary beauty. They are, however, popular as vehicles of religious sentiment, and so read and recited by thousands of Śākta devotees generation after generation. Though these works fall far short of Vaiṣṇavite poetry in diction, imagery and narrative skill, one comes across passages of metaphysical profundity.

Particularly significant of the period is a corpus of panegyrical poems composed by poets attached to the courts of kings, ministers and noblemen, lauding their patrons' heroism, victories, munificence and magnanimity. The Ahom kings and nobles were generous in digging tanks, building roads and erecting temples, and in this connection many dedicatory verses glorifying their piety and charity were composed. These court poets were masters both of Sanskrit and of Assamese. Naturally, in the *praśastis* or panegyrics, the poets used a specific diction abounding in sonorous and metaphorical Sanskrit expressions presupposing a knowledge of *Paurāṇik* mythology and legends.

The science of erotics (*Kāma-śāstra*) was very much cultivated and fostered in the Ahom court, and some of the Sanskrit texts on *Kāma-śāstra* were translated into Assamese. A versified treatise on erotics was compiled by a poet named Kaviśekhar Bhaṭṭācārya for the entertainment and instruction of Prince Charu Singha Gohain, son of King Rajeswar Singha, and of the Prince's consort, Princess Pramadā Sundari Aideo. It became the practice to engage scholars to read out to queens, princesses and high-born ladies popular *kāvyas*, love-romances and erotic *śāstras*. That *Kāma-śāstra* exercised a tremendous influence is evident from the fact that a large number of *Mantra-puthis*, books on charms relating to love-making, were compiled during the period. These *Mantra-puthis* contain nostrums, charms and conundrums on the art and practice of love-making, of winning love, exciting passion in woman, beautifying and removing physical defects in woman, and increasing virility.

As observed earlier, this period was characterised in particular by a new and rising interest in historical writings. Popular poets evinced antiquarian interests. *Barphukanar Gīt* is a most important historical ballad which narrates events centering round Badancandra Barphukan, an Ahom viceroy at Gauhati, who invited the Burmese to remove his rival, Purnananda Buragohain, from the prime ministership. This ballad presents a popular version of historical events, and its narration closely follows actual events. *Barphukanar Gīt* is remarkable for its dramatic interest, descriptive quality, vivid characterisation, and racy humour. *Bakharabarar Gīt* and *Padum Kuvarir Gīt* are two other very popular historical ballads composed during the period under review.

Here we may mention a few other poems of a popular nature. Some of them develop the tales from the *Purāṇas*,

Hitopadeśa and *Pañcatantra*. Poets even turned to folklore and fairy tales for inspiration, and found materials that gave their imagination a free rein. Dvija Goswami's *Kāvya-śāstra* is a book in verse containing many fables from the *Hitopodeśa* and some moral observations in rhymed couplets. Another Assamse version of the *Hitopodeśa* was done by Rāma Miśra, author of *Putalā-caritra*, at the instance of Bhadrasen Gohain Phukan, an Ahom general.

Kavirāj Miśra is another story-teller, who flourished about 1616. He was an itinerant minstrel, going about reciting his verses on *Siyāl Gosāin* (The Fox-Saint) and thereby obtaining food and raiment.

The story centres round a legendary figure, Siyāl Gosāin by name, who was thrown away under a *ketaki* plant soon after his birth through the intrigues of his stepmother, Kundalatā. Chandotarā, his mother, was blindfolded at the time of her delivery. The baby was picked up by a newly littered vixen who suckled him and brought him up among her own young ones. The boy grew up among the young cubs and imitated their habits of howling at night and of retreating to their lair at the approach of men. On his return from pilgrimage, Dharmadeva, his father, who traced his origin to the twelve famous Bhuyas, was informed by his wife Kundalatā that Chandotarā had borne no child and the *dais* (midwife), heavily bribed by Kundalatā, confirmed the lie, which he believed. But one day, on his way to the bathing-ghat, he happened to notice a child retreating into a den at the sight of him. This struck him as curious and, apprehending foul play somewhere, he vigorously questioned the *dais* on his return and elicited the truth that Chandotarā had been delivered of a male child. Next day he had the child, the mother fox and the young cubs all dug out of the hole and taken to his house. The boy, when he grew up, came to be known as Siyāl Gosāin.

Furthermore, love-romances were composed by the court poets from episodes culled from the *Purāṇas* and folklore. Kavirāj Cakravartī, who was the court-poet of both King Rudra Singha and King Siva Singha, in his *Śakuntalā-kāvya*, narrated the familiar story of Śakuntalā but to heighten the romantic effect added to it the love episode of Candraketu and Kāmakalā. In this story, King Candraketu saw in a dream Kāmakalā, the beautiful daughter of the king of Bhadrāvatī, and soon fell in love with her. The king engaged a parrot as go-between, and with its help succeeded in marrying Kāmakalā. But they could not enjoy married life very long. One day, both the king and the queen went to a forest, and then the queen was separated from her husband when the latter went away pursuing a deer. In grief and remorse Kāmakalā wanted to immolate herself by burning. A voice from above prevented the tragedy and assured their reunion after a year's time. This incident offers the poet an opportunity to describe the seasonal characteristics of the twelve months (*Bāra-māha*), and the descriptions aptly emerge from the lips of the lovelorn heroine Kāmakalā. At the end of the twelve months, with the return of spring, the lovers were reunited. Kavirāj Cakravartī in his *Tulasī-carit* or *Śaṅkhāsura-vadha*, an episode adapted from the *Brahmavaivarta Purāṇa*, made much of the love-theme relating to Śaṅkhāsura, his marriage to Tulasī, and the rape of Tulasī by Nārāyaṇa. Dīna Dvijavara wrote the elegant love poem *Mādhava-Sulocanā* from the story of the same name in the *Kriyāyogasāra* canto of the *Padma Purāṇa*. By erotic language and skill in romantic narration, the author in his adaptation replaced the original devotional ideas with sentiments of Anacreontic love and earthly passion.

Some poets searched for fresh love-themes in new literary pastures. One such new love-romance is Rāma Dvija's *Mṛgāvatī-caritra*, a work corresponding to the Sufi work of the same name written in 1500 by Kutban. It also appears that the poet was familiar with some elements of Jayas's *Padmāvat* and the Jaina poet Maladharin Devaprabha's *Mṛgāvatī-caritra*, a work based on the popular Udayana legend. The plot of the Assamese *Mṛgāvatī-caritra* is briefly this: The prince of Kundilanagar saw four nymphs bathing in a lake and instantly fell in love with the youngest of them. The nymphs flew away, and the love-lorn prince passed his days pining for his beloved. Fortunately, next time when they came again to bathe, the prince was successful in capturing the youngest one, and lived with her happily for some time. One day, when the prince was away, the nymph managed to escape. She, however, left the name of her city with her matron. The prince was mortified when on return he learnt of her departure. He immediately set out in search of his beloved. In his wanderings, he met with many vicissitudes and performed many miracles, and at last arrived at the city of Rukem where the nymph lived with her companion-nymphs. The latter celebrated his marriage with their youngest companion with great merrymaking. Here the poet takes the liberty to describe graphically the erotic sports of the couple with much zest. Another mediaeval Sufi poem similar to *Mṛgāvatī* is *Madhumālati* by Manjhan. This was also adapted in an Assamese *kāvya* of the same name by an unknown author. It should be noted that in both the Assamese poems the original Sufi ideal is completely shorn off. The purpose of the Sufi poets is to depict the soul's love and aspiration for God and its ultimate union with Him. To the Sufi poets, the story of human love is only an allegory. The Assamese poets, however, made their lovers suffer for the sake of their beloved. They emphasised earthly and human love and treated love both in union and in separation. Naturally, in the Assamese *kāvyas* erotic tendencies predominated, and they are replete with passages describing intimately every feminine charm and treating of love dalliances with an easy frankness.

Many secular Sanskrit texts were also translated into Assamese prose under royal patronage. They deal with medicine, astronomy, arithmetic, dancing and architecture. In these books Assamese prose was employed for the first time for the discussion of utilitarian knowledge. Most of them were written by Sanskrit scholars. It was natural, therefore, that Sanskrit would leave its stamp on them, because a sufficient number of *tadbhava* and racy *deśīya* (indigenous) words with clear-cut usages had not yet been evolved. The study of Sanskrit texts for the cultivation of knowledge was indeed indispensable but Sanskrit words were even more necessary to enrich Assamese prose vocabulary. It must, however, be added that, although *tatsama* words were borrowed, the Assamese writers used a straightforward and direct style suited to scientific expression. For the same reason these books are, generally speaking, clear and intelligible. Apart from their value as literary and technical documents, they afford most important specimens of scientific prose in the Ahom period. The chief one among them is *Hastividyārṇava* of Sukumār Barkāth. This illustrated book was written in 1734 under the orders of King Siva Singha and his consort, Queen Ambikadevi. The illustrations were drawn by the painters Dilbar and Dosai. The book contains descriptions of several kinds of elephants, the ways of training them, their diseases and their cures. The book also specifies the different categories of elephants to be used by men belonging to different social classes. The materials of *Hastividyārṇava* are stated in the text itself to have been taken from *Gajendra-cintāmaṇi* of Sambhunātha. The prose of *Hastividyārṇava* does not differ from the prose of the chronicles. It has similar sentence formation and vocabulary. The orthography is phonetic, and the structure of sentences follows that of every-day speech.

The *Ghorā-nidāna*, a treatise on horses, is another book of the same genre. A printed edition of this valuable book has been published by the Government of Assam. This has been edited (1932) by Tarini Charan Bhattacharyya. In the preface to *Ghorā-nidāna*, Dr. S. K. Bhuya observes: "These two representative treatises (*Hastividyārṇava* and *Ghorā-nidāna*) reveal the richness and variety of the Assamese pharma-copoeia, and their literary value consists in the presentation of a very large number of expressions now thrown into disuse." Side by side with the texts on medicine, books on astrology and divination were compiled in both Sanskrit and Assamese. Even treatises on medicine include chapters on astrology inasmuch as they discuss the nature of diseases, astral in origin, and therapeutic charms and incantations. Divination was also resorted to for treatment and cure of diseases. *Mantras* or spells were practised to cure diseases. *Mantras* were further used to scare away devils and evil spirits who were supposed to be the cause of human ailments, to cure snakebite, to remove the bad effect of dreams, to secure release from misfortune, to protect the fields from the evil eye, for the prosperity of the home and the harvest, and for a hundred and one other purposes.

The Ahom chronicles as well as the reports of Muhammedan

historians testify to the use of charms and incantations for bewitching hostile armies, and even oppressive officers were sought to be killed by means of charms or witchcraft. An Ahom *Buranji*, while recording the proceedings of a trial for conspiracy and subversive activity for the overthrow of the State, reproduces the following deposition of a witness· "I am told that one Baga possesses an old *puthi* with the help of which all can be subdued, including the king and his subjects." A bulk of writings on *mantras* was, therefore, created in both prose and verse. An idea of the volume and variety of *mantra* literature can be had from the titles of some of these books. Significant among these *mantra-puthis* are the following: *Sāpar-dharaṇī-mantra* (Snake-catching charm), *Karati-mantra*, *Sarva-dhāk-mantra*, *Kāmaratna-mantra*, *Bhutar-mantra*, *Khetra-mantra*; the list might easily be extended. It is true that these *mantra-puthis* have no literary value, but they are important as documents of popular beliefs and superstitions. Among other books of useful knowledge, *Śrīhastamuktāvalī* of Subhaṅkara must be taken into consideration. The original Sanskrit texts deal with the movements of human body and its different limbs, while acting, in the minutest detail. All the texts are elegantly rendered into Assamese with the utmost precision. The translator has tried to give, as far as possible, suitable Assamese equivalents for Sanskrit words. Kavirāj Cakravartī's *Bhāsvatī* is a text on astronomy. If he is the same person who wrote *Śaṅkhāsura-vadha*, *Śakuntalā-kāvya*, the metrical *Brahmavaivarta Purāṅa* and the translation of *Gīta-govinda*, then he must be a contemporary of King Siva Singha (1714-1744). *Bhāsvatī* is an epitome of the Sanskrit *Sūrya-Siddhānta*. Of the books on arithmetic mention must be made of *Aṅkar-Āryyā* of Kāsīnāth. The book treats of arithmetic, including rules of land measurement and the method of finding the square root of figures. At places the book contains Sanskrit verses. There were also treatises on architecture, road-construction and such other subjects.

From the number of prose works composed during the period, between the time of Bhaṭṭadeva and the composition of *Hastividyārṇava*, it is easy to see how Assamese prose literature developed enormously in several directions. The influence of Sanskrit was, of course, there, particularly in the case of serious philosophical and religious treatises which were mostly translations done by Sanskrit scholars. Assamese had not till then developed an adequate number of *tadbhava* and racy *deśīya* words, nor was their use standardised. Except Sanskrit there was nothing that could serve as a pattern of grammar and style. Therefore imitation of Sanskrit on the part of the new-born Assamese prose was not merely necessary but also inevitable. Though modelled after Sanskrit texts and commentaries, Assamese prose had done away with flamboyant expressions and profusion of compounds, and had thus attained clarity. Its aim was the spread of useful knowledge amongst average men. Hence its limpidity and simplicity. Everywhere in these books ideas are expressed in an exact, logical, relevant, and, whenever needed, concise manner. Apart from their value as literature, these books are worth recalling for a proper appraisal of the intellectual activities of mediaeval Assam.

As stated earlier, the most important development in Assamese literature under the Ahoms is the *Burañjīs*, the chronicles of the Ahom court. The *Burañjīs* were compiled under royal edicts and under the decrees of the high dignitaries of the state, for they alone could grant access to State documents on which the chronicles had invariably to be based. These documents were principally the periodic reports transmitted to the court by military commanders and frontier governors, diplomatic epistles sent to and received from foreign rulers and allies, judicial and revenue papers submitted to the kings and ministers for final orders, and the day-to-day annals of the court which incorporated all the transactions done, important utterances made, and significant occurrences reported by reliable eye-witnesses. (*Asam Burañji*, Introduction).

The *Burañjīs* were at first written in Ahom, the language of the rulers. Later, however, they came to be compiled in the Assamese language. The *Burañjīs* constitute an unprecedented and glorious chapter in Assamese literature. It will not be an exaggeration to remark that it is from these *Burañjīs* that modern Assamese prose emerges. Commenting on this unique historical literature, Sir G. A. Grierson observes: "The Assamese are justly proud of their national literature.

In no department have they been more successful than in a branch of study in which India, as a rule, is curiously deficient. The historical works or Buranjis are numerous and voluminous. A knowledge of Buranjis was an indispensable qualification to an Assamese gentleman." (*Linguistic Survey of India*).

The compilation of a *Burañjī* was a sacred task, and, therefore, it was customary to begin it with a salutation to the deity. The chronicles were prepared generally by men who had a comprehensive knowledge about state affairs, and we have several *Burañjīs* whose authors were high government officials. Hence the language of these chronicles is dignified and graceful. As they are factual records, they have been put in a language which is ordinarily free from sentimental rhetoric. They are simple, easy, unpretentious, and unquestionably charming.

All these vast historical writings have not yet been completely brought to light. Dr. S. K. Bhuyan has published some of them under the auspices of the Department of Historical and Antiquarian Studies, Government of Assam. The prose chronicles published so far by the said Department are *Āsām-Burañjī* by Harakanta Barua (1930), *Deodhanī-Āsām-Burañjī*, a compilation from several sources (1932), *Tuṅgakhuṅgīyā-Burañjī* by Srinath Duara (1932), *Kachārī-Burañjī* (1936), and *Asam-Burañjī* (1945). Two other important chronicles, viz., the *Puraṇi-Āsām-Burañjī* (1922) and *Pādśvāh-Burañjī*, have been published by the Kāmarūpa Anusandhāna Samiti and edited respectively by Pandit Hemachandra Goswami and Dr. S. K. Bhuyan.

The dates of composition of all these *Burañjīs* have not definitely been ascertained; they were perhaps compiled over a long period, beginning from the late sixteenth to the early nineteenth century. Chronologically speaking, *Puraṇi-Āsām-Burañjī*, edited by the late Pandit Hemachandra Goswami, may be taken to be the earliest. Goswami considers the work to have been compiled in the reign of Gadadhar Singha (1681-1695). Another chronicle, *Svarganārāyaṇdeva-Mahārājār-Ākhyān*, now published under the title *Āsām-Burañjī*, also appears to have been compiled, according to Dr. S. K. Bhuyan, during this period.

Pandit Goswami also came to the conclusion that *Kathā-Gītā* was composed at some time after 1594. So the time intervening between the composition of *Kathā-Gītā* and *Purani-Āsām-Burañjī* is roughly about one hundred years. *Purani-Āsām-Burañjī* shows clearly how during these one hundred years Assamese prose was shaping itself. It is true that Bhaṭṭadeva broke away from the conventional ornamental style and, for the first time in the history of Assamese literature, adopted the spoken language. But he was not completely free from the influence of the ornate and cultivated Sanskritised style. As already pointed out, Bhaṭṭadeva indeed succeeded to a large extent in using an Assamese vocabulary in spite of the classical learning that encumbered him. But in the structure of his sentences he could not completely get away from the Sanskrit model, and a large percentage of *tatsama* words made their inroads into his writings. The language of the *Burañjīs*, however, is completely free from classical influence as they were written on subject-matter which was entirely different in tone and accentuation. The *Burañjīs* have no association whatsoever with scriptural texts. They are annals of royal families and intimate portrayals of the contemporary scene, compiled by wise and experienced men of affairs imbued with the sense of historical perspective. They give us chronological accounts of the court life, the royal routine and the proceedings of the royal court. For these reasons the language of the *Burañjīs* cannot but be the polished language of the courtiers. Based as it was on the cultured language of the court, it is admirable for its richness, and clarity and is well fitted for historical narration. "It is curious how the Assamese intellect," observes Dr. S. K. Bhuyan, "nurtured on the extravagance of Vaiṣṇava poetry, could pin itself down to the chronicling of grim realities and hard facts in a colourless and impersonal fashion. The bridge between the two phases of the intellect labouring in the realm of fiction or of fact was afforded by the model set forth in the *Burañjīs* written in the Ahom language, the chroniclers of which enjoyed immunity from the influence of imaginative poetry and who were subjected to rigorous discipline and supervision as their works were compiled as a matter of official routine."

Though there was no need for literary airs and graces, yet the *Burañjīs* are not wholly devoid of them. In this connection another remark of Dr. S. K. Bhuyan, made with reference to the literary flavour of *Pādśāh-Burañji*, may also be applied to other *Burañjis* with equal force. He observes, "The historical narrative is not a dry bone. One notices in it thought and emotions too. Hence it ascends to the level of pure literature. It will not be too much to say that such a confluence of history and literature is not to be found in any modern Indian literature in the pre-British period. What would otherwise be a dry historical narrative, has in the hands of the writer become an entertaining historical literature punctuated to the reader's satisfaction by such elements of style as simile, analogy, illustrations, episodes and diversions." Scattered throughout the entire *Burañji* literature are numerous instances of worldly wisdom and original thoughts. The secret of the literary success of the *Burañjis* lies to a great extent in sentence construction, local idiom and the expressive cadence of the spoken language. The writers are adepts in expressing themselves in short sentences and simple and homely phraseology.

The *Burañjis* contributed largely towards the enrichment of Assamese vocabulary in its various ramifications in diverse fields. They incorporate a large number of administrative and legal terms current in the Ahom court. Words from the Ahom language are also not rare. Such words are used to denote things and institutions which are distinctly connected with Ahom life and culture. Words of Arabic and Persian origin also have been laid under contribution, particularly in ambassadorial and diplomatic deeds and documents.

These *Burañjis* were mostly written in the eastern dialect of Assamese (*Ujaniya bhāṣā*), which from this time began to rank as the standard literary speech. This development was due to the predominance of eastern Assam as the seat of the Ahom court and administration, and centre of trade and commerce: a fact which made eastern Assamese the language of affairs. It was after the pattern of this prose that the easy and simple prose of the *Aruṇoday* (1846), the first periodical in Assamese, developed in the early years of the 19th century.

There is another class of historical writings composed in both verse and prose and generally known as *Vaṁśāvalīs*. Besides recording the genealogy of the different families of the nobles, the *Vaṁśāvalīs* give sketches of their lives and careers. It seemed important for various reasons to preserve an authentic record of the noble families for receiving royal grant and office. These *Vaṁśāvalīs* thus supply information which is not available in the *Buranjis*. Such a *Vaṁśāvalī* is *Darang-Rāj-Vaṁśāvalī* composed in verse by Suryakhari Daivajna during the latter part of the eighteenth century under the patronage of Samudra-narayan, Koch king to Darang. The original manuscript of the book was embellished with beautiful illustrations. "The *Darang-Rāj-Vaṁśāvalī*" writes Dr. S. K. Bhuyan, "has been an invaluable source book for all studies connected with the early history of the Koch rulers."

The six hundred years of Ahom rule present a panorama of growth in all departments of life. The most distinctive aspects of the period, as noticed earlier, were the geographical and racial unification of the country, stabilisation of the political institutions, organisation of the economic, social and religious systems, and the rise of cultural nationalism. Contributing to the growth of nationalism were such diverse factors as the invasions of the Moghuls, the coming of Islam, the expansionist tendency of the kings and a general awakening in the country. The rationalistic temper of the age had a direct effect on arts and literature, which contributed a good deal to the life of the people. The intellectual and artistic expression of the period may be known alone from the production of enormous manuscripts. The manuscript-production, which demanded much calligraphic and orthographic ability, was itself a magnificent achievement. The production of a manuscript was a laborious process involving leisure and money. A large number of manuscripts could be produced only with royal munificence. Each manuscript produced in the royal court is even now a priceless treasure of art for its calligraphy and even for the material on which the words are written. These manuscripts were prepared on barks of *cañci* trees or on aloe wood, and the preparation entailed various processes of seasoning, polishing and painting before the material could be used for writing. It should also be noted that with the manuscript-production was intimately connected the art of painting. Some of the magnificent manuscripts produced during the period are *Gitagovinda*, *Śaṅkhāsura-*

vadha, *Bhāgavata*, *Darang-Rāj-Vaṁśāvali*, *Hasti-vidyārṇava*. The paintings in these manuscripts do not consist exclusively of religious pictures but also abound in lively portraits of kings and court life.

From the standpoint of literary history, however, the distinctive features of the age are the growth of prose and secular literature, the tendency to exalt the individual, particularly saints and kings, and the emergence of scientific curiosity. It is a significant feature of the age that along with the development of prose literature, interest in utilitarian subjects and the scientific temper also gathered a fresh momentum. The study of mathematics and architecture was the first step in this direction. Astrology and 'the donkey and the steed of Apollo' were cultivated, and in the treatises on *Jyotiṣa* the authors described natural phenomena with the limited knowledge they had at their command. The tomes on *Ayurveda* are full of pharmacological and zoological observations.

When, however, we turn to literature proper we do not gain an inspiring impression. It seems that never before so many flower-plants were nurtured with so much zeal, but there are very few flowers blossoming with perfumes and colour to count with. The output of literary productions was doubtless great and books were composed practically on all branches of literature, but the majority of writings, both religious and secular, are stereotyped, etiolated, imitative and laboured, and do not rise above the level of mere verse-making. Their poetic forms are also traditional or repetitive of earlier models, and they do not show any spontaneity and originality. It is true that a few poets handled fresh motifs and themes, but their works, too, lack intense feeling and emotion and are consequently anaemic in their final impression. The period produced a large number of poets and writers, but we do not get a saint-poet of Śaṅkaradeva's genius, a devotee-philosopher of Mādhavadeva's eminence or a scholar of Rāma Sarasvatī's greatness.

CHAPTER VI

BEGINNING OF THE MODERN PERIOD THE AMERICAN BAPTIST MISSION

THE Ahoms ruled in Assam from the beginning of the thirteenth to about the middle of the nineteenth century (1826). The closing decades of the Ahom rule were fateful years in the history of Assam. The whole country was torn with internal strife. In the struggle for ascendancy between the two forms of Hindu worship, the Vaiṣṇavite and the Śakta, that had been going on since the fifteenth century, the latter had so far succeeded as to become the court religion of the Ahom kings, who extended patronage to its adherents on a large scale. This did not matter much as long as the kings themselves exercised religious tolerance. But during the last days of King Rajeswar Singha's reign (1714-1744), the queen, who wielded immense power, persecuted a section of the Vaiṣṇavas. The latter rose in revolt, and the rebellion gathered such force that it shook his administration to its very foundation. His successor, Laxmi Singha, was not able to improve the situation. The administrative machinery of the state, already none too strong, began to show distinct signs of decadence and disintegration.

On account of the Vaiṣṇavite revolt and other political feuds the administration finally broke down during Chandrakanta Singha's reign, and in 1817, on the invitation of Badan Barphụkan, an Ahom Viceroy, the Burmese invaded and plundered the country. They revisited it the following year, tempted by the wealth of the country, and decided to conquer it and finally took possession of Assam in 1820. In 1826 the Burmese came into conflict with the British in Cachar and, being defeated, surrendered Assam to the East India Company under the Treaty of Yandabu (1839).

The British were strangers to the land and had no knowledge of the local tongue. So people from other provinces of India began to pour into Assam and settle down as interpreters and clerks of the British to enable them to carry on the newly established administration. Under the influence of these men, recruited mostly from Bengal, the British administrators made Bengali the language of the court and the medium of instruction in the schools of Assam. It was in 1836 that Assamese was thrown out of the law-courts and schools and Bengali was installed in its place. The same year that Assamese thus lost its official position two remarkable members of the American Baptist Mission, the Rev. N. Brown and O. T. Cotter, arrived in Assam with their families. Among other things a printing-machine was part of their missionary equipment. Realising at once that to instil the love of Christ in the heart of the people they must approach them through the medium of their mother tongue, the missionaries immediately set about learning it, and within three months of their arrival in Assam they produced the first Assamese primer for use in the schools which they had established. Even before their arrival, the English Missionaries Carey and Marshman had started work in this direction from Serampore near Calcutta, and in collaboration with an Assamese Pandit, Atmaram Sarma of Kaliabar (Nowgong District), they had translated the entire Bible into Assamese and published it from Serampore in 1813. This was the first Assamese book in print. The missionaries were not literary men. Their chief aim was the spread of Christianity and of Western education along with it. So they wrote mainly Christian literature and text-books. These books dealt in general knowledge, stories from history, geography and the world of science, as well as the lives of Christian saints and apostles. In addition to these they also compiled dictionaries and wrote texts on Assamese Grammar—both essential for learning the language. In 1839 was published *A Grammar of the Assamese Language* by Mr. W. Robinson from Serampore. This is the first Assamese Grammar. In 1848 the Rev. Brown published from Sibsagar his *Grammatical Notice of the Assamese Language*. From the same place was published Mrs. Cutter's *Vocabulary*. In 1894, Mr. G. F. Nicholl published, along with his *Manual of the Bengali Language*, an Assamese Grammar. All these grammars of the Assamese language were written in English and were intended for English-speaking people who wanted to learn Assamese.

Inevitably they were influenced by the method of English grammar, but they represent the first scientific attempt at studying the Assamese language.

In 1867 was published Mr. Bronson's *Dictionary in Assamese and English* from the Baptist Mission Press at Sibsagar. This is the first published Assamese Dictionary. Sri Jaduram Barua had compiled a Dictionary even earlier but unfortunately it did not see the light of day.

Bronson's spelling was based on the spoken language which does not always conform to the written style. Hence his Dictionary does not have much practical utility today. Regarding the other contributions of the missionaries, Mr. P. H. Moore, a missionary and linguist, observed as early as 1907: "The modern literature in Assamese whether Christian or non-Christian may be said to be the product of the last sixty years of the 19th century. Brown, Bronson and Nidhi Levi are the trio of names that stand out pre-eminently as the founders of Assamese Christian Literature."[1]

Of the missionaries, Brown was the greatest single benefactor of Assamese literature. Together with O. Cutter, he established the first printing press in Assam in 1836, and from this press was published in 1844 the first newspaper in Assamese—*Āruṇoday* (The Sunrise). Reference has already been made to his *Grammar of the Assamese Language*.

Another contribution of Brown was his Assamese version of the New Testament. It has, however, to be noted that though the Bible is a great and sacred book, its Assamese version has not left any impress whatsoever on Assamese language and literature. Written in an artificial and defective idiom by men with imperfect knowledge of Assamese, and dealing with an absolutely different set of saints, apostles and religious beliefs, the New Testament could not strike root in the minds of the common people who found in it nothing to approach the immortal epics, the *Rāmāyaṇa* and the *Mahābhārata*. In addition to the Christian tracts and psalms, which he composed and published, Brown also arranged for the publication of some old Assamese manuscripts. His wife too wrote a few text-books and stories in Assamese.

[1] V. H. Sword, *Baptist in Assam*, Conference Press, Chicago, Illinois, 1933.

Among the local talents who assisted the missionaries, Nidhi Levi Farwell's name is noteworthy. He published a number of articles and poems in the *Aruṇoday* and tried to standardise Assamese spelling and grammar. He also translated from Bengali in 1855 *Natural Science in Familiar Dialogue*. The book explains, in fourteen different dialogues, such phenomena as planetary motion, the atmosphere, the origin and mystery of man, the evolution of animals, plants, creepers and minerals. The book illustrates the earliest prose dialogue of modern Assamese, which was developed in the later prose dramas. Farwell's general treatises on science together with the flexible prose style he developed for scientific expression in Assamese are, in a sense, *sui generis*. Mention may also be made of *Yātrikārar Yātrā* (Assamese rendering of *The Pilgrim's Progress*) and the novels *Kāminī Kānta* and *Phulmaṇi Aru Karuṇā*, which the missionaries published. Though scriptural in tone, *Kāminī Kānta* by G. S. Gurney (1877) is the first modern Assamese novel. The missionaries wrote several books, all in prose, for the spread of Christianity. Though most of these books were translations from English and as such lacked originality, through them was evolved a prose style capable of expressing varied interests.

The missionaries adopted in their compositions the spoken language of the people. They had no extensive or intimate knowledge of the genius of the language. The result was that their writings were artificial and sometimes even amusing for their malapropisms. On the whole their writings failed to attract the people.

The missionaries definitely achieved one thing. Up till now Assamese literature was more or less an oral literature confined to the villages and the Ahom court. It now takes a definitely urban complexion, and at Gauhati, Sibsagar, Nowgong and such other headquarter towns literary circles sprang up. The old religious tone was replaced by a more secular one, and there grew up a literature dealing not with a mythical world of gods and nymphs but with the life and society of the 'mortal millions' here and now. Western ideas began to spread along with the progress of English education in the land. In every town a literary society was born. Old beliefs, ways and concepts yielded place to new ones. The influence of Western ideas began to be keenly felt in the domain of literature, which now enters a period of varied creative activity.

To this spread of new ideas, the widening of horizons and enrichment of literature, the press and the newspapers made an invaluable contributions, particularly the Baptist Mission Press of Sibsagar and its periodical, the *Aruṇoday*. Most Assamese books of the mid-nineteenth century were published from this press. The printed books and newspapers brought literature within the reach of the average man, and not only helped in its advancement but also enabled the growth of a standard language understood by all.

In this connection mention must be made of some Assamese litterateurs of the time, who had a community of interest and whose efforts supplemented the work of the missionaries. Among them Anandaram Dhekial Phukan was the leading figure. Dhekial Phukan agitated for the reinstatement of the Assamese language in the schools and courts and published several spirited articles on the subject in the *Aruṇoday*. Phukan's *A Few Remarks on the Assamese Language*, a pamphlet of force and power pleading for the re-instatement of the Assamese language was published in 1849 from the Baptist Mission at Sibsagar. Of the other works of Phukan, the *Asamīyā-Lorār Mitra* (The Assamese Boys' Companion, 1849) deserves commendation. Though devoid of literary merit, his writings provide specimens of the transitional modern Assamese prose style that was gradually evolving. His untimely death in the prime of life cut down a promising literary career.

The next major writer who tried to advance Assamese language and literature was Gunabhiram Barua (1837-95). Like Anandaram Dhekial Phukan, Gunabhiram was also educated at Calcutta. The two principal works of Barua are *Biography of Anandaram Dhekial Phukan* (1880) and the *Asam Burañjī* (1884), both models of the modern scientific spirit in biography and history respectively. Gunabhiram had skill in sifting and re-arranging details to bring out the soul of the man he wrote about and the spirit of the time he touched on. He made a breach with the tradition of the religious biography of the Vaiṣṇava period. His history is also the first comprehensive modern history of Assam covering not only the political but also the religious, the social and the cultural aspects. His descriptions are charming; his language, devoid of rhetorical flowers, is elegantly simple and appealing. Gunabhiram also edited a monthly journal, the *Asām-Bandhu* (The Friend of Assam, 1885), from Calcutta, to which he himself contributed a number of valuable articles on Assam's history.

In Gunabhiram Barua's hands Assamese prose attained a perfection not reached before. While his predecessors had made Assamese prose flexible enough to express all kinds of ideas and the Christian missionaries had employed it not only for Christian theology but also for secular knowledge including science, it was Gunabhiram who made it a full-fledged literary and artistic medium. What was till now largely an instrument for proselytisation became in his hands a weapon of strength and beauty. He fostered literary culture amongst his friends by encouraging them to write, and was thus the central figure of much fruitful literary work. His dominating literary personality and his long literary career made his contemporaries regard him as the literary dictator of the time. He reminds one of Dr. Johnson.

Another literary stalwart of the 19th century was Hemchandra Barua (1835-96), who has rightly been called the father of modern Assamese language and literature. He brought great devotion to his work coupled with organisation, assiduity and diligence. His *Grammar of the Assamese Language* (1856) and *Hemkoṣ* (Dictionary), the first standard work on lexicography, laid a sure foundation for the future development of the language. The language now had a systematic grammar which among other things laid down clear-cut rules for spelling and syntax, leaving no room for obscurity and confusion. The *Hemkoṣ* became a standard lexicon giving the etymology of words and their English equivalents and clearly setting forth what each word in the Assamese language really meant. His Grammar and Dictionary remain even today standard texts.

Hemchandra Barua, a descendant of an orthodox Brahmin family of Sibsagar, learnt English secretly at home with the assistance of the missionaries. He was a gifted contributor to the *Aruṇoday*. He began his literary career as a writer of school texts, of which the *Ādipath* and the *Pāthmālā* remain even today two of the best specimens of Assamese prose style. Of his other works, the *Bāhire Raṅ Caṅ Bhitare Kovā Bhāturi* (All That Glitters Is Not Gold) is a novelette where the satiric or critical spirit was for the first time introduced in Assamese literature. Though himself a high-class Brahmin, Hemchandra Barua was an outspoken critic of Hindu orthodoxy and was pitiless in exposing its many social and moral hypocrisies and hide-bound conventions. He mercilessly lays bare in the novelette the immoral practices of Gobardhan Satradhikar, a Hindu pontiff, who professes to be religious but is in fact lecherous, secretly indulging in all sorts of immoral liaisons, and even going so far as to seduce the wife of a low-caste disciple of his.

In 1861 was published his *Kāniyār Kīrtan* — a social farce dealing with the evil effects of opium-addiction. Incidentally, he also exposed in this farce how in the name of religion the Gosains and Mahantas, who were entrusted with religious administration, perpetrated immoralities, and how Assamese peons of the British in their overweening pride used Hindusthani in preference to their mother tongue for no other purpose than to mystify the common folk and to cut impressive figures. The whole farce is full of bitter satire and biting sarcasm. Though somewhat lacking in dramatic vigour, its reformatory appeal and entertaining dialogue make *Kāniyār Kīrtan* an outstanding literary achievement. Indeed, it actually won a prize from the Government. In the evolution of Assamese prose style Hemchandra Barua's has been a profoundly wholesome influence.

CHAPTER VII

POETRY

As a result of the spread of the Western system of education and the consequent impact of Western ideas on the minds of the people, Assamese poetry underwent radical changes in both form and content. These changes began to be noticed in the last decades of the 19th century. Assamese literature was influenced by the Romantic Revival in England, and the result was a new and unprecedented florescence of Assamese literature, rich and varied, vital and vigorous. The old and narrow outlook yielded place to catholicity, formalism to a variety of attractive and new patterns. There were innovations in diction, rhythm and imagery, potent instruments of poetic consciousness, and what emerged from these innovations was something novel, invigorating, powerful and brilliant. Assamese poetry entered into a romantic period of large and lofty dreams of Utopias and El Dorados, daring hopes and sky-scraping aspirations. The new poetry sang of freedom for all from political dependence, social injustice, religious bigotry, of the dignity of the individual, and of the unity of the nation.

In Assamese, as in other languages, poetry was the earliest medium of expression. No wonder, therefore, that the new spirit of romanticism also found its earliest articulation in verse. As one modern poet remarks, "Burdened with the complexity of the lives we lead, fretting over appearances, netted in with anxieties and apprehensions, half smothered in drift of tepid thoughts and tepid feelings, we may refuse what poetry has to give; but under its influence serenity returns to the troubled mind, the world crumbles, loveliness shines like flowers after rain and the further reality is once more charged with mystery." This is pre-eminently true of modern Assamese poetry over which the influence of the English Romantic Revival was doubtless very wholesome. Its love of beauty developed in the Assamese poets a fuller appreciation of the scenic grandeur of their country. Similarly, its interest in antiquity imbued the Assamese poets with a deeper understanding and a more intense love of the national heritage.

A leading poet of this new movement was Kamalakanta Bhattacharya (1858-1936). In the poetry of Kamalakanta Bhattacharya there is the triple strand of the patriot, philosopher and social reformer. For the first time in Assamese literature, he sounded the clarion call of liberal patriotism. His patriotism, however, consisted not only in rousing a forgetful, sleeping but puissant nation to the glories of their ancient culture, but also in urging it to march with the times and follow the methods of Western nations. He was inspired by the examples of Garibaldi and Mazzini:

Then will be born hundreds of Mazzinis,
    Out of neglect stones,
And hundreds of Garibaldis too
    To shed lustre on the soil of India.

Two notable collections of Kamalakanta's poems are *Cintānal*, 1809 (Burning Thoughts), and *Cintātaraṅgiṇī* (Waves of Thought). The lack of freedom and the accompanying ills of the country roused him to poignant protest. The sad contrast between the lofty and sunny past of the country and the benighted present was a recurring theme in most of his poetic raptures. The poet reminded his countrymen that they alone had fallen into disgrace while the country remained still as lovely and delightful as of old. Some poems of *Cintānal*, such as the *Udagani* (A Word of Cheer), the *Pūrṇimār Rātilai Cāi* (On Looking at the Full-Moon Night), *Eino Āsām Nahayane Śmaśān* (Is Not This Assam a Grave yard?) and *Jātīya Gaurav* (National Glory) are especially devoted to the illuminating juxtaposition of two pictures, one of the golden past and the other of the contemporary iron age of a crippling and stultifying bondage. His poems exhale, as flowers exhale fragrance, a new ideal of nationalism, new values of life, and the culture of the Upaniṣads. He was proud of being an Indian, and in this pride resides chiefly the power and charm of his stirring songs. He was extraordinarily sensitive to Assam's glory.

In *Pāharani* (Forgetfulness) the poet, after narrating how Assam's ancient glories have sunk in oblivion, dwells on how those glories can be revived to exalt her to her deserved place of honour in the comity of nations. These patriotic poems of Kamalakanta inspired the succeeding generation of educated and enlightened youth to delve deep into the rich mines of Assam's magnificent past.

In *Himālayar Prati Sambodhan*, 1919 (An Address to the Himalayas), the poet addresses the mighty mountain and narrates in the form of a highly imaginative and fascinating dialogue, the annals of India's glorious antiquity, contrasting them with the woes and throes of the present. In the Vedic age, the Brahmins were worthy custodians of light and culture, whilst the Kshatriyas performed their ordained task of administration and defence of the country, and the Vaisyas, that of economic enrichment of the country through commerce and industry. But at present all of them have deviated from their well-ordained duties with the result that ignorance, illiteracy, discontent, iniquity, corruption and misery stalk the land. The poet has, of course, faith in a bright future and the poem ends on an optimistic note:

> A new earth will now be slowly born,
> And envy and hatred will yield to love
> And peace will possess the world.

More than any other writer Kamalakanta has through his stirring verses excited the imagination of the Assames people and created in them a fresh interest in life and stimulus to progress. Kamalakanta has emotion and fire but his rhythm is not always smooth, polished and disciplined. His is not a chastened muse. Generally speaking his poetic texture is somewhat loose and inorganic.

Bholanath Das (1858-1929) was another early lyricist, and his *Cintā Taraṅgiṇī* (Waves of Thought, 1884) contained some fervent and noble lyrics. He also wrote the first Assamese epic in blank verse, *Sītā-haraṇ Kāvya* (1888), based on the *Rāmāyaṇa* story, in which the influence of Michael Madhusudan Datta is broadly discernible. His diction was an uneven mixture of Sanskrit words and compounds, together with mediaeval inflexions of Assamese words, and hence it lacked chastity and felicity. At places the poet shows eloquence and verve which make up for the defect in diction. Occasionally there are memorable observations. While describing Śūrpaṇakhā, the poet reflects about women in general:

> Who in the whole universe can know the mind of a woman?
> The soft face of a woman is not an index that the mind is as soft.
> Who can fathom the minds of women? They may be silent and pliant; but are their hearts as pliant?
> Hard nuts abound in their hearts,
> Where the bees do not get honey.
> The lotus-faced women shed lusture to conceal dark minds within,
> Like the flame that sheds light and yet bears a dark core.

Lakshminath Bezbarua (1868-1938) is universally acknowledged to be the greatest figure in modern Assamese literature. He was an excellent poet, a gifted essayist, and a distinguished journalist. Assamese poetry in the hands of Lakshminath broke all its traditional fetters. He not only struck new notes and opened new vistas of thought but introduced fresh forms and diction. He wrote outstanding love-lyrics, nature-poems, narrative verse and ballads. He is thoroughly imbued with the romantic spirit, and visualises two poles for the world of poetic consciousness — the sweetness of the saddest thought and the beauty of colour and sound pervading the whole world.

In his patriotic songs and poems, as in *Amar Janma Bhūmi*, *Mor Deś*, *Asam-saṅgīt*, and *Bīṇ Barāgi*, Lakshminath sets forth the glories and the greatness of Assamese culture and history with glowing love and admiration. He looks with wondering eyes upon the past history of the country and bursts into splendid paeans of praise for the faded grandeur and the forgotten national heritage.

Romantic idealization of the past stimulated Bezbarua's nationalistic sentiments. Needless to say, Lakshminath's patriotic poetry shed lustre on and lent courage, faith, confidence and strength to the downtrodden and oppressed people of the country during their last freedom-fight. His song,

O My Own Land, O My Beautiful Land, is justly regarded as the national anthem of Assam.

A meeting-ground for various races and tribes, Assam naturally has become the cradle for various cultures and the treasure-house of vast lore arising from the peoples' genius. Her folk-literature has always exercised a weird fascination over the minds of all lovers of letters. Lakshminath not only collected ancient lays in Assamese and conserved the other literary treasures of the country but also distilled their wealth of passion, imagination and expression into his own compositions. He skillfully recreated in his poems the body and soul of many an old ballad and many a mediaeval pastoral song. He was endowed with the eye of a painter and the ear of a musician. His *Nimātī Kanyā* (Dumb Bride) is a picture in words. *Dhānbar aru Ratanī*, a ballad about a rustic youth and a maiden, is a unique piece of literary creation. *Kiyano Ānili Māne ai Badan Tai*, a sombre pastoral poem which deals with the catastrophic treason of Badan Barphukan, the Assamese Minister at whose invitation the Burmese invaded Assam in 1816, is full of melancholy, sadness and despair.

Padmanath Gohain Barua also composed some lyrics, and his *Phular Cānekī* (Sample of Flowers) is an anthology of descriptive nature poems. The poet is attracted by the silent profundity of Nature. Gerald Manley Hopkins observed that the world is charged with God's grandeur which shines forth everywhere as from 'shook foil'. Gohain Barua subscribes to the same view and affirms that all Nature points to God. The sun, the trees and creepers "sing the hymns of God". From this point of view, his poem *Kartavya* (Duty) is noteworthy. In the poem, *Uṣā* (Dawn), the poet speaks of the birth of new life as a result of the union of Dawn and Nature. Gohain Barua's vocabulary is racy of the soil, he being extremely loyal to orthodox and meticulous Assamese. *Līlā* is a long autobiographical poem in blank verse, describing domestic felicity. The poem glows with charming descriptions of the natural beauties of Assam.

Chandrakumar Agarwala (1867-1938) is another votary at the shrine of Beauty. His poetry breathes a love of beauty, a joy in living and a spirit of optimism, issuing forth from a warm, sympathetic and tender heart. He did not follow the beaten track, and in his poetry there are some new trends. While older poets believed beauty to dwell in the ambrosial bliss of the heaven of the hereafter, modern poets discover the same beauty in the heart of Nature. Chandrakumar went a step further and maintained that it dwells in man's tender affection, cordiality and grace. *Pratimā* (The Image) is a small collection containing beautiful nature poems such as *Sandhyā* (The Evening), *Prakṛti* (Nature), *Niyar* (The Dew), etc., in which the poet gives glowing pictures of Nature's mysterious and awe-inspiring beauty and conveys the profound appeal that she makes to the mind of man. Romanticism, under whose wings he had come during his younger days, also directed his thought to folklore. His *Ban-kumvārī* (The Woodland Nymph), *Jal-kumvārī* (The Sea Nymph), *Tejīmalā* (The Creeper Nymph) and other such poems are pregnant with a supernatural beauty and mystery. Here is a 'Celtic' touch with which old popular beliefs have been made to yield poems of matchless craftsmanship and charm. Another element of his poetry is his wide humanity and the recognition of the basic equality of men. In recognising the dignity of man as man everywhere, he was influenced by the French philosopher Auguste Compte. In his poem *Bīṇ Baragi* (The Ministrel) he sings of the glory of love for man. He sees beauty and truth in the relations of man in his everyday life, and finds glory and excellence in human affection and sympathy in the face of common suffering. The poet wants to metamorphose our tabernacle on earth into a blessed heavenly abode by sweeping away all the dirt and inequalities of the earth.

Ananda Chandra Agarwala (1874-1940) translated poems from English which read like the original. He also wrote several narrative poems of absorbing interest based on folk-tales.

Hiteswar Barbarua (1876-1939) wrote long narrative poems in blank verse and a number of sonnets, modelled after English types. His earliest collection, *Dhopākali* (The Bud, 1902), contains poems composed in early youth. The long poem, *Kamatapur Dhvaṁsa aru Birahiṇī Bilāp Kāvya* (The Fall of Kamatapur and the Sorrows of Parted Lovers), was published in 1912. The theme is taken from mediaeval Assamese history. It describes how ancient Kamatapur (situated near modern

Cooch-Behar) was sacked, during the reign of King Nilambar, by the Nawab of Gaur through the conspiracy of Nilambar's own minister. Divided in fifteen sections, the poem is mostly dramatic. Another historical narrative poem is his *Tirotār Ātmadān* (Woman's Self-Sacrifice) in which the poet describes how the illustrious Ahom Princess, Jayamati, held as ransom by a tyrannical despot, the Lara-Raja, willingly embraced death through torture for the cause of her husband and the country. The poet, while maintaining fidelity to facts, pours out all the wealth of his imagination whenever there is opportunity to do so. He often stops and indulges in impassioned apostrophes to such things as Imagination, Tears, Dewdrops, Sleep, etc. apostrophes which almost become independent lyrics of rare charm and beauty.

Yuddhakṣetrat Āhom Ramaṇī ba Mula Gābharu (An Ahom Heroine in the Battle-field or Mula Gābharu) is another long, narrative poem by Barbarua. Based on the sixth and seventh invasions of Assam by the Moghuls of Delhi in 1532 and 1533, the poem describes the exemplary courage, unswerving heroism and sacrificial love of the Assamese heroine, Mula, who joined the army, fought the Moghuls, killed two Moghul generals, and thus avenged the death, at their hands, of her own husband, a general killed the previous year in action. Mula was herself subsequently killed on the battle-field. There is soul-stirring patriotic appeal throughout the poem; Barbarua's lines on love of the father-land have become proverbial in Assam:

> Whoever lays down his life on the battlefield,
> Fighting for the freedom of his father-land,
> Gets immortal bliss after death.
> Death is, in his case, eternal rest,
> Full of happiness, on the lap of the Mother Universal.
> To him fire is mellow as moonlight
> And the bed of clay is flower-bed,
> And the piercing spears falling
> Are but flowery showers.

He was widely read in European literature which he admired very much and which influenced his literary practice. He modelled his *Añjali* after Goldsmith's *Vicar of Wakefield* and based his *Desdemonā Kāvya* on Shakespeare's *Othello*. Profuse quotations from famous European writers are interspersed in his works. The *Ābhās* (Outline, 1914) is a collection of twenty-one lyrics devoted to the lives of as many illustrious women, including such diverse figures as Yasoda, Boadicea and Joan of Arc.

His *Mālac* (1918), a collection of 128 sonnets, is the first sonnet-sequence in Assamese. Covering in its narrow compass a very wide range of topics such as Iśvara (God), Kalpanā (Fancy), Ihakāla (This Side of the Grave), Sapon (Dream), the sequence contains, besides, poems addressed to Shakespeare, Kalidasa, Sankaradeva, Sakuntala, Miranda and other figures, real and imaginary, dear to his heart. Barbarua had known several bereavements in life, and apparently some of his sonnets are keys to unlock his agitated and afflicted heart. We have some splendid sonnets on Yātanā (Tribulations), Kandon (The Crying), Sāntvanā (Consolation) and Cakulo (Tears).

Cakulo (Tears, 1922) is another sonnet-sequence of Hiteswar Barbarua composed on the death of his youngest son. The sonnets express the bitter grief of the father. If the test of genuine poetry is to move, there can be no more genuine poetry than these sonnets. There is something in their language which brings tears to the reader's eyes. The title, *Cakulo*, is thus an apposite one. The sequence contains, in addition, a number of elegiac poems, which deal not only with the recurring grief of the bereaved father but also with ultimate problems like Life, Death, Soul, Heaven and the like. In such poems the poet succeeds in refracting the actual into the prophetic.

A scion of an ancient Ahom royal family, Hiteswar Barbarua knew intimately the pageant of Ahom history. This he collected into a book called *Ahomar Din* (The Ahom Days), which unfortunately yet remains to be published. His *Mālitā* is a novel with the same purpose, lined on a more fanciful canvas, and gives a faithful picture of some aspects of Ahom aristocracy in its heyday.

As a sonneteer Durgeswar Sarma also occupies a high position in Assamese literature. His sonnets together with other lyrics have been published in two collections—*Añjali*

(Flower Offerings) and *Nivedan* (The Supplication). A poet of strong moral and religious feeling and of elevated thought, Durgeswar Sarma occupies himself with the life fleeting and the Godhead eternal and the restless craving of the soul for self-realisation.

Many of his poems are sensuous and contain idyllic descriptions of sylvan youths and maids and of external nature. Picturesque in content and musical in phrase, symphonies of colour and sound weaving themselves into strange and rich melodies, Durgeswar Sarma's poetry reminds one of the English Lake poets whose influence is discernible in it.

Chandradhar Barua (1878-) is among the pioneers of Romanticism, but his reputation rests more on his dramas than on his verse. His *Rañjan* is a collection of poems containing, besides love and nature poems, hilarious ones composed in a light vein. *Smṛti* (Reminiscence) is a happy performance, alike for thought and feeling, where nature becomes the background for his love-emotions. The poet here expresses his belief, that the nectar-like touch of his departed beloved is there now everywhere in Nature. He says that in this uncertain and fickle life reminiscence alone is certain, and this reminiscence is vouchsafed protection by Nature only.

Raghunath Chaudhari (1879-) is known as the bird-poet of Assam. His very first collection of poems, *Sādarī* (The Darling), shows a preference on the part of the poet for birds, flowers and gardens. This was followed by two long poems published separately viz., *Keteki* (The Indian Nightingale) and *Dahikatarā* (The Wag-tail). In these two poems, the bird-theme, firmly established in the mind of the poet, is projected with admirable skill and penetrating vision. In *Sādari* poems like *Bahāgīr Biyā* (Marriage of May), *Govān he ebār mor Priya Bihaṅginī* (Wilt thou sing but once, thou darling Bird?), and *Keteki Carāi* give vivid and charming pictures of bird-life and the plant world. He finds sermons in stones and books in the running brooks. His nature poems fall into two categories—those that give objective descriptions of Nature and her objects, and those in which Nature is an ornamental filigree for the human fabric. In the former, Nature luxuriates in her abundance and ecstasy, while in the latter she generates enthusiasm in man. His *Bahāgīr Biyā* is a recreation of Nature's own festival. The bride, Bahāgī (May), daughter of Spring, is to be given in marriage. On this auspicious occasion, plants and shrubs and trees have put forth new foliage and blossoms, while birds and insects are piping and dancing in overwhelming joy. The poet exploits this scheme to describe the beauties of Nature that have appealed to him. The central idea of his *Ketekī* is the renaissance of Nature with the return of the bird to earth. The song of the *Ketekī* is some "unbodied joy", a delightful symphony of perfection incomprehensible to man. The poem begins in this attitude of wonder and mystery, and is sustained through five sections. After the wonder of the first section is over, the poet tries to grasp the inner truth of the bird's song. Through intuition the poet realises that in this world of cares and miseries, wherever there is any joy, that joy is nothing but an echo and effect of the bird's song. The second section contains many charming pictures of the love and joy that the bird's song generates in the world of nature and man. These pictures, by their fidelity to Assames life and nature, easily captivate the mind.

> Hearing thy voice, the bashful bride
> Stops weaving at her loom,
> And forgets to shuttle
> Listening dumb-founded.
> That self-same note
> Intoxicates the maiden,
> Thrilling and filling her with joy,
> Her spinning wheel comes to a stand-still,
> And the thread-ball drops down to the spindle.

In the third section the poet imaginatively visualises the flood of delight that the bird's song let loose in the legendary and mythical world of man. Sakuntala in Kanva's hermitage, Princess Damayanti of Vidarbha and Ushadevi of Sonitpur, the newly-wedded Yaksha of Alaka, and the Gopinis (milkmaids) of Gokula—all became engrossed in and overwhelmed with love by the bird-song. In the fourth section the poet finds that the bird's music has charmed not only people of the past nor only objects at all times, but has thrilled the life-stream running tirelessly around, above, below, and flowing through everything. The bird's music it is that calls forth rumbles of clouds and sparks of lightning, the dance of milkmaids, and the ebb and tide of the river Yamunā. In the fifth section the structure raised by the poet's imagination topples down, the bird disappears, and the poet is again aware of sordid realities. The poem runs a full cycle returning finally to the bosom of Nature whence it first emanated. Campbell and others rightly observe that such 'cyclic poems', taxing the poet's highest technical skill, are very difficult to compose. The *Dahikatarā*, composed in 1910, is a love lyric, singularly free from any sensuous taint. The poet imagines this bird as his beloved throughout the poem. It should be remembered that the poet is a life-long celibate. That Nature becomes endowed with beauty when the beloved comes in is, of course, an old poetic convention. Our poet adopts the same convention, but here a bird replaces the beloved of other poets. Besides, the bird brings to the poet's fancy a memory of the past, which, like a flower now past its springtide of beauty, has become faded and withered.

Raghunath Chaudhari was largely influenced by Sanskrit literature. He has not only made the traditional use of nature for comparison and contrast but has also adopted numerous Sanskrit fables, anecdotes, allegories, episodes, similes and image. Of the Sanskrit works, again, those of Kalidasa cast a remarkable spell over him.

Ambikagiri Roychaudhari (1885-)has been a life-long fighter for national liberation and social regeneration. A sincere patriot, progressive reformer and indefatigable worker, Ambikagiri is also a noted musician, brilliant orator and powerful writer. Love of his country is a strong undercurrent in his poetry, blending effectively with his urge for national awakening and social reform. He has often given himself out as a rebel and a revolutionary. He was incarcerated for taking part in the national liberation movement. He wanted not merely to liberate the country from foreign yoke, but also to liquidate the caste-system, inequality, envy, hatred, jealousy, vanity, meanness and selfishness that poisoned the roots of society. That was his mission in life. In his poem, *Mai Viplavī Mai Tandavī* (I am a rebel, I am an iconoclast), the poet unfurls his banner of revolt and charges hollowness and hypocrisy.

In the collection *Anubhūti* (Feelings), there are a number of poems calling upon people to cast off sloth and wake up from their deep stupor. His latter-day poems are influenced by realism and wage a relentless crusade against the numerous social evils that came in the wake of World War II. They are permeated with robust patriotism and a strong note of rebellion.

The poem, *Jiban Kihak Kai* (What Life Should Mean), gives a succinct statement of his life-philosophy. The mediaeval poets believed that the 'summum bonum' of life was enjoyment and rest, because life was regarded as a short span of wakefulness between two endless states of oblivion. At best they advocated an idle pursuit of the arts. But Roychaudhari's life and gospel are one of stress and storm. Life fulfils itself in a ceaseless stream of untiring activities for the common good. According to him

The lust for power and pelf
Has swallowed up man's humanity;
The soul's hunger has been trampled;
The sex impulse has been exalted,
Till it has maddened men;
The sense of duty has been drowned
In the clamour for rights.
I shall come there to stir up mutiny
And shatter these evils to pieces.
In the most perfect and fruitful life,
There is the fiercest friction
With pain, sorrow and tyranny;
And fire breaks out over
The phosphorescence of universal cataclysm
—Mad, colossal and time-conquering—
Reducing to ashes
The free emotions of creation—
The errors and blunders—
The rotten jetsam of things—
Giving birth to a new heaven and earth,
A new rhythm of indefatigable industry,
Over the debris of sloth and disintegration.

His poetry written prior to his incarceration, however, was neither political nor fiery. Politics entered into his writings after 1920-21 when the Non-co-operation movement started and he was sent to gaol. *Tumi* (Thòu, 1915) is a profoundly philosophical poem of remarkable charm and carftsmanship, and enshrines the poet's highest spiritual beliefs. In it the poet sees the image of the universe. It is in seven sections. The first three abound in descriptions of God who pervades everything. God is inherent in the beauty of the girl, the affection of the mother, the love of the spouse, and the beauty of Nature. The fourth section establishes that this all-pervading God is the essence of all religious creeds. The remaining sections are devoted to determining the poet's relationship with God, and describing the bliss and profound contentment that has come over him as a result of this realisation of the universal God. *Tumi* is a noble performance alike for its ideas and for its imagery and music. Every quatrain is rich in suggestion, bright imagery and appealing melody.

Jatindranath Duara (1892-) is a lyric poet. Banikanta Kakati held that among the poets who had dealt with the complex ideas of the twentieth century in effective Assamese, Jatindranath Duara was the greatest. Duara is a subjective poet who, in modern times, sang about his own soul earlier than others of Assam. The poet is concerned solely with himself, and tosses about ideas and toys with them as his shifting emotions and moods direct him. He himself is the minstrel and the listener rolled into one.

Duara is essentially a love poet, a devotee of Beauty, who 'dreams of love, and writes of the same stuff'. To him, love and beauty are but the indivisible colour and fragrance of the same flower. Where love is, there is divine beauty. He has vainly sought for this love in the haunts of men. Unalloyed love is difficult to find in human society. There love is attended with pain, suffering, separation, grief, neglect, calumny, oppression, and despair, and thus it presents the spectacle of a rainbow. In a like fashion Duara's poetry is rich in variety. There are desire for union, regret at repulse, the despair of the unblest, the sigh of unrequited love, and the pang of separation in his poems. Unable to obtain untainted beauty and unalloyed love in the world, the poet, ever hungry for love and beauty, seeks and finds them in the objects of Nature with which he wants to establish intimate relationship. The all-pervading beauty of the universe ravishes the poet's heart and evokes in him manifold pleasant responses. The sweet ditties of birds, the humming of bees, the comeliness of flowers, the purple glow of sunrise and sunset, the flash of lightning, the murmuring of brooks, the moon-lit islets of the Brahmaputrȧ shining silvery, the majestic movement of summer clouds—all these raise in the mind of the poet super-sensuous feelings.

If we examine all the wealth of diversity in romanticism, two common qualities appear in bold relief. They are the love of adventure and the passionate pursuit of Beauty. The former manifests itself in the poet's hunger for an ideal landscape. Both these qualities irradiate Duara's poetry. A ceaseless quest for sublime beauty and an endless incessant voyage towards and beyond the land of the sun-set—*Ei bāte Nāhibā Dunāi* (Do not tread this Road again)—these are the chief philosophic burdens of Duara's poetry. With the help of three symbols—the river, the boat and the helmsman—the poet gives a religious interpretation of life. This invites comparison with the Buddhist concept of the universal flux of things. The storm and the stress, the clouds and the despair, the trials and tribulations have failed to bear down the poet. Undaunted, he pursues his love to the ends of the earth and embarks on a ceaseless journey in search of golden land. His poetry is a record of this twofold quest.

Duara was attracted especially by English literature, which has exerted a wholesome influence over his mellifluous poetry, particularly in the matter of music, smoothness and fluency. Duara's metrical skill is unusual. Verse comes naturally to him, and his sense of form never fails him. In fact his lyrics have served in Assamese as models of that species of poetry for the last half century. His *Āpon Sur* (My Own Songs) and *Banaphul* (Wild Flowers) contain lines which, albeit exquisitely appropriate, are actually echoes from English poets like Shelley, Tennyson and others.

Duara has also brought out a matchless version of the Rubaiyat of Omar Khayyam in Assamese. Another novel work from his extraordinarily facile pen is the *Kathā-Kavitā*, which he claims to be poetry but is written in impassioned prose. This book has resemblance with Turgenev's Poems in Prose. The 'poems' are written in poetic idiom (firmly grounded in the naked thews and sinews of the Assamese language), and have remarkable suggestiveness. As in some of his poems, here too sorrow and sadness are dominant, and the pieces are very characteristic of the poet.

Like Chandrakumar Agarwala, Ratnakanta Barkakati (1897-) is also a remarkable poet; but the beauty of his poetry chiefly resides in earthly love between men and women. Most of the poems of his *Śevāli* centre round Anacreontic love. His lady-love has, inch by inch, appropriated to herself all the beauty of the world, and has thus become peerless like Tilottvamā.

The poems of the *Śevāli* give, in addition to the description of the body beautiful of the lady-love, a passionate expression to the doubts and fears, pangs and sorrows, separation and despair, that earthly love involves. These sentiments of earthly love are composed of words "as subtle, as complex, as full of mysterious life as the body of a flower or of a woman".

A few poems of this collection are devoted also to the poet and his relationship with poetry. Poets are extremely sensitive creatures who are endowed with supreme awareness enabling them to see the significance of happenings where (in consequence of the film of familiarity and selfish solicitude) the common people find none. They are emotionally more responsive and react deeply to happenings in life and Nature by showing beauty in unlikely places, the jewel in the boar's snout, the flower on the dunghill. So great is their emotional tension that they see cosmic sublimities and cannot help bringing them within hail of common life.

In his poem *Sakiyani* (Appeal), the poet turns to the pedestrian rabble and asks :

> To me, this Nature, ever appeals.
> Does she not give you any tidings?
> Does not the Bakul flower stir you?
> The wild flower, and the Kokil bird?
> Do they bore you?

Barkakati's poems deal also with the complex facts of life and existence, harmony and discord and experiences of being. In the poem, *Kijāni Nahai Bhul* (Fallibility is but a Guarantee), the poet believes that man's fallibility is but a guarantee of his superiority and a pledge of his salvation. Inferior life has no freedom of action. It goes wheresoever Nature leads it. Man's freedom is not so restricted by Nature.

> Hence it is that man errs
> And commits countless mistakes at every step.

The whole poem is a tribute to the creative powers of man, for whose imperfections the poet has the most generous sympathies.

Apart from the philosophic content of his works, Barkakati stands unrivalled for his artistry. The haunting melody, the resonant rhythm and the spontaneity of his utterance make him the most musical of our poets. In his poetic technique Barkakati was considerably influenced by Rabindranath Tagore.

Nalinibala Devi (1899-) is a notable modern Assamese poetess. She became a widow rather early in life. This cast a deep gloom over her life, but she weathered the crisis in the characteristic way of enlightened Indian womanhood. In her search for consolation and light she enquires into Indian philosophy, more particularly the *Gītā*, the *Upaniṣads* and the literature of the Assamese Vaiṣṇavite saints, and these studies foster in her a serene meditative mood and deep faith and hope in God. She is also attracted by the poetry and philosophy of Rabindranath Tagore whose influence can be detected in her thought and diction. A mystic poetess, Nalinibala Devi has an undefined restlessness — a craving for something which eludes definition and specification. This same central theme informs all her three poetical collections — *Sandhiyār Sur* (The Music of Sunset), *Saponar Sur* (The Music of Dreamland) and *Paraśmaṇi* (The Philosopher's Stone). Running through all her poems there is the deep feeling of a heart lacerated by the sorrows and sufferings of life, and a marked characteristic of many of her poems is a purity of soul achieved through suffering. There is also an over-powering desire for union — the union of the individual soul with the universal and supreme soul. This latter is conceived sometimes as her beloved and sometimes as the Infinite and the Beautiful. She feels a touch of this eternal Beauty in all the objects of

Nature, whose pied beauties are collectively the beauty of their maker. The seasons and the ever-changing loveliness of external Nature are but manifestations of that universal spirit, between whom and the poet Nature herself acts as the point of contact and the medium of union. The lightning, the Ketekī's lenitive song, the gentle zephyr of the dawn, the profound silence of the night, the smell of the wild jasmine,— all these give her intimations of the Supreme Deity, and not only serve as offerings to Him but also deeply humanise her. These help her in explaining the supreme truth, and add to the beauty of her poetry.

Writing about *Saponar Sur*, Shri Krishna Kanta Handiqui has observed that these poems are not pessimistic but actually disclose a deep faith in man's infinite future and the immortal nature of the spirit of man.

Param-Tṛṣṇā (The Supreme Thirst) is a single long poem of Nalinibala Devi, in which there is an explicit statement of some of her philosophic beliefs. She believes that the soul of man, especially that of a poet, has an eternal thirst which does not let him rest, although he may be surrounded by infinite riches and beauty, and that the journey of life is not a new thing. Like God, His creations, including human life, are also endless. That same eternal nature of the stream of life has made it inevitable that man's relationship with Nature should be as old as creation. The same spark illumines both Nature and Man. Hence it is that fragrance and buds, breeze and brooks, hold out so much meaning for man. *Param-Tṛṣṇā* is, however, not a bundle of wilfully esoteric or uncritically glorified philosophy. It abounds in vignettes of nature, which are not a mean source of the pleasure of the poem.

Nalinibala Devi's father, the late Nabinchandra Bardoloi, was a front-line leader of the Indian Freedom Movement. She has written a fine biography of her father. As was to be expected, she imbibed her father's patriotism and wrote some patriotic poems in which her love of the fatherland and its glorious past is expressed with an intense and insistent passion. The beauty that was Bharat is disclosed side by side with the beauty that Assam was. *Bhāratī* (Indiana), *Rabindra Tarpan* (Homage to Rabindra), *Mahānadar Atma-kāhini* (Autobiography of the Great River Brahmaputra) are some such patriotic poems. *Janmabhūmi* (The Land of Birth) is a matchless expression of the poetess's intense and overflowing love for her motherland. She wants to be allowed to serve, even after her own death, the land of her birth which is admittedly superior even to heaven.

A word must be said regarding her technique. The roll, the rise, the carol and the evocation of her poetry are exquisitely musical. She has copiously drawn on the rich treasure-house of Sanskrit, and her similes, imagery and vocabulary are enriched by the sublimity of that literature.

Dharmeswari Devi Baruani (1892-) is another venerable figure in Assamese poetry. She is a life-long invalid. About this, she has written in a memoir : "Rheumatism attacked me in the prime of my life. My dear husband and other kith and kin gave me all possible medical aid, but to no purpose. The ailment refused to be controlled. Gradually I began to be confined to bed, and that became my life-long place of rest. Ever-continuing treatment and never-declining disease began to torment my mind which my beloved husband tried to console by speaking words of encouragement. 'Don't brood over your disease and languish; better write down your thoughts in verse.' I cherished his advice and began to put down my thoughts on paper recording them as faithfully as I could : . . ."

Dharmeswari Devi Baruani has two published collections of poems — *Phular Sarāi* (The Basket of Flowers) and *Prāṇar Paraś* (The Soul's Touch). Both are expressions of a profound pantheism and the desire of the individual soul to get merged in the universal soul. The poetess does not believe that God resides in heaven, which to her is a figment of man's imagination. He is present in all things, both great and small. We behold Him around us:

> Art thou the sweet azure sky,
> The moon, the sun and the little star?
> Art thou the play of lightning between clouds
> In the lap of space?
> Art thou the enchanting hope that
> Dwells in the bosom of men?

Art thou the bright glow
Of the beloved's sweet enjoyment?

The divine spirit and motion she finds everywhere and in all the objects of the world, and it is these which endow everything with peerless beauty and inexhaustible meaning.

Though an invalid, and widowed early in life, Dharmeswari has none of the melancholy of Nalinibala Devi. With robust optimism she awaits the day of supreme union. Hence her poetry, issuing from a heart truly deep and passionate, is the sweet reflection of silent womanly self-surrender, love-lorn tenderness and sincere devotion, undimmed by the clouds of adulation or controversy. Although her subjects are limited in range to the most common themes like God, nature and the human heart, she possesses the sensitiveness and insight to endow them with fresh beauty and lovely diction. There is in her poems a deep sympathy and reverence for life and worldly things.

The late Banikanta Kakati aptly remarked that Nilamani Phukan (1880-) is the only modern Assamese poet of lofty spiritual aspirations. Remarkable is the fact that Phukan published his collections of poems, *Jyotikaṇā* (A Spark of Light), *Mānasī* (Intellectual Beauty), *Sandhānī* (The Seeker), and *Guṭmāli* ('The Jasmine'), in his sixties and seventies. If poetry is to be regarded as application of ideas to life, undoubtedly Phukan's poetry is unique. But unfortunately ideas, when they predominate in poetry, become an obsession, and in such cases the poetic flame is not steady but adventitious, though intensely incandescent at times. *Mānasī* reveals the poet's thirst for beauty and his *Sandhānī* is, in similar manner, a quest for truth and beauty. The collection *Guṭimāli* contains homely sketches of the life of poor, ordinary men and is lit with human love and feeling for nature.

The poet was gaoled in 1942 for taking part in the August revolution, and his prison experiences have been incorporated in his *Jiñjiri* (The Shackles). He wrote, "In search of God, I entered the temple of liberty. What I saw, heard and felt there had to be put down in writing to gratify my strong desire. I add introspection to them, and offer them as suggestive poems." Almost all the poems of *Jiñjiri* are optimistic in tone, and behind the poems, there is a powerful and healthy mind that is not deterred by the struggle or the storm. Rugged, bare and cryptic, rather prose-looking in dress, resembling the rattling of a milk-cart, his lines have beneath the surface a deep philosophic core.

Nilamani Phukan's prose is as passionate as his poetry. It lacks however analytical acumen and restrained or disciplined imagination. He cultivated the rhetorical, ornate and sonorous prose style. His *Sāhitya-Kalā* is a book of original essays on diverse aspects of literature.

Sailadhar Rajkhowa's *Nijarā* (The Brook) is a collection of poems composed at different times and on a variety of themes. He did not discover anything "far more deeply interfused" in nature nor did he propound any philosophy about her. He is enchanted with the objective beauties of Nature. He had the most profound regard for places of historical interest. He wove historical myths around those places, thereby enhancing the general effectiveness of the nature descriptions. His *Pāṣāṇ Pratimā* (Image of Stone) is a remarkable achievement of this type. The poem has the historical background of the invasion of Assam by the Burmese. Two Ahom generals, who bravely fought and laid down their lives, had by their inspiring heroism and valour attracted two damsels — Phularā and Chatalā by name. The damsels accompanied their beloved heroes to the battlefield and joined the ranks. On the death of the two generals, Phularā and Chatalā, now about to fall into the hands of the enemy, were metamorphosed of their own free will into stone images. Sailadhar's love lyrics are delicate and touching, depicting the longing and the sadness of the human heart.

Lakshminath Phukan has been a dilettante and a life-long journalist, associated with several English newspapers. For the last ten years he has been editor of the *Assam Tribune*, the English daily of Assam, and in this capacity he has shown great ability. An editor of a daily newspaper has not much leisure. Yet, Lakshminath Phukan found time for literary activity. Most of his poems were written in his youth and hence they largely deal with love, but his love has nothing sensuous about it. He is attracted by beauty and is enthralled by it. His beloved is no earthly creature, but an unbodied being.

A restless desire for beauty is the key-note of all his poems. In *Maraṇ-Belikā* (At the Time of Death) the poet says that he is not confronted by fate and that even death is an opportunity for contacting the beautiful. He has none of the usual fears for death and desires none to disturb his mind even for a moment.

Dimbeswar Neog's (1900-) poems broadly divide themselves into two categories — youthful effusions and patriotic poems. The collection *Indra-Dhanu* (The Rainbow) contains love-poems of considerable strength, bearing on different aspects of that primal passion. This side of Assamese romantic poetry is best illustrated in his poems. The Non-co-operation movement, started under the leadership of Mahatma Gandhi in the early twenties of the present century, had launched in the land a powerful patriotic movement and young poets were caught in it. Neog dived deep into the vanished glories of Assam and found much in them to inspire him. The poem *Burañjī Lekhak* (The Writer of History) is notable in this group and is charged with emotion. The *Śāpamukta* (Freed from Curse) is a poem in which love of the beloved has coalesced with love of the mother country. The poems of the collection *Thāpanā* (The Flower-stand) are meant for children. Neog's poems display varied metrical skill.

Binandachandra Barua (1906-) had a sonorous style which he employed in writing a series of powerful, patriotic verses much in the line of the Bengali revolutionary poet, Nazrul Islam. Most of the poems of the two collections, the *Śaṅkhadhvani* (Clarion Call) and *Pratidhvani* (The Echo), deal with the glorious past of Assam as contrasted with her precarious present. The poet, however, does not yield to despair. If he rakes up the ashes of the past, it is only to find sparks of courage, inspiration, and light for the present and the future. He remembers the noble sons and daughters of the past, and invites the rising generation to emulate their examples, break the shackles of foreign rule and misery, and rear up a prosperous Assam, advanced in all spheres of life. Language, culture, literature, industry—everything has to be revitalised. His youthful, iconoclastic and optimistic poetry rings into the maddening clarion call —

Rise! you fledglings of power
O my young countrymen
Awake from your sleep,
Let steaming blood race through your veins.
Dazzle the world, you heroes of action and strength!
None is big, none small,
All heroes are equal.
Remove obstacles;
Drive them away like the tempest.
Shake up the earth like the thunder-bolt.
And as the rays of the sun,
To this task, march forward,
And ever forward.

Binanda Barua concerns himself chiefly with Assam, and of that again, the glorious period of Ahom rule. In such poems as *Rongamuvā* (The Red-faced), *Rongpur*, *Gargaon*, *Brahmaputra*, *Śmaśān* (The Cremation Ground), against a dramatic background and in dramatic monologue, the poems describe historical places and personages in an inspired manner and a fluent style.

He has also adapted a few English anecdotes and episodes in Assamese. One such adaptation is the *Agiathutir Bīr* (The Hero of Agiathuti) which reminds one of the English poem, *The Incident of the French Camp*. Inspiring patriotism, sonorous rhythm, racy phrase and homely imagery make his poems happy reading.

Devakanta Barua (1914-) shot like a meteor in the firmament of Assamese literature and, by the innovations he wrought, created quite a stir. In subject-matter, attitude, technique and ideas he carved out a new path for himself which is indicated in his poem *Āmi Duvār Mukali Karon* (We Open the Doors). He does not appear to have been much indebted to any single predecessor in style. His youthful collection, *Sāgar Dekhicha* (Hast Thou Seen the Ocean?) contains poems of great intellectual variety.

His love poems, however, have none of the traditional content of describing the physical charms of the beloved or passionate attachment to her. They are hymns to intellectual beauty, and delineate the reactions in the mind to reciprocation as well as rejection. Each poem raises a different psychological question. What appears to be failure in love to others, is nothing of the kind to the poet. He finds success and contentment where others see only frustration and despair. Non-fulfilment brings a new pulsation of life. Even as pity for the killed curlew distilled itself into marvellous verses from the lips of Vālmīki, so the tender touch of some maiden's love caused the young poet to sing out in rhyme. Says the poet in his *Premar Uttar* (Love's Reply) —

> Darling! the silent gift of bountiful love,
> Which thy soft heart offered me,
> Has only this return
> —These my meaningless rhymes.

His beautiful beloved awakened his feelings, intensified them, and suddenly disappeared. This cruel desertion does not make him angry or reproachful. His mind is unsullied by dark clouds. His association with the beloved, very transient though it was, gives him perpetual joy and satisfaction. What is life but a constant shifting of brief scenes? Momentariness seems to be the law of life. The loveliness of the flower and the sunny youth of man are all short-lived. With ardour and enthusiasm is the Goddess Durga invoked on the sixth day of the new moon in October, but on the tenth day, do not all hilarity and boisterous mirth come to an end with the immersion of the idol into the waters? Hence the poet does not set much store by victory, achievement and acquisition. His joy is in the endeavour. One beautiful beloved may desert him; but there are a thousand others as charming. Failure in individual love leads him to seek universal love. In his poem, *Deva-Dāsī* (Temple Maid), the poet discovers in the dancing girl of the temple a specimen of exploited and trampled humanity. He wants to liberate the maid from the tyranny of her cruel god, so that her love can be bestowed on all men. Similar ideas prevail in the poems, *Sāgar Dekhicha* (Hast Thou Seen the Ocean?), *Rāṅga Eti Karabīr Phul* (A Red Oleander), and *Kalang Pārat* (By the River Kalong).

Devakanta has cast his poems into the mould of the dramatic monologues, such as was practised by Robert Browning. They cannot be regarded as dramas by any stretch of the imagination. There is neither dramatic conflict of character or ideas, nor clash of wit, nor dialogue, nor indeed anything else pertaining to the traditional drama except that some one is speaking all through to an imaginary second person. The very title *Sāgar Dekhicha* (Hast Thou Seen the Ocean?) signifies this. All the conflict that it portrays is in the mind of the protagonist, and in the verses the protagonist speaks through the poet in a rare intimate tone.

Devakanta Barua has the credit of having introduced this art-form into Assamese for the first time. If his poetic thought was influenced by D. H. Lawrence, his poetic diction was no less influenced by the art of Rossetti and Swinburne.

Another well-known poet of love and beauty was Ganeshchandra Gogoi (1910-38). Life is rich, according to him, because of love and beauty. 'The world around love is the lasting world of beatitude', he says in his poem, *Svapnabhaṅga* (Shattered Dream). He wanted to dedicate his life to the realisation of beauty, for which he had enough love and ardour.

The *Pāpḍi* (Petals) is an autobiographical love-poem of Ganesh Gogoi. The girl who inspired the poet in his youth and in whose beauty 'he bathed and learnt to find new beauty in this world', forsook him heartlessly. Life often involves an entaglement with some 'belle dame sans merci' who looms larger than life; her unkindness makes the loving poet write in agony.

Ganesh Gogoi died young a little beyond his teens. Hence his output was rather small in quantity, but the greatness of the little that he wrote demonstrates the immensity of loss his death occasioned. By their sincerity, emotional depth and effective diction his poems of love and separation have endeared him to a widening coterie of young admirers.

Dandinath Kalita (1890-1950) is a comic poet, and his collections — *Ragaḍ* (Fun), *Rahagharā* (House of Jest), and *Bahurūpī* (The Masker) — contain poems which are justly renowned for their sparkling wit, boisterous humour and penetrating satire. A consummate skill in the selection of words and arrangement of matter makes his verses enjoyable. He holds up to ridicule contemporary superstitions and foibles which were growing apace like ill weeds, without making any personal attack on or flinging mud at any individual, group, or community. Some of the poems are like poniard-thrusts at old superstitions and prejudices.

One revolutionary Assamese poet of the class of the Bengali poet Nazrul Islam is Prasannalal Choudhury, who is an iconoclast, out to erect the edifice of a brave new world upon the ashes of the old. He is the king of the destitute and celebrates his accession by urging them to rally to his standard. Passionate and powerful, his poetry glorifies patriotism and incites the people to rebel and re-build so that the spirit of man may function freely. His collection, *Agnimantra* (Fire-Chant), bears a significant title expressive of the idealism of the poet. The fire that burns and sanctifies is symbolic of the poet's urge to purge off all the accumulated dross and filth of the centuries, and the poet is a rebel against everything that is ugly and sordid.

Prasannalal's desire for freedom is not confined within the frontiers of India but concerns all colonial peoples. In several poems of his *Agnimantra,* the poet speaks of the sufferings of the working class everywhere sweating in travail and urges them to unite, rebel and establish new values. The poem, *Nangalar Gīt* (Song of the Plough) speaks of the wide sympathy which the poet felt for the riff-raff of the streets in general and the tillers of the soil in particular.

Humanistic ideas dominate the poems of Ananda Barua (1908-) included in *Pāpaḍi* and *Ranjana Raśmi.* Ananda Barua feels that life is an adventure of the soul in the realm of beauty. Barua has translated some poems of Hafiz and so his humanism has been a blend of aesthetic emotion with Sufi theory.

While writing about verse, mention must also be made of songs which have exercised tremendous unbounded influence in Assamese literature—ancient and modern. They are the *Bihunāms* and *Biyānāms*—lyrical ballads of spring and marriage which are sung even today and which have left their indelible stamp both on the tune and phraseology even of modern compositions. The 'ballad tune' occupies a distinct place in Assamese song and dance. In the middle ages, the Vaiṣṇavite and Śākta reformers composed songs for the propagation of their faith and some of these songs, known as *Bargits* are peerless and paramount improvisations alike for their gravity and high moral tone as for their craftsmanship and melody. They hold the religious field even today. These *Bargits* have been imitated and songs patterned after them began to emerge even in the early years of the present century.

In the present century, Lakshmiram Barua is the pioneer song-composer. His collection of songs, the *Saṅgit-koṣ* was published in 1911. Though religious in tone, these songs differ widely from the older *Bargits* in phraseology, tune and subject matter. His songs betray some indebtedness to the *Gītāñjali* of Rabindranath Tagore.

Padmadhar Chaliha is another song-composer. The song and poems contained in his *Phulani* (Garden, 1915), *Gīt-Laharī* (Symphony, 1921), and *Sarāi* (Vase of Verse, 1928) were at one time very popular. They were mainly devotional, patriotic, amatory or didactic.

Kamalananda Bhattacharya was himself a good singer and actor. The songs contained in his collection, the *Bauli* (The Dishevelled) display a penetrating intellect, the vigour of a genius newly awakened to a more intense life and honeyed and lingering melody. He recounts with regret the vanished glories of Assam. He is a panegyrist of her bountiful beauty. His voice is occasionally lifted in praise of God, and he sings with the subdued glow of a lyricism that is vague and mystical of his separation from the divine lover and the soul's craving for reunion. His last songs chronicle his experiences of the prison cell whereto his love of his motherland and independence took him. Kamalananda's first lines were magnificent:

> The lotus-petals glitter in the lake,
> And water sparkles on the lotus leaf...
>
> * * *
>
> O Mother dear, I love thee profoundly...
>
> * * *
>
> Again and again I bow down to thee, O Assam,
> The land of my birth,
> Though art sacred over everything...
>
> * * *

In melody, felicitous expression and captivating imageries, Kamalananda had few rivals. In his poetry, the measure and the idea, created in one and the same act, move with equal freedom, force and felicity and are consequently very forceful and striking in their happy synthesis; here form comes as the natural dress with which ideas are spontaneously invested.

Umeshchandra Chaudhury has left behind over three hundred songs and poems on a variety of topics and some of these have been published in the three collections, the *Pratidhvani* (Echo), the *Devadhvani* (Divine Music) and the *Mandākinī* (The Divine River).

Most of the religious and spiritual songs have a tone of non-attachment, self-abnegation, and renunciation, and the quest of the Ultimate. The *Mandākinī* is a collection of graceful love poems—love of the earthly kind. Umeshchandra is now known more for his patriotic songs, some of them by the clarity of thought, the direct energy of the expression and smooth movement are chiselled for immortality:

Ever loveable is my mother tongue...

* * *

Oh mother, Assam! thou art peerless...

* * *

Work the oar, and ply the boat...
A thousand times are you welcome.
O you assembled devotees!
You enlightened devotees, in service.
Of the motherland...

Umeshchandra's songs have the true magic touch. The flowing music, the poetic imageries, and the chastened emotions make them the very best in modern Assamese poetry. Umeshchandra Chaudhury was a reputed poet too. The poem, 'Mantra-Sādhanā' (Resolution Made) contained in his collection the *Amṛta-manthana* (Churning for the Nectar) is informed with virile patriotism and wide and ample human sympathy. The poet wants to establish a new order based on equality and justice:

We are the new generation,
We bring new enthusiasm,
And march forward to establish
Equality, Liberty and Fraternity.
We embrace the high and the low,
The depressed, the poor, the alien;

We untie all unholy knots,
And cut the roots of diplomacy.

Another poem the 'Kabir Kareng' (Poet's Palace) contained in the collection *Triveṇī* (The Three Streams) describes how the palace of art in which the poet led a cloistered life away from the tears and toil of real life, crumbles like a pack of cards and the reverie is over when he comes in contact with a beggar-woman—the symbol of down-trodden humanity. The poet's extravagant pre-occupation with art and isolation in an ivory tower now appears in a different colour. He sees around him:

The worn-out body of the cultivator and his famished condition;
The bruised limbs of the labourer;
The ignorant, starving millions
Breaking down under exploitation;
The heart-rending cry of the unfed and the sick,
And the dry lips of ignorant, superstitious and neglected masses.

Umeshchandra's poems reveal at times a concentrated force of virile reflection and a singularly grave pathos animated often by a philosophic ardour; but they lack polish in their style.

The note of pathos sounding dirge-like through the whole gamut of moving song, is conspicuous by its absence in the songs of Ambikagiri Roychaudhuri, in whose hands for the first time grief, lamentation, and regret yield place to robust resolution. In his poetry we have a new note—of an indomitable will for self-determination and survival. Replete with eloquence and verve, these songs are a clarion call to awake and arise to fulfil one's destiny. He wants individual independence to shape one's destiny according to his free will and to develop to his fullest stature and he stands for a better world free from exploitation, injustice and inequality.

The three ideas, viz, independence, love of the fatherland and a juster social order—are powerfully vocal in the compositions of that wizard of the Assamese lyric, Jyotiprasad Agarwalla. Assam's natural beauties, her glorious past and rich cultural heritage have inspired him. Like Hanumanta of the *Rāmāyaṇa* who crossed the channel by virtue of spiritual power, the poet wants to conjure a powerful spirit from Assam's past and with its help not only free Assam from foreign yoke, but also to resuscitate and modernise her politically, socially, and culturally so that a really charming Assam may be born. And to this task he invited in maddening songs the youth of the land. For their moving eloquence, exalted ideas, apt imageries, and delicate melodies, Jyotiprasad's songs are matchless. 'The world conquering youth', 'It is Time, Oh brother Assamese, to get ready', 'Mother's temple is empty', 'Why dost thou not light the lamp?', 'We are young, We defy Death', 'On the River Luit'—poems like these will echo and re-echo in the hearts of Assam's youth for all time.

With the installation of the Shillong-Gauhati centre of All India Radio, a fresh stream of inspiration for song-composition has overflowed in Assamese and there have come to light a good number of song-books such as Mahesh Goswami's *Amaya*, Malin Bora's *Reṇu* and *Surar Kavitā*, Bhupen Hazarika's *Jilikāb Luitāre Pār*, Lakshyahira's *Sur Setu* and *Prathamā*, Taffazul Ali's *Mandākrāntā*, Kamal Choudhury's *Gītāvalī*, Surjya Bora's *Sur-Sandhānī*, Alimunnisa Piar's *Sur-Nijarā* and Deben Sarma's *Salitā*. These modern Assamese songs deal not only with the traditional themes of devotion, love, patriotism and the beauty of Nature but also with the common man's struggle to approximate to the ideal of freedom and equality. The latter theme is conspicuous particularly in the songs of Bhupendranath Hazarika who has wrought not only renovations in the form and content of Assamese songs but entirely broken away from the classical style of music and tunes. His songs depicting the unenviable lot of the ordinary railway workers '*Jhāt jhāt jhāt rail cale*', the hard life of the stone-breakers '*Bhāṅg bhāṅg śil bhāṅgotā*', the misery and disgrace of the palaquin-bearers '*He dolā he dolā bar bar mānuhar dolā*', the misfortune of Rangman, the fisherman '*Rangman māchalai gol*', the sufferings and superstitions of the tea-garden labourers '*Eti kali duti pāt Ratanpur bāgicāt*', and the like show that Bhupendranath is an effectual organ-voice of plain humanity. In addition, the influence of folk-music and local itinerant singers is writ large over these songs. Hardly less successful in this respect than Bhupendranath is the promising poet Keshav Mahanta whose lyrics are to a considerable extent an articulate language of the common man's heart. An excellent case in point is the song

'*Jeuti tolai manat pare*' (Jeuti, I remember you) which recounts the feelings of young postal peon living far away from his dear wife, Jeuti. One word more must be said about these songs—the songs of plain humanity. They are intensely touching but not pessimistic. On the contrary, they hinge more or less on a love for life and faith in a good earth. This love for life and the earth has found expression in the first song of the *Mandākrānta* (Mild Movement) by Taffazul Ali:

> Seven-colour'd is the rainbow of the sky,
> But our earth is fairer still.
> The beauteous Sun's seven colours
> Sport upon the cloudy bosom,
> And our life goes amaying in soil's sunny breast,
> And ever green is our heart full of love.
> The light uncheck'd upon our earth
> Is a gift from the sun bountiful,
> Who gave the rainbow its seven colours
> And gave us life;
> Hence on the earth's bosom
> Our life is so lovely.

Distinct from, but not disconnected with, this love for life on earth is the remarkable recurring idea of a yearning for the Sun's lustre expressed chiefly through magnificent images in the songs composed particularly by Keshav Mahanta and Nabakanta Barua: 'The glimmering flash of fresh sun-shine'; 'O sun, where have you got this smile of pure gold?' 'All in expectation of you, my eyes were sleepless all the night'; 'We go in quest of light'; 'Cleaving the cloud, let us go to the fair of colours'; 'O ye sky, give us a little sky'—such images are not merely present but conspicuous in modern Assamese songs. It is, therefore, not too much to say that modern Assamese songs embody, among other things, a longing for the sweetness of the earth below and a wistful yearning for the light of the sun above.

NEW POETRY

Poetry is impassioned writing and all writing is a way of thinking. Obviously, thinking is moulded by the dominant metaphysics of the age. Modern Western literature is almost a penumbra around the dynamic ideas of Darwin, Freud,

Jung and Marx. Freud, by emphasising the vital role of the unconscious and exposing the operation of repression, and Jung, by emphasising the primordial images of the collective unconscious, upheld individual sensibility and made a complete shift from the naturalistic to the surrealistic point of view. Thanks to these psychologists, poetry came to be regarded as a voice of a disembodied spirit, something akin to dream experience. Jung also renewed our interest in myths which were no longer considered figments of one's deliberate invention but came to be regarded as the residuary of racial wisdom. Following this interpretation, W. B. Yeats invented myths to serve the needs of his mind and employed them as symbolic sign-posts of his emotions.

A considerable body of modern verse is also inspired by the gospel of Marx. This class of sociological poetry, though narrow in outlook, opens an ill-tended social parterre, about to be broken up by some colossal revolution. Assamese poetry today, particularly the poetry written by budding poets, is strewn with psychological thought and dialectical materialism.

The two world wars intensified the note of individual sensibility in modern poetry. One is familiar with the mood of disillusionment and bewilderment caused by the confusion and welter of the first world war and how this is reflected in the writings of Franz Kafka, Thomas Mann, T. S. Eliot and others. The Eliotean note of disillusionment has also crept into modern Assamese poetry. There is a historical hiatus between the young poets writing today in Assamese and tradition, because they are writing more with contemporary European literature than with their own tradition in their bones.

Disillusionment born of scepticism is then the new chord struck in Assamese poetry. Modern poets have developed a sceptical attitude to all that went before — love, beauty, religion, justice. They have assessed them anew in accordance with the time-spirit. They have lost the old faith, and a new faith has not yet come. One poet writes, "God, art thou then the X of Algebra?"

To this loss of the old faith, psychology and social anthropology contributed in no small measure. Freud's theory of libido suppression has affected not only the texture of poetic diction but the texture of poetic thought as well. This libido suppression finds expression in dreams, which, according to Freud, are only symbols of more comprehensive desires. To the modern poet words are similar symbols denoting parts of a vaster experience. Like the apparently incoherent dream-symbols, vocables in poetry today also appear unconnected. There seem to be no logical sequence except, of course, the emotional sequence. The presence of one particular symbol or image, by association, is made to suggest another desired image. And these images, like dreams, may mean not one thing but several. This has brought in the element of imaginative ambiguity in modern poetry.

Freud's 'libido' and 'complexes' show up 'love' in a different colour. The poet has lost faith in the eternal and beautific nature of 'love'. The naked warm-blooded woman has caught his eyes.

Marxist philosophy and egalatarian ideas have influenced another school of our poets. These poets have held up to ridicule the love, faith, culture, etc. of a decadent society. In their hope to bring about a brave new world, they have sought to make nothing of older, emaciated faiths. Some poets have altogether despaired of the entire mechanical civilization, and compared the future to death.

The majority of modern poets are widely read. They have drawn copiously from the various cultures of the world. This gave them not only delight but also insight. Hence we find in their poetry wise sayings of the East and the West, history, legend and what not. In their search for meaning, they dive deep into the literatures of the world. This has made the language of their poetry a little overladen with foreign words, phrases, and allusions, rendering it stiff and obscure for the average reader. The pre-war poets wrote chiefly about the beauty of the countryside. Rural life in all its beauty and happiness, sorrow and poverty figured in their poetry. But modern poets are town-conscious. Towns are the nerve-centres of modern civilization. Here the middle-class people live and work and enjoy themselves. Some of the poets have written about the ugly side of town life — its uncouth life of sexuality and indiscipline. In their poetry is depicted the immature love of young collegians, which, to the poet, is as unrealistic as their acting on the stage.

The poetic diction also has undergone revolutionary changes. The first change is the use of prose rythms. The ordinary speech form is made to coagulate with the verse form. The difference between prose and verse is done away with. Prose constructions together with rustic words and contemporary speech-rhythms are utilised for poetic use. They believe that conventional phrases and epithets, like old coins, have passed out of currency. They have lost the power to evoke emotion or administer a shock. They can no longer convey modern sensibilities. They have discarded old epithets and metaphors. Even when they use one, they attach a new significance to it.

The pictures in this modern poetry are not those of static scenery only. They are sensuous too. By a kind of friction and interchange of the different sense-feelings, an insight vouchsafed by psychological insight, a novel sense enjoyment is achieved. Their 'moon-light darkness and tears give out odours', 'the sun teases with shrieks', 'their sky is soft', and 'their earth is rough like the rough skin of an old man', etc., echo, one might suppose, from the poetry of Dame Edith Sitwell or Rilke.

In the first quarter of the twentieth century the chief influence on Assamese poets was that of the English poetry. But after the War, the influence of the French, Russian, German, Japanese and Chinese poetry began to be discernible. In our new poetry, one notices the adoption of images, symbols and music such as one meets with in the poetry of Baudelaire, Paul Valery, Stephane Mallarmé and Rainer Maria Rilke. The new poets attempt even springing rhythm. They have so much been tinged with these foreign colours that they appear to belong to an international community. Their language has arrived at the *Esperanto* stage. Like impressionist poets, their poetry is full of symbols and images, sometimes so contrasted that it is difficult to discover their natural inter-links. Anything of any country or of any time or culture may come up suddenly and an uneducated reader can never hope to find the full meaning; and references to history and geography are never without symbolism. This may be interpreted from Hemkanta Barua's poems. The pyramids, Hiroshima, Nagasaki of Hemkanta's poetry are no mere names, they are the grave-yards of civilizations. They indicate moral decline. Hemkanta's references to the figures of the epics denote more than meets the eye. The scion of the family of Santanu, Vṛhannalā, etc., are epic names for modern eunuchs, people who are found in society today. The noted Saties (chaste women) Kuntī, Śākuntalā and Damayantī, have figured in a new context in his poetry and they mean things far different from those of the epics. The old mythological figures assume strange kaleidoscopic shapes in the inclined mirrors of his symbolism. This is well illustrated in the following lines from his poem: *We Can Never Rest:*

Let us compose our hearts
With crimson courage. The epic Sītā
Lies entombed under our ploughshare.
The gold-spotted deer beckons to us,
And the gold of our body, O Śakuntalā,
Beacons to me. I burn into ashes.
There are the white crows in Korea,
And the black paddy too, My love, our harvest
Is full like your youth, and the spindle moves
In your fingers sifting the cotton.
Our sun is asleep in the green-room
Of history, the slogans we raise disturb
The deep silences of the sand-banks of time.
There are the people marching out,
And what are these slogans about?
There are a thousand like us,
And the hunger of ages battles
In our stomachs. Let us come,
And dye once more the waters of
The mighty Brahmaputra with our
Heart-blood. There is the call of life
In it. For whom? For you. For me.
And for a million like us.
Come, sit near me. Let the dead noon
Die in the flames of your eyes,
Eyes sharper than those of a leopard.
Our path quivers with the lights of ages,
And beacons.

O Śakuntalā, the poetry of struggle
Cannot die, and we can never rest.

This technique adopted with a cynically satirical vein has been brought to bear devastatingly upon the hollowness and hypocricies lying concealed in the modern civilization. The new poets' wide range of studies of the East and the West, of the ancient and the modern was laid under contribution and hence quotations and references abound in their poetry. These quotations may come from such widely different sources as European literature, the *Upaniṣads*, Vaiṣṇavite literature, or the Assamese folk songs. Often, the romantic tradition of Assamese poetry is held up to ridicule. But the poets do all this with a more positive aim. They want to administer to the educated and cultured section of the readers an emotional shock as does the psychiatrist to the neurotic patients in order to restore their mental equilibrium. The poets' shock consist of paradoxical and astounding statements of known facts in a kind of telescopic language. But unfortunately, very often, these learning-ridden, cryptic sentences produce very little emotion in the common reader.

Navakanta Barua has also established his reputation as a promising poet of the age. Navakanta's three published books of verse are *He Araṇya*, *He Mahānagar* (O Forest, O Metropolis) *Eti Duti Eghārati Tarā* (Counting up Eleven Stars) and *Yati*. Navakanta has been influenced more deeply by T. S. Eliot than by others. Like Eliot he also believes that poetry requires a language distinct from that of prose, a language rich in suggestions both to the senses and the intellect. Naturally, Navakanta's poetry tends to become difficult. In this respect, the Assamese poet also holds that poets in our complex civilisation must be difficult. Our civilisation comprehends great variety and complexity, and this variety and complexity, playing on a refined sensibility, must produce various and complex results. The poet must become more and more comprehensive and more allusive, in order to force language into his thought. Navakanta's stay in Calcutta and at Santiniketan in connection with his higher education brought him also under the influence of Rabindranath, Jivanananda Das, Amiya Chakravarty and some other modern Bengali poets. One can catch, here and there, in Navakanta's poems a music akin to that of Tagore. He is an experimenter in verse-form with a delicate sense of rhythm and symphony of words. He has shown admirable skill in handling metres, rhymed or free or mixed. Like Eliot, Navakanta is aware of the monotony and dichotomy of the modern age and the snobbery of the middle class. But he is never caustic. Acceptance of life is the key-note of his poetry. The poet's feelings and realisations have beautified and ennobled the earth which is no metaphor to him but a warm reality. Even after departure, the poet will ever seek to return to the earth (*The Poetry of Return*). His love and desire for a fuller and ampler life under the broad blue sky is beautifully expressed in his prayer to the night sky (*To the night sky: prayer through the window.*)

> Helpless I am, even if mine
> Is only the luxury of supplication;
> Hear my prayer, O sky,
> Tell me what issue falls like an arrow
> From the moon's amber-crescent?
> Give us a little more room, O sky,
> For our sky is too, too narrow.

Modern poetic diction is marked by a great economy of words. In common with other modern poets Navakanta also has used a diction where there are semantic disturbances, words of different levels, and the juxtaposition of difficult Sanskrit and English vocabulary, and dialect words, producing contrast images. Phrases, quotations, pictures and symbols of the European and Indian literatures are freely employed by him to convey a complex sensibility. His symbols are ambiguous, they do not definitely convey one idea, but a spectrum of ideas. Their beauty and circumambience vary in proportion to the cultural and emotional range of the reader.

Sayed Abdul Malik is better known for his short stories. He writes poetry also with left-wing political affiliation. Among the new writers, he is close to the masses not only for his sympathy for them but for the sake of his poetry too. He finds the subjects of his verse in the common experience of man, and to communicate his ideas clearly, he uses the common man's language and idioms with considerable ease and melody.

Birendrakumar Bhattacharya has also rallied round the left wing banner, and his poetry is pungent criticism of the present day social order. He is the editor of the monthly magazine, *Rāmdhenu* (The Rainbow), round which all new poets gather as members of a family. *Rāmdhenu* has created not only a congenial atmosphere for new poetry but also a growing circle of admirers for it.

Obscurity, shocking images and a good deal of literary allusions are the notable features of the poems of Hari Barkakati and Mahendra Bora. Both of them are considered to be intellectuals, and they register in their writings impressions mostly of modern life with emphasis on cosmopolitan elements. Mahendra Bora has recently compiled a selection from the writings of twenty young poets and calls it *Natun Kavitā* (New Poetry). The sixty-eight short poems in *Natun Kavitā* of varied contents and metres reveal to what extent these new poets have freed themselves from the bondage of traditional themes, verse-patterns, techniques and taboos.

Homen Bargohain writes short stories and poetry with equal felicity and distinction. His poetry dwells mostly on sex themes and Bargohain's fondness for sex imagery is reminiscent of the poetry of Dylan Thomas.

The other younger poets Dinesh Goswami, Nilmoni Phukan (Junior), Bireswar Barua, Mahim Bora have used novelty of themes, new symbolism and imagery, and have thus generated scepticism and a high pitch of social consciousness in their poetry.

In the large body of Assamese poetry written today, to ascertain what poems will endure for tomorrow, is a moot-point. One only feels that there is abundance of rich ore in the slag.

CHAPTER VIII

DRAMA

THE theatre has been a popular national institution in Assam since the time of the Vaiṣṇavite movement, and thus the theatre in Assam, like its counterpart in other parts of India and in England, is ecclesiastical in origin. Even today, in the village Namghars one-act plays composed during the Vaiṣṇavite period are enacted and witnessed with great eclat and enjoyment. Rooted in popular faith, these plays have their impact on the religious and social life even of today. The incentive for modern drama—the realistic, psycho-analytic and problem plays—came, however, from the West. Although professional public theatres to cater to highly cultivated tastes are still to develop, amateur dramatic clubs have sprung up almost in every Assamese town and village. These clubs are at once repertoire-theatres and centres of culture, and with them all educated people of the neighbourhood are associated and under their auspices all social festivals, including the staging of dramas, are organised and celebrated. In most places, barring a few, men perform the feminine roles. Since the attainment of independence, the standards of histrionic art have risen considerably, thanks especially to the encouragement given by the Sangeet Natak Akademi. During the winter of 1954, the Sangeet Natak Akademi sponsored the first National Drama Festival in Delhi during which about 25 plays in 14 recognized languages were enthusiastically staged. The drama festivals have since become an engaging annual feature of the modern cultural renaissance in India.

All the plays written since the beginning of the British rule were meant for the stage, and hence in them the poetic impulse is subordinated to stage exigencies. These modern plays may be broadly divided into four classes—mythical, social, historical and romantic. The plots of the mythical plays are based chiefly on various pleasing and graceful episodes from the two epics—the *Rāmāyaṇa* and the *Mahābhārata*. The social group of plays may be sub-divided into serious pieces and light ones. They focus attention on Assamese social and domestic life. In the lighter social plays incongruities and failings of daily life are mirrored to excite mirth and laughter. The historical plays are an illustrious gallery of portraits drawn from Assam's history, particularly of the golden Ahom period. The Muslim invasions of Assam during that period, the heroic resistance of the people, the courage, heroism, and statesmanship displayed by kings, generals and soldiers, the supreme patriotic self-sacrifice of individual sons and daughters of Assam, and occasional court intrigues and wars and revolts and struggles for succession and such other episodes are treated with animation and verve. The romantic group of plays—rather small in number—contain lyric dramas filled with dance and song.

Of the modern mythical group of plays, mention may be made of *Vaidehi Vicched* (The Exile of Sita) by Debanath Bardoloi, *Sītā-haraṇ* (The Abduction of Sita) by Ramakanta Chaudhury, *Haradhanu-bhaṅga* (The Breaking of Siva's Bow) by Purna Kanta Sarma, *Abhimanyu-badh* (The Killing of Abhimanyu) by Bharat Chandra Das, *Dakṣa-Yajña* (The Ritual Sacrifice of Dakṣa) and *Dūryyodhanar Urubhaṅga* (The Breaking of Duryyodhana's Thigh) by Benudhar Rajkhowa, *Pārtha Parājaya* (The Defeat of Pārtha) and *Bāli-badh* (The Destruction of Bali) by Durgeswar Sarma, and *Bṛsaketu* and *Guru Dakṣiṇā* (Homage to the Master) by Durga Prasad Majindar Barua. In these dramas the scriptural themes were faithfully rendered into drama without any great alteration, to inculcate in the mind of the ordinary spectator the religious tenets of the scriptures and a veneration for them. To make these attractive to the vulgar, lighter scenes were introduced, and these comic interludes later developed into full-fledged comedies.

Of the earliest social plays of the British period mention may be made of *Rām Navamī* by Gunabhiram Barua, *Bangāl-Bangālanī* by Rudraram Bardaloi, and *Kāniyār Kīrtan* by Hem Chandra Barua. The play *Rām Navamī* emphasises the necessity of widow-remarriage, by dramatising the tragic sequel to its prohibition. A child-widow Navami, a Brahmin girl, falls in illicit love with Ram. She becomes pregnant, and, unable to stand up against the social odium and apprehensive of social ostracism, both Rām and Navamī commit suicide. *Bangāl-Bangālanī* also deals with illicit love, scoundrelism and knavery. *Kāniyār Kīrtan* is a propaganda-play dealing with the evil effects of opium-addiction. The play also exposes the moral hypocrisy, falsehood and shams of those who profess to be guardians of religion and social ethics.

In his play *Maharī* (The Clerk) Durga Prasad Majindar Barua paints the wretched life of an ill-paid, overworked clerk of a tea-garden. The clerk's life contrasts sharply with the riotous and licentious living of its rich English manager, Mr. Fox. These farces of rollicking fun are like two-edged knives in their scornful condemnation. They slash the superstitious beliefs of the local people, they also assail blind and silly imitations of the West and strip naked the ragged follies of the time. One thing must be said at least for truth's sake: many of these earlier farce writers sought to give realistic pictures of a corrupt society and they emphasized vices rather than virtues and consequently gave us low-toned plays without much moral significance.

The historical group of plays is larger in number, and more popular. These plays afford greater scope for dramatic action—in the fights, the heroic deeds and the like with which history abounds, and which make a drama more captivating to the laity. Their prevalence also indicates the love of historical literature for which Assam has a unique reputation. The playwrights depict the glorious past of the land, her valiant and chivalrous sons and daughters whose exploits form an immortal saga of heroism. Out of them a new demand is made upon the heroism, sacrifice and faith of the present generation for liberating the fatherland from foreign yoke. The historical play thus contributed in no small measure to the re-awakening of the people to their social and political problems.

Lakshminath Bezbarua has to his credit three historical plays and four farces. He began by writing farces for which he was naturally gifted, and sufficient material offered by the incongruities of Assamese social behaviour easily caught his observant eyes. The farce *Litikāi* (1890) is based upon the humour of a situation created by foolery, deceitfulness, and pretentiousness, and has brilliance in its drollery. In *Pācani*

(1923), Pāncani's hospitality, expanded to ridiculous proportions, clashes with his wife's parsimony, giving rise to a humorous situation. The *Nomal* (1913) presents the old rickety Naharphutuka who, because of his gawkiness and foolishness, returns strongly mortified from the temple to which he had repaired to seek his son's welfare. In *Cikarpati Nikarpati* (1913), two thieves display the tricks and methods employed by them in larceny, and this display, together with the corruption of the judiciary, creates situations which force laughter. Exaggerated situation, irony of thought and words, malapropisms and humorous dialogues—these are the characteristics of these farces. There is hardly any development of plot. The humour is low because it is invariably one of situation. Exaggeration is the very breath of these farces and hence they are often unreal.

Bezbarua's three historical plays are *Jaymatī Kuwarī*, *Cakradhvaj Siṁha* and *Belimār*—all composed between 1914 and 1916. In *Jaymatī Kuwarī* is shown the dazzling self-sacrifice of the martyr, the Princess Jaymatī, who willingly laid down her life for the welfare of her dear husband and her country. *Cakradhvaj Siṁha* deals with another very glorious chapter of Assam's history. It shows the Moghul invasion of Assam during the reign of Swargadeo Chakraddhaj Singh, and how that invasion was successfully repulsed on the battlefield of Saraighat by the Assamese army under the leadership of the great general—Lachit Barphukon. Here is a full-flavoured realistic commentary on the military strategy and patriotism of the general, the disciplined efficiency of the Assamese forces, and the noble spirit of their king Chakraddhaj Singh. It may be regarded as the Assamese national anthem in five acts. *Belimār* depicts the decline of Ahom Imperialism, and its final, sad collapse as a result of three successive Burmese invasions. In all the three dramas, the dramatist has not taken any liberty with history. He has however shown excellence and originality in inventing companion episodes that help in recreating and reinforcing history. With the help of dramatic contrast and comparison the dramatist has thrown his characters in bold relief. Though the medium of expression for ambitious dramatic works was at the time blank verse, Bezbarua adopted prose instead. He has, like a truly great master, avoided all sentimentality and excess. In these dramas, the influence of Shakespeare is noticeable. The characters of Gajpuriya and Priyaram in *Cakradhvaj Siṁha* easily remind one of Falstaff and Prince Hall in Shakespeare's *Henry IV*, after whom they have been patterned. Bhumuk Bahua and Pijou of *Belimār* are also echoes of the Fool in *King Lear* and Ophelia in *Hamlet*. The dramatist has afforded comic relief by inserting lighter scenes in the midst of tragic ones.

Padmanath Gohain Barua has left behind eight dramas, four historical, one Puranic, and three farcical. *Jaymatī* (1900), *Gadādhar* (1907), *Sādhanī* (1911), and *Lācit Barphukan* (1915)—these four plays are based on Ahom history. *Jaymatī* and *Sādhanī* are tragedies while *Gadādhar* and *Lācit Barphukan* are comedies. The first three have blank verse as the chief medium of dramatic expression, and their leading characters invariably speak blank verse. In *Lācit Barphukan* and the later Puranical play, *Bān Rajā*, blank verse has been replaced by prose. *Jaymatī* is a tragedy dealing with the supreme self-sacrifice of Jaymatī, who was tortured to death by the tyrannical Ahom King—Lora Raja—because Jaymatī, taken by the King as a hostage, would not divulge the whereabouts of her absconding lord—Prince Gadādhar. This she would not because Gadādhar was not merely her dear consort but also the guarantee of a prospective good Government. Though the earliest of the author's tragedies, *Jaymatī* sustains a tragic atmosphere and delineates characters much better than *Sādhanī* does. While the heroine of the former, Jaymatī, has extraordinary endearing traits in her character, Sādhanī, heroine of the latter, has no such graces. Sādhanī, is an easy, simple-souled dove, without individuality, and she is a scapegoat of other people's failures. There is not much of either complexity or logical development of plot, and hence the drama falls short of the orthodox, classical requirements of a tragedy. *Gadādhar* is a kind of pendant to *Jaymatī* but far less successful. The leading character, Gadādhar, disappoints the reader. There is more of dialogue than of action, sentimentality than sense, and empty vaunt than skill in plot-weaving.

In plot-development the dramatist pays scant attention to economy; unnecessary sentimentality, tedious descriptions of occult matters, an effusive love of Nature, purposeless and prolix dialogue, and irrelevant comic scenes do not contribute towards the organic growth of plots in the drama. There are a few historical anachronisms too in these plays. The materials are completely historical, and, in their exposition, the playwright does not show any new attitude or throw any new light. *Bāṇ Rajā* is based on the *Harivaṁsa*, and the dramatist does not take any liberty with the original anecdote. Prose is employed here all through, though, in view of the very mythical nature of the theme, verse would be more justified here than in the other historical plays. The language is artificial, being heavily Sanskrit-laden, and there is very little of characterisation or ingenuity.

Gohain Barua shows great skill in drawing low life and rustic scenes, but he signally fails in dealing with scriptural anecdotes and in recreating history. He has not that creative imagination and that knowledge which are especially necessary in recreating historical periods and interpreting historical figures.

The *Gāobuḍhā* (The Village Headman, 1890), *Teṭon-Tāmulī* (1908), the *Bhūt Ne Bhram* (Is it Spirit or Hallucination?, 1924)—of these three farces, the last-named is a collection of some pictures, with a definite purpose. The author wants to effect a reform in rural society oppressed by a preposterously superstitious dread of evil spirits. But this is stressed again and again in a very direct manner without an eye on plot-development or characterisation.

Teṭon Tāmulī is a full-fledged farce of the picturesque variety. In describing how the sly Teton converts his very defeats to personal advantage, in creating situations, and in adjusting the talk and behaviour of the characters, the author displays intimate knowledge of rural life. The success of the farce and its popular appeal depend largely upon its brilliant wit.

Gāobuḍhā, though the earliest of his farces, is yet the best. It gives a realistic picture of the British administration of the closing decade of the 19th century. Like Dinabandhu Mitra's *Nīla Darpaṇ*, *Gāobuḍhā* is a play with a set purpose and, like that too, it is a meritorious play—a notable contribution to Assamese comic literature. The drama depicts the miserable life of Bhogman, the village headman, who holds the responsible, burdensome, but honorary post of the headman, and whose own affairs come to the verge of ruin on account of his extreme pre-occupation with his official duties, for which he gets not only no money but actually insult from one and all—big and small. Beneath the mirth and fun there is a pathetic and tragic undertone, and this increases the appeal of the play. The dramatist displays uncommon skill in drawing such typical rural characters as Bhogman and Rongdai. The play is better described as a light comedy than a farce. Here we realise the gifted author's sharp faculty for irony and epigram. His serious dramas have become rather stale; but the comedies and farces are realistic and perfect alike for their characterisation and for stage management.

Another leading dramatist of this century is Benudhar Rajkhowa. His *Seutī Kiraṇ* (1894) has been influenced to some extent by Shakespeare's *Othello.* Another tragedy is *Ūrubhaṅga* (The Breaking of Thigh). But he has earned wider fame as a writer of farces, the chief being *Kuriśatikār Sabhyatā*, 1908 (The Civilisation of the 20th Century), *Tini-Ghaiṇī* (Three Wives), *Aśiksita Ghaiṇī* (The Uneducated Wife), *Topanir Pariṇām* (The Consequences of Sleep) and *Corar Sṛṣṭi* (The Creation of Thieves). In the first is depicted the hypocrisy of youths with half-baked Western education. They are sceptical about the older and time-honoured faiths of their land, but have not realised the plenitude of the newfangled Western faiths either. They are atheists and do not believe in the caste system. Yet they respect it outwardly for fear of society. The farces on matrimony deal with co-wives and illiterate wives who make the husband's life a bed of thorns. The *Topanir Pariṇām* is a vivacious representation of how Topani, a young man, seduced a young dame and was forced to marry her. The story is borrowed partly from old folk tales. The *Corar Sṛṣṭi*, a lighter comedy, is patterned after Shakespeare's *Comedy of Errors.* The two husbands, Dhumuha and Mauram, lead unhappy lives with their respective wives due to temperamental incompatibility. One night a thief who enters their house gets to be aware of this unhappiness. With the help of a charm which he knows, he gets the wives exchanged. The two men now enjoy their new loves to the full. In spite of the presence of several scenes to provoke laughter, the story resembles a folk-tale. The author's aim is reformed, and this cannot be missed in any of his plays. The weakest spot of the plays is the presence of too many unintegrated songs and feeble dialogues.

Chandradhar Barua's fame as a writer depends chiefly on his dramas. Two of his major dramas deal with Pauranic anecdotes. *Meghnād-vadh* (1904-5), and *Tilottamā-sambhav*, both in blank verse, deal respectively with the killing of Indrajit (son of Rāvana) and the mutual destruction of the two demons, Sunda and Upasunda, through their rivalry for the hand of Tilottama. In plot-development and descriptions, the dramas disclose the influence of Michael Madhusudan Datta. There is like emphasis on the characters of Rāvana and Meghnād, which have been drawn with special sympathy. The character of Lakṣmana has been neglected while Rāma has been drawn as a great and large-minded hero. Our dramatist has, with great success, drawn Meghnād's wife, Promilā, as of greater charm and interest than even the Sitā of Michael. *Tilottamā-sambhav* deals with the mutual destruction of the demons and the way virtue is secured thereafter in the world. Lust or animal desire can never lead to the realisation of beauty. Beauty, when subjugated to desire, only brings about downfall. This final downfall of satanic ways is the central theme of *Tillottamā-sambhav*.

Tilottamā-sambhav may be called a verse drama. The flowing verse, the sweet rhymes, and the songs with which this drama abounds make it look like one long poem, and the author points this out in the preface and asks the reader to accept it as such. There is not much of characterisation, and the introduction of rural and light scenes in which the writer elsewhere displays considerable skill, has not, in this case, helped to give better effect. The episode of the poor Brahmin's wood-boy, Kolia, in heaven, though meant to give relief, is jarring in tone against the august background. Chandradhar Barua's diction is easy-flowing and happy and his blank verse is flexible.

Bhāgya Parīkṣā (Fate Decided) is a farce in which the relative merits of fate and affluence are assessed in a lighter vein. For Barua fate resides not in occult power but in moral earnestness. Where this earnestness is, there are riches and power. The author brings this out through the changing career of Paniram. The farce abounds in coincidences and accidents, and as such is a mixture of both real and unreal matters. The faintly connected narrative is nearly throttled at places by these accidental coincidences, leaving the impression that here situations count for much. The writer displays skill in depicting varied pictures of rural life. Paniram and Maniki, man and woman, are living characters. In a similar way, the characters of Kewaliya bhakat, fishermen, money-lenders, etc. are realistic and representative of their classes, both in their behaviour and speech. *Bhāgya Parīkṣā* is thus a notable farce in Assamese.

Amongst living farce-writers Mitradeva Mahanta occupies a prominent place. *Biyā-Biparyaya* (The Marriage Debacle, 1924), and *Kukurīkaṇār Āṭhmaṅgalā* (The Reception of the Purblind Son-in-law, 1927), are very popular, and at one time these two were warmly received at every theatre in Assam. In recent years he has written and published a few more farces such as *Eṭā Curaṭ* (One Cigarette), *Tengar-Bhengar* (The Clever Rogue), *Leklau Lam*, *Cenchā Jvar* (Cold Fever), *Acin Kāthar Thorā* (The Unknown of Caste and Creed),*Bom-Phuṭukā* (The Bluff-Giver), and others. But in dramatic and literary virtues his earlier farces are definitely much better.

Incongruous situations and behaviour are the sources of mirth in his *Biyā Biparyaya*. The playwright holds up to ridicule such evils of rural life as child-marriage, dowry, and superstitions, and this he does with the help of dramatic exaggerations.

Indreswar Barthakur is known chiefly as a dramatist, and has written a number of thoughtful articles on ancient Indian drama and acting. His great work is *Śrībatsa Cintā* (Śrībatsa and Cintā). Based on a Puranic episode, the play displays admirably the author's craftsmanship. In giving variety to incidents, in developing characters, and in generating dramatic pathos, the dramatist's success is the more remarkable because of the episodic theme which ordinarily does not allow variety. While faithful to the Puranic story, the author has given us characters who possess charm and vitality. It seems that he finds a native medium when his imagination wanders in the world of mythology. This fact is revealed when we survey his work in other forms of literature. The *Indra-Mallikā* (Jasmine) is a collection of poems on varied themes. A lover of Sanskrit literature and old Indian culture, Barthakur has not only written many articles on them but has also composed poems to glorify them. *Bhāratī* (Indiana), *Śarade Namas* (A Salutation to Autumn), *Durvāsā*, *Vālmīki*, *Vedavyāsa*, *Urvasī* and such other poems testify to this characteristic of the writer.

Atul Chandra Hazarika began as a poet, and although by writing poems and stories based on Puranic episodes, which he is doing at present, he is making a notable contribution to children's literature, yet his chief claim to reputation rests on the dramas he has written. He has a fairly large number of them to his credit. His dramas divide themselves into three classes—those based on Puranic episodes and anecdotes, those on historical events, and those on miscellaneous topics.

The Puranic group of dramas consists of *Nandadulāl*, *Kurukṣetra*, *Rukmiṇi-haraṇ*, *Beulā*, *Narakā-sur*, *Śakuntalā*, *Niryātitā*, *Campāvatī* and *Śrī Rāmcandra*. Except *Śakuntalā* and *Beulā*, all the others are based on the stories of either the epics or the *Bhāgavata*, and their medium is blank verse. The dramatist has not tampered with the original anecdotes, either by addition or by subtraction. He has only dramatized readymade stories and, where necessary, adapted and intergrated them to and with local scenes, ideals and emotions. Regarding *Śakuntalā*, the author himself has admitted that, except for one or two reorientations of facts, he has followed the original with fidelity. The dramatist has, however, displayed considerable skill in localising the dramatis personae and the settings. The local atmosphere is evident in the portrayal of Rukmini's nuptials in *Rukmiṇī-haraṇ*, the cordon of the bride for groom in *Beulā*, road-construction by labourers in *Narakāsur* and the solemnising of the marriage in *Śrī Rāmcandra*. These establish a close intimacy between the reader or the spectator and the characters taken either from mythology or from everyday life. The household of the clown Vedanidhi in *Rukmiṇi-haraṇ* is a realistic picture of a humble home etched without scoffing or rancour.

In characterisation, the dramatist has not taken any liberties at all; in the very nature of things he could not. Where is the room for characterisation, dramatic tension and suspense when the plot is a Puranic story left undisturbed? In the play, *Kurukṣetra*, the playwright has taken some liberties, and hence he has succeeded in depicting in Gandhari the portrait of a woman who has passed through the vicissitudes of fortune. Gandhari's speech to Krishna after she has removed the eye screen of her husband reads like fine lyric poetry. The easy-flowing lines of blank verse make all the plays happy reading. The prose passages thrown in at suitable places offer effective variety. Some of these Puranic dramas are divided into three acts; others, into four, five, or even seven acts. The play *Sakuntalā* has seven acts. The acts and the scenes follow old conventions, except in *Śrī Rāmcandra* and the *Niryātitā* (The Oppressed), where the beginning and the close are very attractive. In the latter as well as in *Rukmiṇī-haraṇ* the dramatist has blended modern dramatic technique with that of the Vaiṣṇavite era, and, demonstrating thereby the excellences of the older technique, tried to evolve a new national dramatic style. He has paid no mean attention to stage arrangement, especially in plays like *Beulā*.

The historical group of plays consists of *Banij Kowar*, *Kanauj Kumārī*, and *Chaṭrapaṭi Śivājī*. The *Banij Kowar* is an Assamese adaptation of Shakespeare's *Merchant of Venice* in five acts of blank verse. In this adaptation the Assamese dramatist has achieved admirable success where it was least expected, *viz*, in finding an historical Assamese class-conflict comparable in almost all its entirety with the Christian-Jew conflict which is the pivot of the English play. In the Assamese adaptation, Amiya Kumar (Antonio) and Chandanmal (Shylock) are representatives of the Assamese and the exploiters from outside, between whom there is deep suspicion and profound distrust and sometimes even passionate schism on linguistic and cultural grounds. In adapting the play in Assamese, the Assamese playwright has brought to bear a wealth of racy phrases and idioms which gives the work the dignity and strength of almost an original work. The *Kanauj Kumārī* is based upon the family feud between the Indian princes Prithvirāj and Jaycānd, regarding the hand of the princess Samyukta, that ultimately brought about the downfall of the Hindu regime. Though it has no great dramatic excellence, it enriched Assamese literature by introducing into it a momentous chapter of Indian History. As individual characters, Jaycānd, Rana, and Samyukta speak heroic sentiments with ardour, passion and liveliness. In *Chatrapati Śivājī*, the writer was, on his own admission, influenced by the *Gairik-Patākā* of the Bengali dramatist Amritalal Bose. Atul Hazarika has shown how, even in writing historical dramas, it is possible to produce creative plays without meddling with historical detail. He has succeeded in portraying Sivaji in glowing colours. Nevertheless the dramatist does not forget, whenever an opportunity presents itself, to sing the valour of the Assamese army of those days, as also the gospel of Hindu-Muslim unity, as in the dialogue between Emperor Aurangazeb and Ram Singh in Act IV, scene 1, of the play. The miscellaneous group of Hazarika's plays contains *Marjiyānā*, *Mānas-Pratimā*, *Āhuti*, and *Raṅgmahal*. Based on a popular episode of the *Arabian Nights*, *Marjiānā* is a dramatic version of the story of *Alibaba and the Forty Robbers*, and as *Marijyānā* is the central character, the drama has rightly been named after her. *Āhuti* is a drama on social problems, focussing attention on the conflict between two generations of men. Though in a small compass, the idealist Anwar—the hero of the play—has called forth some discussion on certain problems, extraneously thrust on Assam. The introduction of the mediaeval Sutradhara has not helped, but hindered the dramatic action. It is definitely unrealistic in many places. The two playlets, *Kalyānī* and *Mulā Gābharu*, published in the same volume with *Āhuti*, have more or less achieved their central objects. *Mānas Pratimā* is a poetic rendering of the Persian Siri Farhad episode. But the Assamese writer's dramatisation is heterogeneous and his language, prolix.

It must be noted that Atul Hazarika wrote dramas to meet the demand of the Assamese stage which, before he started writing, had been practically monopolised by the dramas of the Bengali playwrights, Girishchandra Ghosh and Dwijendralal Roy. Atul Hazarika liquidated this dependence once and for all and his success inspired numerous writers for the Assamese stage.

Three dramas of Daiba Chandra Talukdar, *viz*, the *Biplav*, the *Bāmuṇī Kuwar*, and *Bhāskarvarmā*, deserve special mention

Biplav (The Rebellion) is the story of tenants rising against a tyrannical zamindar who oppressed and exploited them. The insurgence is led by Parbati, daughter of the poet Chandramohan, and later also by Bipin, the zamindar's own son. The proud zamindar finally yields to his people. The drama ends in universal joy with the union of the hearts and hands of Parvati and Bipin. The plot shows some power of invention although characterisation is weak. There are several inspiring patriotic songs in the play, holding up the picture of a socialistic pattern of society.

Bāmuṇī Kuwar is a historical play dramatizing an attractive episode from Ahom history. The Ahom king, Tyaokhamthi, had two queens. When once the King had gone out on a military expedition against the Chutias, the elder queen, who had been left in charge of the kingdom, took advantage of the king's absence. Incited by jealousy, she exiled the other queen to a place called Habung. The exiled queen sought asylum in the house of a Brahman, where she gave birth to a prince who became celebrated as Bamuṇī Kuwar (The Brahmin Prince). This prince grew up and later came to wield his father's sceptre. Around this central plot based on history, a few sub-plots of an imaginary character have been deftly woven to form a skein of striking beauty. Two imaginary characters, *viz*, Rohdai and Baromi, have been etched with unique precision and bewitching loveliness. *Bhāskarvarmā* is a dramatic representation of the Kamrup Emperor, the redoubtable Bhaskarvarma of the 7th century A.D. In this drama unfortunately chronicle triumphs over drama with the consequent crippling and stilting of characterisation.

Only three plays of Jyoti Prasad Agarwala have been published, and several others are still in manuscript. The three published plays are *Śoṇit-Kuwārī* (The Princes of Sonitpur), *Kāreṅgar Ligirī* (The Maid of the Court), and *Labhitā*. The *Soṇit-Kuwarī*, composed while the dramatist was very young, combined in equal proportions the choicest talents of a budding poet and dramatist.

His second drama, *Kāreṅgar-Ligirī*, is his masterpiece and is a marvellous specimen of its kind in Assamese. The dramatist is no longer in the supernatural world of myths. He is among his own kind. He deals with the conflict between man and environment, old tradition and new outlook, man and destiny, and assails the way in which the ghost of the past doggedly haunts the present. Prince Sundar married Princess Kanchan under social pressure but only to learn that the Princess was already in love with her friend, Anangaram. In a very bold manner, he handed over Kanchan to Anangaram. But this was interpreted as having been prompted by a secret love connection which the Prince was supposed to have with Sewali—the Palace maid. The queen mother got Sewali secretly banished. When the Prince learnt this, he ran to rescue Sewali. Sewali, however, wanted to absolve the Prince from this social stigma. She indicated her self-less love for the Prince and committed suicide by jumping into a river, creating thus a void in the heart of the Prince.

In spirit, Agarwala is a romanticist. Besides romantic and ideal love, there is in his plays an insistence on the elemental simplicities of life. Organisation of scenes and acts follows modern lines, and in every scene, the dramatist gives elaborate stage-directions. The dialogue is lively, clear and spontaneous. Dramatic necessity and economy are always kept in view in providing for scenes and characters. Characters are developed naturally, and dramatic contrast makes them not only clear but also living and forceful. Sundar contrasts with Sudarshan, Kanchan with Sewali, and Rewati with Seuti.

From the ethereal and supernatural world of myth in *Śoṇit-Kuwārī* and the romantic tragedy of *Kāreṅgar Ligirī*, Jyoti Prasad came down to firmer and dustier ground in *Labhitā*. From the realm of myth, fancy, poetry and song, the dramatist comes to deal with the sickening and maddening events of the hard present. *Labhitā* depicts the August revolution of 1942 in which India's millions underwent sacrificial suffering for Independence. It also depicts how this revolution as well as the Second World War shook up Assamese life and fired the imagination of Assamese youths and maidens to blaze the revolutionary trail. The courage, patriotism, and ability of the heroic village girl Labhitā, and ex-soldier of the I. N. A., and her pathetic social life—these move us deeply. Realistic to the very core, the drama is principally one of action and thwarted passion. Character is enlivened by action, and the grim action is directed by the force of circumstances.

Realism is enlarged to such a degree that it even warps the poetic creativity of the dramatist occasionally. Though not a tragedy by orthodox canons, the total impression produced by it upon the reader is one of tragedy. *Labhitā* lacks the romantic beauty of *KārengarLigirī;* but it moves on a more familiar and intimate ground and, by the very breadth of its scope and popular appeal, is more endearing than the rest of the dramatist's published work.

Though he wrote short stories, Nakul Chandra Bhuyan is generally known as a dramatist. Both his dramas, *Badan Barphukan* and *Chandrakānta Simha*, are culled from the crowning glory of Assam's history, the Ahom period. In the *Belimār* of Bezbarua and *Ahomar Din* of Hiteswar Barbarua, a historical play is neither a pure play nor history. In it, historical facts are illuminated by the creation of situations and characters which, though imaginary, tend yet to portray the spirit and pressure of the times and interpret them so as to bring them to life. In *Badan Barphukan* the dramatist has not been able to achieve this. There is a rigid fidelity to facts. The introduction of imaginary characters like the woman Golapi gives some amount of dramatic relief, but the character hangs loosely by, and does not help the central action very much.

In character-sketching the dramatist has a firm grasp over his materials. The proud patriot Badan who, when crossed, turns against his mother country, has been firmly drawn. The characters of the far-sighted Queen-Mother, the towering Prime Minister Purnananda, and the weak Chandrakanta, have been depicted with vision and sympathy. The dramatist has underlined the fact that the ills that befell Assam were due as much to Badan's apostasy as to Purnananda's high-handed state-craft.

The other historical play, *Chandrakānta Simha,* is a sequel and complement to the former, and reiterates the decline and fall of Ahom Rule in Assam. The character of Chandrakānta—weak, idle, selfish, short-sighted, surrounded by selfish, envious, and intriguing officers—has been firmly drawn and dominates the play. The regrets and self-reproach which overwhelm Chandrakānta in the last scene, touch the audience too, and rouse their sympathy for him. The other characters also are more or less successful. The picture in the fourth Act of the

Burmese atrocities and the terrors they perpetrated on the people, has been realistically drawn.

Kamalananda Bhattacharya was a writer of songs, a dramatist and a successful actor intimately associated with the Dramatic Club of Nowgong. Two of his plays, *Nagā Kunwār* (The Nāga Prince) and *Avasān* (The End), deserve special mention. The *Nagā Kunwār* relates the life of the Ahom prince, Kanseng. When Chupimpha was on the Ahom throne, occasional tributes were paid him in his court by a handsome Nagā youth named Khunbao. One day Chupimpha's queen saw him and praised his beauty before her husband. At this the king was enraged and banished her, though she was pregnant, to the Nagā territory of Khunbao. There the queen gave birth to a son known in Assam history as the Nagā Prince. When he came to pay respect to the Ahom king (his own father) he was well received by Chupimpha. The king later made him a Barpatra Gohain or a Minister of State. Kanseng fought the Moghuls when they invaded Assam. The play is full of heroic and love sentiments. *Avasān* deals with the death of Krishna. The destruction of the Yadu dynasty at Prabhash and the death of Krishna at the hands of the hunter are depicted in a touching manner.

Kamaleswar Chaliha's *Dhūli* (The Dust) is a symbolic one-act play. Dhūli—represented in the play as a woman—is the last resort of all. Herself a life-long sufferer, she never fails anybody in his hour of need. Dhūli is struck to death by thunder. Her death is mourned by the affectionate cowherds, and Autumn herself is moved to pity and heaps, through the agency of her sweet, cool breezes, floral wreaths on her corpse.

Parvati Prasad Barua's lyric dramas, *Lakṣmī* and *Soṇar Soleng*, are also symbolic. *Lakṣmī* is an operatic farewell to late summer (Sarat) and welcome to the Goddess of Autumn (Hemanta). The white queen of late Summer (Sarat) is bade adieu to in music and dance by the whiteflower Kahuwa grass and the Sewali flower. The goddess Hemanta (Autumn) is welcomed by the bashful damsel, Fog, enveloped in her veil, and Banti (the flambeau) goes out to receive and escort the queen with due honours. The queen, Hemanta, deity of harvest, comes in the month of Kartik—the month in which plantations over, the Assamese people celebrate the Kartik festival or Bihu. The dramatist has poetically rendered the spirit of the season of agricultural peace and plenty in Assam in this play.

Soṇar Soleng is a collection of several melodious, symbolic songs. Bin Baragi (The Roving Minstrel), the chief character in the drama, is in eternal quest after supreme joy. He interrogates everything that he comes across—the golden swans winging wildly across the deep blue of heaven in search of a golden Utopia, the wind that spreads its white invisible wings against the blue sky, and the mountain stream rolling down and singing mellifluously—if it can instruct him as to where ideal bliss (Soṇar Seleng) can be found. But nobody satisfies his curiosity. At long last Bin Baragi himself realises that Soṇar Soleng (Ideal Bliss) is not something which is to be had without. It is something within which is in life, and in it every minute of life is lived intensely and made eternal. Apart from the symbolism, the songs and lyrics contained in the drama are the very best of their kind in Assamese.

While the influence of the English drama on the artistry of the Assamese has to be admitted, it must at the same time be recognised that this influence was only meagre and superficial and did not permeate to deeper levels. Drama grows and is nurtured against the background of society. Assamese society being different from English, the foreign influence could hardly fructify the Assamese theatre at deeper levels. In the selection of themes, in the delineation of social situations, in the unfolding of historical happenings, respect for national genius and native bias are indispensable. Failing this, drama is bound to be effete. This basic resistance qualifies foreign influences that may have found their way in. Though the character of Gajpuriya in Lakshminath Bezbarua's *Cakradhvaj Siṁha* may have been influenced by Shakespeare's Falstaff, and though weaving of sub-plots in historical plays and disguising of women in men's apparel in Assamese plays are attributable to the same source, yet these must be reckoned as external influences only.

Translations of Shakespeare's plays did not thrive on the Assamese stage, because of this incompatibility between local emotions and Western sentiments, the audience and the dramatic background, and social aspirations and ideals.

The Comedy of Errors was rendered into Assamese as *Bhramaraṅga*, 1889. This was followed by *Candrāvalī* (*As You Like It*) of Duregeswar Sarma, *Tara* (*Cymbeline*) of Nabin Chandra Bardoloi, *Bhīmdarpa* (*Macbeth*) of Debananda Bharali, and *Amarlīlā* (*Romeo and Juliet*) of Padmadhar Chaliha. In adapting these dramas the adapters gave Assamese names to the dramatis personae. But none of them really made a mark on the stage in Assam. No successful playwright visualizes flesh without vitalizing it with life. In the adaptations we have flesh without life; we have uninteresting two-dimensional characters, flat and bloodless. Unfortunately, with a few honourable exceptions, the adapters of English plays are a strangely pedestrian rabble blindly treading the English roads, showing to each other the beauty spots which the English masters built and aimlessly endeavouring to transplant them in an alien soil.

1947 AND AFTER

After the second world war and the attainment of independence, Assamese literature has entered a new era of creativity and writers are exploiting new themes. The most recent dramas reflect the contemporary tastes and movements of the people. Dramas on classical themes suffer a temporary eclipse, and the little, if any, that is based on classical topics is a re-interpretation of life in new light. These are marked by symbolism. As pointed out already, patriotic fervour guided earlier dramatists in the selection of their subject-matter, and the Ahom chronicles proved a vast store-house of such patriotic material. Even so, these dramatists concentrated their art on characterisation and not, as has been the practice in the immediate present, on the propagation of political and social ideologies. The modern dramatist has employed the historical play either to preach Hindu-Muslim unity or to condemn the underhand policies of the British rulers, to extol those martyrs who fought the British, and who died for India's freedom at the hands of a perfidious and tyrannical oppressor. Chandrakanta Phookan's *Piyalī Phukan* is one such anti-British play. Himself an actor, Chandrakanta Phookan has intimate knowledge of the stage, and is imbued with the patriotic spirit with which he invested the play. Hence it has been received well on the stage. Piyalī Phukan, the last scion of the Ahom dynasty, secretly made a serious bid to drive away the British from Assam, and he even managed to set fire to a British ammunition dump. But he was finally apprehended and hanged by the British. Prabin Phookan, another anti-British dramatist, shows in his *Maṇirām Devān* how the Ahom official, Maṇirām Devān, plotted for the overthrow of British rule in Assam, and how he too perished on the British scaffold. In both the plays very modern currents of thought find their expression. Sarada Kanta Bardoloi preaches Hindu-Muslim unity in *Magribar Ājān*. It tells how the Muslim youth, Karim, sacrificed his own life in a bid to save the life of a tribal Hindu girl. The drama tries to give a realistic picture of how in Assam's villages Hindus, Muslims and tribals all live in peace and amity.

But most of these recent dramas deal exclusively with problems of urban life. The motif of social reform of earlier plays has been replaced by the motif of diagnosis of social problems, mostly economic and civic, with which the townspeople are confronted today. The problems of women in the new set-up also figure prominently. Sarada Bordoloi's *Pahilā Tārikh* (First Day of the Month) brings out the precarious economic life of the lower middle class and wage-group whose monthly pay is exhausted on the very pay-day itself in discharging the debts of the preceding month.

After the installation of the Gauhati and Shillong Studios of the All India Radio, one-act plays have become very popular. Some of these one-act plays possess literary distinction. These plays concentrate not on plot but on a single situation, analysing therein the inner conflicts of the men and women of today —conflicts born of economic and social ills. These are illuminating studies of some particular character, situation or problem, and as such they are allied in technique to short stories. The first strongly conceived one-act play in Assamese, *Ebelār-Nāṭ* (Drama of a Half-day); depicts the conflicts of ideals and hopes among the members of a single family—father, mother, son and daughter—some sticking to old values, others holding firmly to new ones, all the happenings being confined to one half of a day. The development of the subject-matter and the arrangement of the dialogue has been so deftly handled that it is difficult to ascribe the incidents and characters to any particular locality or people. The treatment rises above racial barriers, and embraces wider issues. In the years ahead the one-act play will remain the only dramatic entertainment for people of diverse tastes.

CHAPTER IX

THE NOVEL AND THE SHORT STORY

THE novel in Assamese came in the wake of the Western system of education that was introduced by the British Administration, and it drew its inspiration from the literature of the west. In the pages of the *Aruṇoday* itself, an Assamese rendering of Bunyan's *Pilgrim's Progress* began to appear in serial under the caption, *Yātrikārar Yātrā.* We have already written about *Kāminikānta* and *Phulmaṇi Aru Karuṇā*, both dealing with Christian scriptural stories. In 1880 appeared *Sudharmar Upākhyān* of Padmavati Devi Phukanani, which got some publicity as the first novel by an Assamese lady, and which is not without some intrinsic merit. But the first attempt at anything approaching a plot, was Hemchandra Barua's *Bāhire raṅg-caṅg Bhitare Kowā Bhāturi* (Playing in the Parlour, Empty is the Larder). As this is a novel with a purpose directed against the social and religious evils of the time, here for the first time realism and characterisation find fuller development. After the social novel, the historical novel was taken up, and in this genre Lakshminath Bezbarua was a leading writer. His *Padum Kunwārī* is a story of tragic love, between Padum and Surjya, inserted into the story of a rebellion led by two zeminders of Kamrup of great influence and power, Hardatta and Birdatta, Padum's father and uncle, against the Ahom throne. The turmoil and the clash of the rebellion do not hinder the tender love story from proceeding naturally, and the author succeeds to a certain extent in conjuring up the spirit and atmosphere of the times in which the characters move and breathe. Minute details are provided to lend to the story the illusion of reality, and the novelist achieves a pattern marked by skilful weaving, clarity of conception and happiness of blending.

Padmanath Gohain Barua wrote two novels, *Lāhari* and *Bhānumatī*, both centring round love. Both have the background of the Ahom days. Though placed against historical settings, neither novel deals with any history as such. Moreover, neither in plot-development nor in characterisation and psychological analysis do the novels show any distinction.

Though Rajanikanta Bardoloi has contributions to other branches of literature, he is widely known as a great novelist. He had a reverence for the past and for Assam's cultural and literary heritage, and was always inspired by a lofty idealism. His novels aim at rousing a regard for the rich heritage of Assam. He held up high moral standards before people, and for human weakness he had the largest sympathies. Equally disposed to all classes of people, he assayed a Comedie Humaine, darting like a traveller from one swarming city or countryside to another with an abundance of human sympathy. He believed that life after all is one and that mutual regard would not cost anything and would remove unhappiness. Primal passions that ultimately count have their soil in every human heart and do not abide any distinctions of class or caste or community. He was thus the most large-hearted and the most felicitous of our novelists.

Influenced by Sir Walter Scott, and possessing the same pure relish for the charm of the wayside, the same ringing humour and infectious vivacity as of Scott and the great Bengali novelist, Bankimchandra, Bardoloi took up his pen to portray the history and social conditions of a critical period of Assamese national existence, and the work he produced endures for its depth of philosophic comment, descriptive power, fidelity to life, creative imagination and charm of style. Historical novelists usually enjoy only a short sway of immense popularity and are then dethroned. But Bardoloi has never lost his pre-eminence in the field of Assamese fiction. His historical novels are abiding historical frescoes. Like Scott and Bankimchandra, Bardoloi was a mighty potentate of literature. With the exception of *Mirijīyarī*, all novels of Bardoloi have historical settings. The *Mirijīyarī*, written in 1895, is his first novel. It deals with the sad love-affair of two young Miris, and is obviously the first Assamese novel on tribal life. *Monomoti* (1900) is Bardoloi's best work. Placed against the background of the declining years of Ahom Rule, the Burmese invasion of Assam, and the consequent insecurity and unrest, both social and political, the novel deals with the love-story of Lakṣmīkānta and Monomotī. The heroism of Lakṣmīkānta and the womanly dignity of Monomotī are both brought into bold relief, and they haunt our memories. If we may quote an English poet, blessings and prayers in nobler retinue than sceptred king or laurelled conqueror knows, follow these lovers. *Raṅgilī* (1925) has the same dark historical background. Against the Burmese invasion, social and political chaos and court intrigues, the character of an ideal woman sheds its divine and redeeming brilliance. The good and distinguished lady Raṅgilī has her earthly love, but this love is gradually sublimated to divine love. The novelist suggests that the fortitude and nobility of Raṅgilī are no mere casual feature of a single and noble househod, but that suffering like hers is characteristic of the time and symptomatic of the decadence of society. Another historical novel is *Rahdai Ligirī* (Rahdai the Courtmaid), depicting the ideal of pure love. Rahdai, a simple maiden, is in deep love with Dayārām, also an ordinary youth. The pure flame of Rahdai's innocent and profound love for Dayārām burns steadily even in the midst of blinding and overpowering storms of royal displeasure, privations, and temptations. When tyranny becomes oppressive, she takes to *yoga* and thereby not only saves herself but also changes the mind of Dayārām. *Nirmal Bhakat* (1925) describes how Nirmal is taken captive by the Burmese during their second invasion of Assam, and how, after a long exile in Burma, he returned home to find that not only the country but also his own home has changed enormously and that his wife has married another man. Nirmal does not despair of life. He becomes a Vaiṣṇavite devotee and spends the rest of his life in religious peace, whereby, according to the Upanishadic Seer, "what has not been heard of becomes heard of, what has not been thought of becomes thought of, what has not been understood becomes understood."

Historical in setting and with marked topographical lining, the *Tāmresvarī Mandir* (The Shrine of Goddess Tāmresvarī) tells the story of a passionate pair—Dhaneswar and Aghoni—whose union is crossed by several factors, the greatest being the sentient Tantricism of the temple itself. The long-delayed union is finally effected by the victory of Vaiṣṇavism over Tantricism, of all-embracing love over blind ritual. The events belong approximately to the same time as those of *Nirmal Bhakat.*

The *Danduvā Droh* (1919) deals with the revolt of the people of Kamrup against the Ahom rule. Provoked by the misrule and oppression of the Ahom Viceroy, Badan Chandra, at Gauhati, the Kamrup people revolt under the leadership of the two heroic brothers, Hardatta and Birdatta. In the battles that follow, Birdatta dies fighting, Hardatta is captured and court-martialled, and Hardatta's daughter kills herself by jumping into the river Brahmaputra to evade captivity. The introduction of love stories enlivens narratives which are laden with the history of Assam around 1800. *Rādhā-Rukmiṇī* is yet another historical novel of Rajanikanta Bardoloi's. It deals with the revolt of the Mowamaria sect of Vaiṣṇavites against the Ahom rule, which broke out towards the middle of the 18th century. The novel narrates the heroic exploits of two Mowamaria heroines—Rādhā and Rukmiṇī. Though historical in atmosphere, Bardoloi's novels do not aim so much at recreating history as at imaginatively depicting the life of men and women. In doing this he has achieved no mean success. Bardoloi's female characters possess special charm. The love, fidelity, tenderness, mental resourcefulness, resolution and extraordinary courage they display in the face of heavy odds, make his women admirable. Yet the novelist does not show a great inclination to draw their full portraits. He gives, on the other hand, much consideration to plot-construction, to unusual sensational incidents and thrilling action which in its variety is like a rich tapestry. Perhaps one thing more should be said of Bardoloi's novels and that is that they exhibit the goodness, beauty, and moral strength of human life. The novelist further betrays a predilection for Tāntricism and Vaiṣṇavism, and in elucidating Tāntric culture, he seems to have been influenced by Bankim Chatterjee. The plots are ingeniously conceived no doubt; but the writer does not hesitate to draw in upon the beliefs of people including those related to the shadowy deeps of the occult.

Social reform is the aim of two of Dandinath Kalita's novels *Sādhanā* and *Ābiṣkār.* The leading characters of both, Dinabandhu and Mādhava, sacrifice all personal happiness at the altar of social purification. In the two women, Rambhā and

Pratimā, the novelist depicts the problem of fallen women and suggests its solution. Both the novels reflect the social conscience of the tirelessly dialectical novelist and hold up for criticism and analysis social injustices and parochialism. The third novel, *Gaṇaviplav* (The Revolution of the Masses) depicts the Mowamaria revolution which broke out towards the close of the Ahom rule in Assam. There is a faithful reproduction of history, set forth in simple, graphic episodes, but there is not much of creative imagination in characterisation in this novel. There is the same lack of fertile imagination that marks his long poem, *Asam Sandhyā*. Kalita is a realist in his faithfulness to the surface; but he is never concerned with nuances of character and situation that spring from awareness of the growth of the human mind in response to critical stimuli.

Daibachandra Talukdar has tried his hand at all the three literary forms—poetry, fiction and drama. But this lack of concentration on a single form has resulted, as it usually does, in failure to rise above mediocrity. In his novel, the *Apurṇa* (The Unfulfilled) is described the chequered career of a village youth, Premadhar, who wins through the various hurdles and hindrances of life but only to die a premature death. His life's ideals thus remained unfulfilled. The *Āgneyagirī* (The Volcano) delineates the character of another youth, Kanak, who comes in violent clash with society and its customs. *Vidroha* (The Rebellion) is a kind of complementary second, in which the same Kanak is the leading character. In defiance of social customs Kanak marries the widow Āikon, and both of them espouse the cause of national liberation. Whilst Āikon engages herself in rural uplift and reorganisation, Kanak carries on the torch of rebellion from place to place, moving like a hurricane from Sadiya to Lahore. The story does not seem to have any lofty intention or a convincing culmination. The feeble and haggard narrative, not very lucid in style or smart in tone, appears to be tossing about in vain, imaginary heroics predominating. His stories largely are mere pretexts for somewhat wordy homilies.

The output of fiction in Assamese is, however, limited, and did not reach maturity till the last decade. In recent years the standard has gone up and several new and salutary tendencies are discernible. From the old romantic sagas, they have now gone to realistic and psycho-analytic themes. The present-day fiction writers have turned their eyes on those who are neglected by society, and try to assess their unique social value. One of such novels, on the rural life of Assam, is *Jivanar Bāṭat* (On the Highway of Life) by Bina Barua (pseudonym of Birinchi Kumar Barua). In another novel, *Seujī Pātar Kāhinī* (Story of Green Leaves) the author portrays the life and society of tea-garden labourers with sympathy. Dinanath Sarma's *Nadāi* is also a novel on village life. Sarma lays stress on the character of Nadāi, a cultivator, whose whole life is intimately bound up with the prosperity of his own village, and he gives a complete picture of Nadāi's goodness and the hospitality and liberality of his co-villlagers. Hitesh Deka's *Ājir Mānuh* (The Man of the Age) and *Māṭi Kār* (Who Owns the Land?) deal with present-day life and agrarian problems, and an attempt is made to evaluate the political and social rights of man. His *Bhārā Ghar* describes a love story round the ever-growing urban housing problem. Adyanath Sarma's *Jīvanar Tini Adhyāy* (Three Chapters of Life), Chandrakanta Gogoi's *Soṇar Nāṅgal* (The Golden Plough), Govinda Mahanta's *Kṛṣakar Nāti* (The Cultivator's Descendants) are some of the outstanding novels of social study.

Woven round a love story, Navakanta Barua's *Kapilīparīyā Sādhu* depicts the unfortunate tale of the people dwelling on the bank of the river Kapilī, which changes its course whimsically every year. In *Dāvar āru Nāi* (Clouds No More) Jogesh Das portrays the disruptive effects of the last World War upon the ethics and manners of our society. His *Sahāri Pāi* and *Jonākīr Jui* deal with love, the strongest of human emotions, and achieve striking effects by a series of unexpected situations which serve the purpose of fragmentary mirrors in a kaleidoscope. Muhammed Piar mostly writes of town life. His *Saṅgrām* (The Struggle) describes the struggles and sufferings of middle-class youth, while *Herowā Svarga* (The Lost Heaven) depicts the life of a Muslim family. Some psychological novels produced during recent years have made a mark by their realistic technique, depiction of the subconscious motives and urges of the human heart, men and women being seen as jets of emotional energy drawn from the vast, dark tides of unconscious impulse. Praphulladatta Goswami's

Kecā Pātar Kapani (The Quivering Foliage) describes the ideological unrest of a young man who makes a mess of his own life longing for better things and seeking peace in beauty. Goswami's genius is essentially aesthetic and visionary. Radhikamohan Goswami's *Cāknaiyā* (The Vortex) portrays the life of a frustrated young man who cannot adapt himself to the present-day society. His *Bā-Māralī* (The Whirlwind) protests against the whirlwind of modern civilisation that has uprooted our serene village life with all its time-honoured traditions and restful ways of life. Birendrakumar Bhattacharya, in his *Rājpathe Riṅgiyāi* (The Call of the Highway), depicts the life of a young revolutionary who wants to set right the 'wrongs' of society. The entire approach of the author is political and the treatment psychological. His *Āi* (Mother) is a clear cut story of a poor Brahman widow struggling against abject poverty and social insecurity. *Iyanuingam* is a complex and longer narrative on the life of the Tangkhul Nagas. The story begins with the retreat of the Japanese from the Naga Hills, and many social and political problems that appeared immediately after the War are projected in the living images of Naga men and women. Politics also predominates over the story in Syed Abdul Malik's *Rathar Cakari Ghūre* (The Chariot Wheels Move); the novel appears to be semi-autobiographical. In *Chabi Ghar* (The Picture House), Malik covers psycho-analysis and social consciousness. Unfortunately the story is lost in the experiment. *Sūrujmukhir svana* is Malik's latest and most successful creation. This is a romantic tale of Gulas who wants to marry the fifteen-year-old Tara but her mother Kapahi cheats him and herself manages to marry the young man. *Asīmat Yār Herol Sīmā* (Whose Boundary Lost in the Horizon) by Kanchan Barua (pseudonym) is a big novel published recently, where the author seeks to portray an imaginary historical event that took place thirteen hundred years ago, on the bank of the great river Dihing, in the north-eastern region of Assam. The work doubtless has idyllic descriptions in moving language, ingenious invention, and skilfully wrought emotional complexes, but the elements of fantasy, unreality, and anachronism have made it more or less an absurd fairy tale for grown-ups.

In spite of all these new tendencies and endeavours, fiction largely is being written even today on sentimental, erotic and escapist themes to which life does not wholly approximate. These are very popular among a class of readers, particularly among middle-class women, who live a drab, bored, depressed life of domestic cares. Through their reading of these novels they seek to escape from drab realities and to be transported even for a few hours to the sleepy region of fancy. The popularity of this type of fiction grows along with the wide spread of literacy, and it will continue to grow till better books are provided to serve the emotional needs of young readers. It will be, however, unkind if we do not admire a few novels of this class which show competence both in story telling and in diction. Premanarayan Datta's *Praṇayar Suti* (The Stream of Love), *Niyatir Nlrmāli* (The Garland of Fate), and Suchibrata Raichoudhury's *Bā-Māralī* (The Whirlwind) are tolerable productions. For the very same reasons, thrillers have also become best sellers. The thriller or detective fiction is new to Assamese literature. The late growth is due to historical reasons. Assam did not have big towns or cities until recently. Now along with the growth of big towns and development of trade and commerce, emigration to towns and business centres has led to various crimes which are reported in the daily newspapers. These, therefore, provide themes for thrillers. Premanarayan Datta's *Pā-Phu* series is well known. Most of the detective novels have, however, neither much inventive faculty nor skill to render the incredible credible; as a result, improbabilities remain wildly improbable.

The short story is the chief literary type that grew in recent times under the influence of the West. There have been stories, tales, myths, fables, parables and anecdotes in Assamese from very old times. But these differ from the modern short story profoundly in both matter and technique. It was in the period culminating in the first World War that the modern short story emerged as a form to be cultivated separately. It was fostered by the considerable growth of magazines and stimulated by the example of foreign masters, Chekhov, Maupassant, Somerset Maugham and others. The modern short story is marked by realism. It is a criticism of life. The notes that appeared in the *Aruṇoday* gave varied information of life all around us; yet these were not short stories. Lakshminath Bezbarua was the first short-story writer in Assamese who brought an entirely new conception and an entirely modern approach to the short story. By close observation and analytical reasoning, he achieved great success in both matter and technique, and his short stories are admitted even today to be the best of their kind in Assamese. His touching stories depict the nature and life of the people, their joys and tears, their strength and weakness, their sufferings and frustrations, in all their fullness. These stories reveal Bezbarua's profound attention to human sympathy with and wide understanding of the life of Assamese peasantry, which many of our educated people understand so little. Some of his stories are charming and poetic, haunting the memory like romantic lyrics. The pleasant aspect of Nature in *Jal-Kunwārī*, the terror underlying its glory in *Kanyā* and *Ratan Muṇḍa,* Nature's loveliness and sympathy in *Erābāri*, are all described in an animated style. Bezbarua's stories centre round rural middleclass life, and they do not have about them that weird cry of the dispossessed, the oppressed and the hungry which rings so much in recent stories. Occasionally he patterns his story with the crosslights of paradox and satire. The hypocrisy, deceit, vanity, and blind prejudices masquerading as orthodoxy of the higher stratum of society are held up to ridicule in some of his stories. Some other stories ridicule the blind imitation by educated village youth of western habits, dress and customs. He knew Assamese life very intimately; so he could make the uneventful life of the simple villagers the subject-matter of many of his entertaining short stories. The most engaging thing about Bezbarua's tales is the essential innocence and sincerity of his people. His rural stories depict the hopes and fears, simple joys and sorrows, the temptations and weaknesses, the deep piety and superstitions of the rustics as also the fidelity of rural love.

Sarat Chandra Goswami achieved considerable success as a writer of short stories, and the collected editions of his short stories, *Galpāñjali* and *Maynā*, contain powerfully conceived stories happy alike for skilful and conscientious craftsmanship, for building up of atmosphere, and for characterisation. They mostly deal with the drab life of the Assamese villagers, their sorrows and joys, hopes and fears, their simple and languorous love, and their thrifty activities. In *Banariyā Praṇaya* (Wild Love) in the *Maynā* collection is described the romantic love of a Miri youth and maiden, whose union is disapproved by their parents. The pair then plunged together into the mighty Brahmaputra. People think that they have committed suicide. In fact, however, they do not die. Being creatures of water, they swim ashore, reach a distant village, and settle down there as man and wife. The story gives a pleasant picture of the simple life of the Miris. The story *Nadrām* gives a realistic picture of tribal life. The Kachari youth, Nadrām, goes to France in the First World War. During his long absence his wife espouses another Kachari youth, Bhātirām, of the same village. Returning home, Nadrām comes to know of what has happened. He complains to the Deputy Commissioner, who orders Bhātirām to restore the woman to Nadrām. Nadrām wins the case, but is deeply moved at the thought of how the woman would commit suicide if she were torn from Bhatirām. Without malice or grudge and with almost superhuman nobility, he lets her live happily with the man of her choice. Several other stories deal with illicit love, but nowhere is there any lapse into unrefined taste or feeling, nor is there any unnaturalness anywhere. *Yātrī* (The Traveller) is another story dealing with illegitimate love. Godadhar nearly succumbs to the charms of Santi; but the fear of social ostracism proves a powerful deterrent. He flees from her and saves himself. In *Brahmaputrar Bukat* (Into the Bosom of the Brahmaputra) a married woman, who had a secret love affair with a second man, ends her distressed life by jumping into the river Brahmaputra. In more stories than one, Goswami has drawn vivid pictures of the pathetic life of girl-widows. Free from bias and sophistication, sensitive and profoundly realistic, Goswami records his observation of human nature and frailty with the most sober sincerity.

In his stories, Nagendranarayan Chowdhury introduced new subjects and a novel mode of treatment.

Lakshminath Phukan is noted also as a short-story writer. Six short stories, written at different periods, have been collected and published in *Ophāidāṅg* (The Bombast). These stories contain entertaining character-studies of modern educated hollow men and women. The story *Mahimāmayī* (The Glorified Woman) deals with a woman of that name, wife of the head clerk of a tea garden, who practised austere economy at home, but who ultimately, was compelled to spend all her savings through the trickery of a youthful relative of hers. The story is entertaining from beginning to end and contains homely pictures. *Tāipiṣṭar Jīvan* (Life of a Typist) is a sad story of the miserable life of Manik Saikia, a typist. For a pittance this typist over-worked himself, often working extra hours at his office, and ultimately fell ill and died prematurely. The death of his dutiful typist and ideal employee was mourned in the office and a condolence resolution was passed. The proprietor of the Chaudhury Brothers Company, the firm where the typist worked, promised to hang a portrait of Manik Saikia in the office room at a cost of three hundred rupees. A timely dole of one third of this amount would have saved the life of the object of so much of gratefulness and adoration. Lakshminath Phukan uses spoken language and idioms with nice discrimination and great telling effect. A sense of humour is an additional virtue of his fascinating and picturesque writings.

The short stories, written in lighter vein and depicting the life of the middle classes, that are now being written by Mahichandra Bora, have not much of the vitality and graphic quality of his pre-war stories, mostly published in the *Awāhan*. Yet none can deny them literary distinction. The chief feature of Mahi Bora's short-stories is charming description of the healthy, contented middle-class life of Assam, of its capacity to lead an uncomplaining and uninsinuating stoic existence even in the teeth of want, and of life's little ironies. A consummate artist of the short story, Bora has a chaste style and an urbane humour introduced either for just simple amusement or with the object of exposing the absurdity of some character or situation. His stories are matchless in Assamese alike in creating certain types of men and women whom we meet in our everyday dealings, and in their plot-construction, narration, humour, urbanity, and spontaneity and ease in character projection. He has a flood of imaginative energy that breaks through all the dykes of customary solemnity and gravity and carves its own wayward channels of pure and sustained humour or irony.

Another elder short-story writer is Haliram Deka who brings to bear on his writings a deeper analysis of character and satire. *Alakālai Ciṭhi* (Letters to Alaka) is a collection of letters addressed to an imaginary Alaka. Through these separate letters the author has tried to weave an epistolary novel. But the chief merit of the book lies not in its narrative but in its analytical flair. Deka's prose style is dignified and thoughtful.

Lakshmidhar Sarma was prematurely cut off. Most of his short stories lie scattered in the magazine, *Awāhan*. A collection of five stories were published in the form of a book *Vyarthatār Dān* (The Gift of Frustration). The story, *Vidrohiṇī* (The Rebellious Woman), is a fearless statement of the sad plight of the girl-widow Lalitā, and her courageous defiance of the cruel and rigid conventions of society which thwart satisfaction of primary instincts. Here she defies a society that has become static and hypocritically rigid and formal. In another story, *Sirāj*, the love between Sita and Anil, which blossoms gradually, withers suddenly because of Anil's fear of society which has, in the meantime, discovered that Sita was born out of wedlock. She is pitilessly forsaken by the cowardly Anil. The story *Līlā* is a trenchant criticism of modern civilization and irrational social conventions. Lakshmidhar gave the Assamese short story dignity, substance and popularity.

In Lakshmidhar Sarma's stories, for the first time woman and the seemingly freakish workings of her primary emotion find a place. He was succeeded by a host of other writers who also dwelt on the inner movements of impulse in modern women. They were Bina Barua, Roma Das and others. Bina Barua's *Paṭ-Paribartan* (Change of Scene) is a collection of stories mostly on the life of college girls and their shallow, ever-shifting, sentimental love affairs. He has written also on rural life, and the leading story, *Āghoṇībāi*, included in the collection of rural stories bearing that name, is a memorable one, depicting the village woman Āghoṇībāi—ever helpful to every villager, even in the face of personal distress. It contains a rich gallery of vivid portraits of rural life daintily and significantly done. What attracts readers to Roma Das is his perfect craftsmanship as a writer of short stories. Vividness of description, charm of dialogue, solidity of thought, and an extraordinary capacity to record nicely discriminated and artfully proportioned differences of feeling in language—all these make his short stories some of the very best we have in Assamese. Most of his stories deal with departures from accepted social canons and aberrations of conventional love, and to this task the writer has brought psycho-analysis and sympathy.

Trailokyanath Goswami is another distinguished writer of short stories especially of the realistic variety. His two collections, *Aruṇā* and *Marīcikā* (Mirage), contain stories which are veritable slices from life around us. The story *Jayr̄āj*, included in *Aruṇā*, is one of considerable power, and depicts the cruel scorn and social tyranny to which Ratan, born out of wedlock, is subjected. In another story, *Vidhavā* (The Widow), the writer depicts the social tyranny and oppression which victimise a helpless mother and her unfortunate daughter, both widows, and render their lives helplessly tragic. The pillar of the village society, Mandal, is a great tyrant who prevents the villagers from cremating the dead body of Promilā's mother. Mandal's own son, however, brings a ray of hope. Quite disregarding his father's opposition, and in the darkness of a foul night, he carries the dead body to the burning ghat. This opens the eyes of all, including the intriguing father, who, full of remorse, subsequently joins the cremation. The stories of *Marīcikā* are devoted largely to the ills which came in the wake of the Second World War. Goswami's *Jīyā-Mānuh* (The Living Man) is a short novel devoted to the same topic of dwindling social morality and the consequent withering away of all spontaneous and noble feelings that the war brought about, and the reforms that have become imperative in the changed society.

Those short-story writers who wrote after Lakshmidhar Sarma and up to the Second World War, were influenced by Sigmund Freud. To the influence of Freud must be ascribed the breakdown of age-old inhibitions, and the preoccupation with sex which presently became the dominant feature of the modern short story as well as of the novel. Freudian psycho-analysis, which opened the way to the exploration of the sub-conscious and unconscious, gave the short-story writers an opportunity to dwell more and more on the mind of their characters. The sanctity of sex having been removed, the short-story writers accepted illegitimate, uninhibited love-romance and unrestricted sex attraction and gratification without hesitation as if these were as real as the other facts of life. Hence in describing sexual love and advocating freedom in sex-relations, they felt no scruple or doubt or delicacy. On the contrary the sex urges were felt by them as manifestations of a cosmic force which they described in religious terms. They tried to give a new interpretation of the primal relationship subsisting between man and woman against the new social and individual background and in a broad Freudian context.

Since the Second World War, however, this attitude has undergone a change. The short story today is preoccupied with the problems of the middle class, the labourers and the peasants. The new social and economic environment, the incongruities, the inequalities of opportunities—these have become the ordinary postulates of the short story of today. It is concerned with the social, political and moral upheavals brought about by the Second World War, and is trying to assess the new values. It contrasts the contentment of the peasant life of the earlier social order with the discontent, misery, oppression, tyranny and exploitation that labour has to undergo in the new social order and the anger and sense of revenge aroused in consequence.

One of the short-story writers who became popular after the War is Syed Abdul Malik. Unlike most other Assamese story writers and novelists who lack sustained devotion, Syed Abdul Malik has stuck to the short story for nearly the past two decades, and he is just now the most favourite story-writer. His sustained productions show the evolution of his technique which is powerful, individual and adequate. Starting with romantic love, he has covered also psycho-analysis and social consciousness. Most of his stories have a sex appeal, particularly to urban youths and maidens. In them, with the help of psycho-analysis, he arouses inquisitive interest, often forging in the smithy of a fallen soul the uncreated conscience of his age. He shows how different mental states—the weakness and fickleness of modern Eves, their fall from accepted ethical standards and the consequent transitory sense of victory—react against the circumstances. The stories, *Śeṣ Upakūlar Seluwā Pār* (The Mossy Bank on the last Edge of Land), *Prāṇ Herowār Pāchat* (After the Soul Was Lost), *Jowār āru Upakūl* (The Tidal Bore and Coast), and *Marahā Pāpari* (The Faded Petal), contained in the collection bearing the last-named title, are devoted to a psycho-analytical dissection of the female mind. In several stories unlawful but overwhelming love has been treated with sympathy. The author appears to be trying to revolutionise the conventional attitude towards these matters and re-educate the modern Assamese mind by suggesting that ideas about chastity, personal purity, etc., are not absolute but relative to society, time and circumstances. He finds abundant humanity and dignity even in some of the so-called social outcasts, whose fall was but accidental, and in the misfortunes with which life abounds. Some of Malik's recent stories bring out the conflicts of the rich and the poor, of the society and the individual, and the lack of harmony in the middle-class people in the new economic set-up. The story *Sio Maril* (He Too Died) describes in a superb manner how in the unjust economy prevailing in society many a man of genius is subdued and untimely cut off. Malik has brought into the Assamese short story a powerful and new technique. All that he writes is impregnated with a fine, candid and charitable spirit and is marked by subtle distinction in workmanship.

Dinanath Sarma's stories have been published in four collections—*Dulāl* (1952), *Akalśarīā* (The Lonely), 1953, *Kowā Bhāturiā Othar Talat* (Behind False Lips), and *Kalpanā āru Vāstav* (Imagination and Reality, 1955). Most of his stories deal with illegitimate love. A large number of Sarma's stories give ugly and revolting portraits of women. In one single story, *Phetigom* (The Cobra), included in the collection *Kowā Bhāturia Othar Talat*, there are several such galling portraits. It is clear that the writer has no abiding sympathy for the fair sex. There are, however, a few noble exceptions, where the fears and silent sufferings, the helpless wanderings in the labyrinths of a woman's life, the complexes and conflicts, are brought out impressively in a psycho-analytical aesthetic study.

The collection *Kowā Bhāturia Othar Talat* contains several stories patterned after Zola and Maupassant and flavoured with the spices of strange lands from across the seas. These deal with the love affairs of queer people of different nationalities against the background of the Second World War. Except for these, most of Dina Sarma's stories confine themselves to Assam (both rural and urban) and the Assamese. Some stories like *Strīratna* in *Kalpanā āru Vāstav* also contain idyllic description of Assamese villages. Dina Sarma's chief defect is lack of felicitous expression.

Hemen Bargohain is both a poet and a short-story writer, and so far he has brought out two collections of short stories, *Bibhinna Korāc* and *Prem āru Mrityur Kāraṇe* (For Love and Death). Bargohain is mostly preoccupied with the Freudian theory of the libido, and naturally his stories have a strong tendency towards sex and factual realism. He, however, exhibits ability to produce effects with a balanced style and economy of words.

In both his novels and short stories Padma Barkakati too throws off restraints of conventions and makes sex the all-powerful theme. Saurabh Chaliha is another promising writer who writes sarcastically of men and women of a decaying society.

Bhaben Saikia, Lakshminandan Bora and Mohim Bora, this trio, have deep sympathy, insight and understanding of village people and their way of life. In their stories they are keen observers of folk and rural situations.

Reference has already been made to the changes that came over our literature after the War. These changes have been reflected in the matter and technique of the short story too. The short story, appropriate literary entertainment of busy modern life, is popular alike with readers and with writers, who, drawn mostly from young students of schools and colleges, find it easy to handle. Brought up on Western education and influenced by Freud and Marx, these young writers want a new assessment of values—literary, aesthetic, philosophical, religious and social. They want the existing values to be subjected to scientific scrutiny. Social behaviour, aristocracy, purity of conduct and moral earnestness—all these are to be defined again. With the help of psychoanalysis these writers have dived deep into the dark waters of the human mind. The tameness and laxity of conjugal bliss, romance, the craze for novelty, the natural magnetism of unlawful love, the thrill of companionate marriages—these seem to be their paramount concerns. They also inquire into the economic relationship of the rich and the poor, of the landlord and the cultivator, and advocate a better treatment of the have-nots.

These young story writers, swayed by the liberal, realistic currents of European thought and questioning, are equally intent on being true to the life or the incidents of life which they want to portray. They imagine that their salvation as literary artists demands realism in every sphere. So along with realism in their subject-matter, realism in language has also been adopted; and all earlier unwritten taboos against writing of anything which might be regarded as indecent, profane or even vulgar, are deliberately discarded. It is true that if any literature is to go on flourishing, it is bound to emerge from 'the trance of suspended faith'. But it is equally true that mere change is not always a symbol of progress and that every new experiment in literary form or content is seldom a milestone on the road to aesthetic perfection.

CHAPTER X

PROSE : GENERAL

MENTION has already been made of how modern Assamese prose made its beginnings under the auspices of the American Baptist Mission and their Assamese co-workers. Anandaram Dhekial Phukan, Gunabhiram Barua and Hemchandra Barua gave the final stamp to its grammar and made it a vehicle for the spread of education and social reform, and for exposition of history, science, philosophy and metaphysics. Their works were mainly frigid essays, or attempts at prose composition devoid of that flow and style which was to appear later on. It was Lakshminath Bezbarua who for the first time freed Assamese prose somewhat from the weight of ideas and matter, and made it dynamic. Impersonal or objective styles now yield place to personal and subjective ones. To Bezbarua goes the credit of the introduction of sketches and informal essays and the use of humour as an instrument for the correction of social evils. Like Chesterton, Bezbarua succeeded in inventing a form half-way between the essay and the short story, promising light entertainment. It is this that gives his essays their exquisitely amusing quality, turning a multitude of homely topics and daily trifles into material for hearty laughter. Bezbarua created in his essays and belles lettres the character of Kripabar Barbarua, in imitation of the eccentric Tory country squire, Sir Roger de Coverley, and exposed and bantered the foibles and the false arts of Assamese life and manners typified in Kripabar's idiosyncrasies. His delightful series of essays under the caption *Barbaruār Bhāvar Burburaṇi* (Barbarua's Bubbles of Thought) are well known in Assam. They touch upon topical themes for the most part, making fun of the hollow men and institutions of the country. They are sedate and composed, like easy conversation within the restraints of decorum, although they are refreshingly flavoured with humour. Sharp observation brought to bear on contemporary life and problems and fondness for good-humoured banter in preference to heavy and angry satire, make the essays amusingly appealing; they make us happier and wiser when we read them. But his essays have some faults too, the most prominent being the diffuseness such as one finds in Montaigne.

Satyanath Borah (1860-1925) was another leading prose writer. He wrote a number of sketches in which he satirised the little vanities and the social vices of his time. These have been incorporated in his *Kendra Sabhā*. But more representative of his distinctive prose style are his *Sārathi*, *Cintākali*, and *Sāhitya Vicār*. His essays in *Sārathi* (The Guide) and *Cintākali* (Buds of Thought) are thoughtful, close-knit, secular compositions. In these essays on the Universe, Mission of Life, Duty, Determination, Character, Uses of Riches, etc., the writer uses literature as an instrument of progress, education and information. An original and deep thinker, his sentences have the directness, epigrammatic brevity and concentrated wisdom of aphorisms. 'Knowledge removes the darkness of the mind', 'Thought is the digestive organ of the mind', 'Superstition is an obstacle to progress', 'Treasures of books are like hoarded gold', 'The world is merely a stream of life', 'Procrastination loses opportunities', 'Practice dissolves hard work as acid does gold'—such sentences, like those of Bacon, are well-ordered and are free from circumlocution. Through these essays Satyanath Borah standardised the language, rehabilitated the grammar and idiom, and impregnated the Assamese essay with a new, compact, sinewy style and a mature philosophic tone.

Kaliram Medhi was one of those who were dedicated to letters all through life. Besides editing some old Assamese manuscripts on modern lines, he also wrote a comprehensive and comparative treatise on Assamese language and grammar. Medhi has also to his credit a number of antiquarian articles devoted to Assam's ancient literature and culture. A master of a sober prose style, Kaliram reminds us of Satyanath Borah.

Another writer of the class of Satyanath Borah was Padmanath Gohain Barua, of whose poetry and drama we have spoken elsewhere. Like Bezbarua, Gohain Barua also was a founder-editor of *Uṣā* (The Dawn) and the *Asam Banti*

(The Light of Assam), the two periodicals to which the literary activity of the first quarter of the 20th century owes much of its inspiration and guidance. Gohain Barua himself contributed to the pages of these two journals a large number of articles on a wide range of subjects. He also compiled a series of well-written text-books for our schools, and though they may not claim any literary eminence, no one will deny that they have contributed in no small measure towards the creation of a lucid, direct and lively prose style which a young man may easily cultivate. But as a prose writer Gohain Barua's eminence rests on his monumental work, *Śrī Kṛṣṇa*, a biographical teatise on Lord Kṛṣṇa, published in three thick volumes. The book discloses the influence of Bankimchandra Chatterji's *Kṛṣṇacaritra* both in unfolding and in interpreting the Kṛṣṇa legend from a rational and human point of view. Here for the first time in Assamese we find historical analysis and critical enquiry applied to the study of the life of Lord Kṛṣṇa, who is admired and exalted by the author not so much as an *Avatār* or incarnation of God but as a great man.

Kamalakanta Bhattacharya was another forceful writer in whose religious and sociological essays a spirit of rational enquiry is manifest. Kamalakanta embraced Brahmanism; he was a monotheist, and his mind and outlook on religion were liberal. His series of essays known as *Guṭidiyek Cintār Dheu* (A Few Waves of Thought) were written in the spirit of a crusader and they disclose a remarkable power of analysis, argumentation and critical judgment. Kamalakanta's didactic essays are instinct with a sense of social justice and embody a strong reaction and protest against the undue domination of the priestly class. They also reveal his dislike of servile worship of authority, decaying traditions, blind rituals, dead customs, and all that tends to fetter the human mind. He wrote numerous stimulating essays condemning the caste system, worn-out and out-moded social codes and traditions, superstitions, and rigid and preposterous Hindu rituals, and advocating Western education, a liberal attitude to religion, widow re-marriage and so on and so forth. In his *Aṣṭavakrar Ātmajīvanī* (Autobiography of Aṣṭavakra), instead of presenting the Hindu religion as it is in the *Upaniṣads*, the *Gītā* and other scriptures, he interprets it in his own way and reads into it ideas and meanings which will stand modern test and reasoning.

Ambikagiri Roychaudhury's prose writings appeared chiefly in *Cetanā*, which is now defunct, and *Dekā Asam* (Young Assam), two periodicals which he himself edited. Some of the articles are collected in a book, *Āhuti* (Offering). The articles were written on contemporary happenings and political problems, especially those of Assam, and they are informed by a deep love for the Assamese people, their culture and heritage. He has a style of his own, which is very much exhortatory, and its charm is attributed to its deep and stately periods, drawn out and amplified like organ music. Full of verve, skipping, hissing and hitting, his phrases are like explosives, scattering colour and sound about them. Rugged and gaunt, his sentences reveal a personality that is intensely sincere and genuine. His language cannot keep pace with his emotions, and the result, sometimes, is obscurity. Roychaudhury has already crossed the 70th year of his life; but in virility of thought and power of devotion, he easily beats a young man.

Jagannath Borah is one of the thoughtful writers on contemporary social and literary problems. Expository in nature, his prose is marked by clarity of thought, raciness of expression, and idiomatic style.

Hemchandra Goswami (1872-1928) was an antiquarian and historian in his mental make-up. Yet he also published in his youth a collection of romantic poems, *Phular Jhāki*. But later, history proved to him an irresistible attraction, and he brought to light a vast deal of material from the Ahom period. He edited the *Puraṇī Asam-Burañjī*, a charming old chronicle of Assam, and edited and published the *Daraṅg Rāj-Vaṁśāvalī*—an illustrated semi-historical record of the Koch Kings written in the 18th century by Surjyakhari Daivajna. But his monumental work was *Typical Selections from Assamese Literature* in several volumes published by Calcutta University. In this work, Goswami brought together selected specimens of the writings of numerous known and unknown authors, and thus ensured their preservation. Another notable work of his, also published by Calcutta University, was *A Descriptive Catalogue of Assamese Manuscripts*, which is an indispensable guide for any enquiry into old Assamese literature. Goswami also scientifically edited and published the *Kathā-Gītā* (*Gītā* in Prose) of the immortal Bhattadeva of the Vaiṣṇvite period. He contributed articles of miscellaneous interest, scientific, antiquarian, critical, to the different journals of his time. Marked by originality, steadiness, and the scientific spirit, these articles have none of the vague and visionary gleam, the dreamy imagination and poetic rapture found in his verse. Cool reasoning, chaste idiom and precise and incisive phraseology—these make his style eminently suitable for such serious discussion. A new and penetrating precision is Goswami's special contribution to modern Assamese prose.

The general advance in knowledge and the growth of research into national affairs, which are the features of the new age, quickly brought the study of Assam history into prominence, and within a short period there occurred the swift rise of historical literature to a place of importance in the hands of Banikanta Kakati, Surya Kumar Bhuyan, Sonaram Chaudhury, Sarveswar Kataki, Kali Ram Medhi, Benudhar Sarma and others. Surya Kumar Bhuyan has been carrying on researches in Ahom history since his college days. In him critical enquiry reaches its acme. He systematically edited a number of Ahom chronicles and got them published by the Assam State Department of Historical and Antiquarian Studies. Surya Kumar Bhuyan is a poet and story-writer too. The poem, 'Apon Sur', included in the collection *Nirmāli*, is an autobiographical fragment embodying the poet's eternal desire to annihilate space and time and link his soul with infinity and eternity. It is for the unattainable that the romantic poet cries; and that, according to Carlyle, is proof of his greatness. Though he has written a number of things about man's sorrows and joys, the poet feels as if he has not fully realised his true self, and that inadequate expression is poetry's great stumbling-block.

Surya Kumar is, however, known more widely for his historical writings. His essays on Assam's history written at different times are now collected in *Āhomar Din* (The Ahom Times), *Asam-jīyarī* (The Daughters of Assam), *Burañjīr Bāṇī* (The Message Chronicle), *Mirjumlār Asam Ākramaṇ*

(Mirjumla's Invasion of Assam), *Kunwār Bidroh* (The Rebellion of Ahom Princes), etc. In *Kunwār Bidroh*, the author selects a few significant incidents and striking figures from a mass of historical detail and shapes them to most dramatic and stirring narratives. These essays of Suryya Kumar have suggested many historical plays by our writers. Bhuyan has devoted all his life to historical research, and in his investigation and re-construction of Assam's past, he is mostly guided by the Western method of impartial enquiry and objectivity. Moreover, in selection and presentation of subjects he does not confine himself to the study of great historical personages but deals also with the political, social and religious life and cultural milieu so as to give us a full and faithful picutre of Assam during the Ahom age. His literary style is simple and direct and modelled after the Burañjīs. Bhuyan is our noted word-reviver too; in his historical writings many old and obsolete words and expressions from the Burañjīs are wonderfully introduced. Bhuyan also has written a modern biography of the great Sanskrit scholar of Assam, Anandaram Barua. In biographical literature, this is definitely a work of a very high order. The late scholar's life has been re-captured through a proper sifting of a vast deal of material, great and small, and piecing them together in a scientific way.

The tradition started by Hem Chandra Goswami and Surya Kumar Bhuyan has found new adherents, and several scholars have engaged themselves in research into Assam's past history and literature, and in editing and publishing old manuscripts. Of them Benudhar Sarma is the sturdiest. The essays contained in his *Dūrbīṇ* (The Telescope) exhibits the author's historical sense and fondness for original sources of information. In depicting the lives of the Ahom kings, generals and princesses, the author uses these materials in a fascinating manner and makes the narrative of absorbing interest. He has also written an entertaining biography of Maniram Dewan, the earliest revolutionary leader of Assam, who first rose against the British in the 19th century. Here too Sarma's historical imagination prevails, and as a result we not only come to know much of the revolutionary hero and patriot but also visualize that soft and bewildered age in which Maniram Dewan hoisted the banner of revolt and inspired his countrymen to heroic sacrifice. Master of a rich, varied and racy prose, Benudhar Sarma has distinct individuality in his style and has a strength of his own.

Alongside these various forms of prose there has also developed a body of literature with the object of interpreting literature. Literary criticism was not known in Assamese till the impact of the West. This critical literature as a type was first begun in the pages of the *Aruṇoday* and is continued later on by other journals. But the early criticisms were mere catalogues of the merits and defects of men and books. The first major critical book was L. N. Bezbarua's biographical treatise, *Śaṅkaradeva*. In this critical study, Bezbarua gave not only a just estimate of the life and teachings of Śaṅkaradeva in a rational and restrained way, but also a brilliant appreciation of the literary works of the Vaiṣṇavite reformer.

Banikanta Kakati is another major literary critic to appreciate the growing status of Assamese literature as a subject worthy of serious study. His studies in ancient Assamese literature were published in instalments in the periodical, *Cetanā*. He studied some modern poets also. An eminent scholar and professor of English literature, Kakati had deep knowledge of Sanskrit too. His monumental work, *Assam, its Formation and Development* (in English), bears testimony to his profound erudition. This book happens to be the only scholarly and authoritative work on Assamese language and grammar. A scholar of wide study and great depth, Kakati knew both the oriental and the occidental ideals of life and ways of critical judgment, and this knowledge made his critical appreciations weighty, rich and attractive. His essays on ancient Assamese literature are the finest of their kind in Assamese. Master of a terse, well-chiselled and dignified style, Kakati, in these essays, explores not only the literary beauties, philosophical heights and technical excellences of Assam's ancient literature but also the social, religious and cultural background of the people of those times. The spirit of the age, an intense and permeating interest in religion, seems to be with him in these studies. The result is that these essays have brought to light the comprehensive spiritual history of the Assamese people of those times, as nothing else has. His second set of studies, *viz*, of the modern Assamese poets, is obviously on Western lines of comparative criticism, and in this his vast Western studies are freely laid under contribution. These studies are remarkable for their amazing fertility of wit, profound and penetrating ideas, and full maturity and perfection of a prose style pre-eminently suited to critical analysis. His contributions, however, do not end here. His articles on Assam Vaiṣṇavism published one after another in the monthly magazine, *Bijuli* (The Lightning), established Kakati as a dialectician of the first order, and before his scholarship, home-thrusts and precision his adversaries found it difficult to hold their ground in the controversy which occasioned the essays. A scientific spirit informs all his critical studies. In his hands Assamese prose style attained its maturity and became a worthy vehicle for the expression of high and abstract thought.

Dimbeswar Neog has written several histories of Assamese literature, old and modern, and these contain valuable information. He has also published some studies of individual authors in his *Asamīyā Sāhityar Jiliṅgani* (Glimpses of Assamse Literature). These studies are coloured and attuned by the spirit and sensibilities of the writer under discussion rather than by those of the critic himself.

The first noteworthy treatise on pure literary criticism was, however, *Sāhitya Vicār* by Satyanath Borah in which both Indian and English methods of literary assessment were briefly described. Nilmoni Phukan's *Sāhitya Kalā* follows his own standards and methods and one cannot but recognise a new and original approach in it. Birinchi Kumar Barua's *Kāvya āru Abhivyāñjanā* is a more standard text in which he follows Benedetto Croce, the Hindi author Lakshminarayan Singha, and several other English, Hindi and Bengali authorities. In *Kāvya Bhūmi*, Umakanta Sarma studies the philosophical basis and background of art. In *Sāhitya āru Samālocanā* Trailokyanath Goswami deals with literature, in the manner of Hudson, in a simple and lucid style. While admitting both Indian and European standards, he illustrates his points with extracts from Assamese literature, which makes his book easy of approach. Hem Barua, in his *Ādhunik Sāhitya*, studies certain periods of English literature with particular reference to modern trends. The work discloses the deep learning of the writer in modern English literature. Hem Barua's *Sānmihali* (Assorted), a collection of essays written on different occasions, is at the same time delightful and serious, ranging from Egyptian history to Einstein, open-air theatre to feminine beauty. Yet these essays are so much flavoured with personal opinions and pedantic allusions that the reader's interest in the subjects is naturally swamped. Lightness of touch and personal charm make his travel books more endearing. His *Sāgar Dekhichā* (Have You Seen the Sea?) and *Raṅgā Karabīr Phul* are absorbing diaries of his travels in America and Russia respectively. They are written in the literary style by a sensitive observer of men and manners.

Sāhityar Rūparekhā by Atul Chandra Barua is a good introduction to the study of literature in all its ramifications.

The present age has been particularly marked by a growing interest in the study of Assamese literature, history and culture, and after the attainment of independence several scholars have considered it to be a serious national duty to enquire into the past, in order to find out and retain all that was best in it. Upendra Chandra Lekharu, in his critical treatise, *Asamīyā Rāmāyaṇa Sāhitya*, studies, on modern lines, the Assamese version of the *Rāmāyaṇa* by Madhava Kandali and examines both the subject-matter and the poetic technique of the great poet. Birinchi Kumar Barua enquires into the origin and evolution of Assamese prose in his *Asamīyā Kathā Sāhitya.* Barua's *Asamīyā Bhāṣā āru Saṁskṛiti* (Assamese Language and Culture) is a collection of original essays about various aspects of Assamese life and culture untouched so far by other writers. Barua has also edited some rare books, *Aṅkīyā Nāṭ*, *Mahāmoha Kāvya* and *Śrī Rām Ata āru Ramānandar Gīt.* In the prefaces to these books, he has critically examined the characteristic features, traditions, and excellences of old Assamese literature. Harinarayan Datta Barua, Maheswar Neog and Satyendranath Sarma also have edited some old Assamese texts on modern scientific lines and have thrown considerable light upon them. Neog's *Puraṇi Asamīyā Samāj āru Saṁskṛiti*, *Asamīyā Gīti Kāvya* and *Asamīyā Premgāthā*, are collections of well-written essays on early Assamese literature and society, incorporating the results of the author's own investigations. Through their writings these scholars have charted the growth and development of the Assamese language and culture, and have discovered the continuity of the Assamese genius.

Interest in the cultural and folk life of the Assamese people was first shown by Lakshminath Bezbarua, Nakul Chandra Bhuyan and Dimbeswar Neog in their collections of folk tales and songs. In recent years, there have come out many valuable and impressive writings on folk literature, notable among which is Praphulladatta Goswami's informative and entertaining *Asamīyā Jana Sāhitya*.

Books on philosophy and popular science have begun gradually to make their appearance, and a few thinkers and writers have already established their reputations. Radhanath Phukon is an outstanding writer of philosophical treatises, and Rohinikanta Barua has been enriching Assamese literature with his writings on scientific subjects.

Literary journals, newspapers and periodicals have come to exercise a great influence on modern trends in Assamese literature, and some of the different literary epochs have been named after leading journals like *Aruṇoday*, *Jonākī*, *Bāhī* and *Āwāhan*. Each new journal is the rallying point of writers of a new school of thought, and in successive monthly issues their views and literary ideals are enunciated, expressed and practised. These journals thus define the age and give it its name.

Mention has already been made of *Āruṇoday*—the earliest of the modern monthly periodicals, published by Christian Missionaries from Sibsagar. The Assamese *Āruṇoday*, like its Bengali and Oriya counterparts, not only published current news but also contained material of varied interest—educational, cultural, literary. In addition to news items it also published stories from far and near and matters of general information, scientific knowledge, and useful knowledge of everyday life. It is in the pages of *Āruṇoday* that we find the first florescence of modern Assamese literature. The magazine gave literary status and dignity to the spoken language of the people in both poetry and prose, and, broadly speaking, the language thus evolved continues to be the standard language of Assamese literature even today.

The next major literary journal was the famous *Jonākī* (Moonlight, 1889), with which were associated stalwarts like Chandra Kumar Agarwalla, Lakshminath Bezbarua, Hemchandra Goswami, Kanaklal Barua, and others. Through this journal, the writers spread in Assamese the ideas of the English romantic poets. *Uṣā* (Dawn, 1907) appeared under the editorship of Padmanath Gohain Barua, while the *Bāhī* (Flute, 1909) was edited by Lakshminath Bezbarua. These two literary magazines with different ideals ran parallel and were frequently engaged in longdrawn polemics on literary and sometimes social problems. But such controversies under the stewardship of two great masters contributed in no small measure to the enrichment of Assamese literature. Prose, poetry, the short story, the historical dissertation, the essay—all the types were cultivated in their pages.

Next came out, in 1929, *Āwāhan*, published from Calcutta for about ten years, that is, up to the outbreak of World War II. This magazine was most popular and creditably maintained a high literary standard. It created a reading public, intensified popular interest, served as a model, and also reared a band of enthusiastic writers. New ideas and fashions in literature, the short story, scientific literary criticism—these were the special merits of this magazine. Speculative, philosophic, reflective and argumentative prose, which has declined today in Assamese, was greatly fostered in the pages of *Āwāhan*. Another journal, *Jayantī*, published just before the War, created a stir by encouraging young writers to experiment in various forms of literature. In its pages for the first time we see the flashes of the new poetry.

After the war were born the two newspapers—the daily *Natun Asamīyā*, and the weekly *Asam Bāṇī*, as well as the monthly magazine, *Rāmdhenu* (Rainbow). The review of books and other feature articles published in the Sunday issues of the *Natun Asamīyā* reflect the new ground made by writers of today. *Natun Asamīyā* has largely contributed to the rapid growth and enormous popularity of what is known as *ramya racanā* or *belles lettres*. Dr. Hem Barua, Lalit Bora, Tilak Hazarika, Hem Chandra Sarma, Bhadra Bora are some of the regular contributors to its columns. Unfortunately most of our young writers have neither the patience nor the ability to think clearly and write precisely because they trust in genius. When we survey their writings we are tempted to quote Dante: "Therefore let the folly of those be confuted who, devoid of art and knowledge and trusting in genius alone, rush forward to write poetry."

Asam Bāṇī publishes articles of varied interest for both adults and children, including feature articles, short stories, poems and belles-lettres. The most up-to-date trends of Assamese literature, particularly the work of young poets, short story writers and critics, are reflected in the vigorous monthly magazine, *Rāmdhenu.* This has been the pivot of a modern intellectual and literary movement—a movement which may be likened to a great river embracing many small and apparently insignificant tributaries, all of them ultimately converging by winding courses into the great stream and thereby enlarging and reinforcing Assamese literature in all its variety and profundity.

INDEX